Critical Reflections on
Research Methods

RESEARCHING MULTILINGUALLY
Series Editors: **Prue Holmes**, *Durham University, UK,*
Richard Fay, *University of Manchester, UK* and
Jane Andrews, *University of the West of England, UK*

Consulting Editor: Alison Phipps, *University of Glasgow, UK*

The increasingly diverse character of many societies means that many researchers may now find themselves engaging with multilingual opportunities and complexities as they design, carry out and disseminate their research. This may be the case regardless of whether or not there is an explicit language and multilingual aspect to their research. This book series proposes to address the methodological, practical, ethical and other options and dilemmas that researchers face as they go about their research. How do they design their research methodology to account for multilingual possibilities and practices? How do they manage such linguistic complexities in the research domain? What are the implications for their research outcomes? Research methods training programmes only rarely address these questions and there is, as yet, only a limited literature available. This series proposes to establish a new track of theoretical, methodological, and ethical researcher praxis that researchers can draw upon in research(er) contexts where multiple languages are at play or might be purposefully used. In particular, the series proposes to offer critical and interpretive perspectives on research practices and endeavours in inter- and multi-disciplinary contexts and especially where languages, and the people speaking and using them, are under pressure, pain, and tension.

All books in this series are externally peer-reviewed.

Full details of all the books in this series and of all our other publications can be found on http://www.multilingual-matters.com, or by writing to Multilingual Matters, St Nicholas House, 31-34 High Street, Bristol BS1 2AW, UK.

RESEARCHING MULTILINGUALLY: 1

Critical Reflections on Research Methods

Power and Equity in Complex Multilingual Contexts

Edited by
Doris S. Warriner and Martha Bigelow

MULTILINGUAL MATTERS
Bristol • Blue Ridge Summit

DOI https://doi.org/10.21832/WARRIN2555
Library of Congress Cataloging in Publication Data
Names: Warriner, Doris S., 1969-editor. | Bigelow, Martha, editor.
Title: Critical Reflections on Research Methods: Power and Equity in Complex
   Multilingual Contexts/Edited by Doris S. Warriner and Martha Bigelow.
Description: Blue Ridge Summit: Multilingual Matters, [2019] | Series:
   Researching Multilingually: 1 | Includes bibliographical references and index.
Identifiers: LCCN 2018039095| ISBN 9781788922555 (hbk :alk. paper) |
   ISBN 9781788922548 (pbk :alk. paper) | ISBN 9781788922586 (kindle)
Subjects: LCSH: Linguistic minorities – Study and teaching – Case studies. |
Ethnology – Study and teaching – Case studies. |
Linguistics – Study and teaching – Case studies.
Classification: LCC P40.5.L56 C75 2019 | DDC 306.44072 – dc23 LC record available
at https://lccn.loc.gov/2018039095

A catalog record for this book is available from the Library of Congress.

British Library Cataloguing in Publication Data
A catalogue entry for this book is available from the British Library.

ISBN-13: 978-1-78892-255-5 (hbk)
ISBN-13: 978-1-78892-254-8 (pbk)

Multilingual Matters
UK: St Nicholas House, 31-34 High Street, Bristol BS1 2AW, UK.
USA: NBN, Blue Ridge Summit, PA, USA.

Website: www.multilingual-matters.com
Twitter: Multi_Ling_Mat
Facebook: https://www.facebook.com/multilingualmatters
Blog: www.channelviewpublications.wordpress.com

The policy of Multilingual Matters/Channel View Publications is to use papers that are natural, renewable and recyclable products, made from wood grown in sustainable forests. In the manufacturing process of our books, and to further support our policy, preference is given to printers that have FSC and PEFC Chain of Custody certification. The FSC and/or PEFC logos will appear on those books where full certification has been granted to the printer concerned.

Typeset by Riverside Publishing Solutions.
Printed and bound in the UK by Short Run Press Ltd.
Printed and bound in the US by Thomson-Shore, Inc.

Contents

Contributors

Nimo M. Abdi is an assistant professor in the department of Curriculum and Instruction at the University of Minnesota. She received her PhD from Michigan State University in Educational Administration. Her research focuses on immigrant and refugee education, particularly as it relates to cultural, racial, and religious diversity. Her primary methodological approaches are phenomenology, decolonization theory/methodologies, and discourse analysis. Her work examines Somali educational experiences in urban United States, United Kingdom, Sweden and The Netherlands.

Michele Allen is an associate professor in the Department of Family Medicine and Community Health, and Director of the Program in Health Disparities Research at the University of Minnesota. Her research focuses on using community-based participatory approaches to develop and implement health promotion and tobacco and other substance use prevention interventions for adolescents and their families. She has led multiple studies funded by the National Institutes of Health, American Cancer Society, and other large foundations. Dr Allen completed medical school at the University of Minnesota, and a Master's Degree in sociology from the University of Wisconsin, Madison.

Katie A. Bernstein studies language learning in young emergent multilingual children, attending to the multiple layers of context in which their learning is embedded: from the immediate context of peer social interactions, to the classroom context shaped by teachers' beliefs and preparation, to the broader political, ideological, and policy contexts. Katie's interdisciplinary research draws on methods and theories from the fields of education, applied linguistics, and anthropology and has been published in journals such as *TESOL Quarterly* and *Linguistics and Education*. Katie is an assistant professor of education at Arizona State University and a former preschool teacher.

Martha Bigelow is Professor in Second Language Education at the University of Minnesota, USA. Her research focuses on equity in language teaching and learning in the United States and abroad. She works in the areas of research ethics and state and national level language policy implementation. She has engaged in transformative and sustainable curriculum projects in Vietnam, Costa Rica and India. She is internationally recognized for her work in the areas of teaching immigrant- and refugee-background youth and multilingual/modal critical literacy instruction.

Christopher Browder is a teacher, professional developer, and education researcher. He has been teaching English to Speakers of Other Languages (ESOL) since 1993 and has taught in five different countries. He currently manages a US high school ESOL program with over 850 students in an immigrant gateway community near Washington DC. He is particularly interested in the role English learners' educational backgrounds play in their educational achievement in US public schools. He has spoken at conferences and published articles on the topic of students with limited and/or interrupted formal education.

Jenna Cushing-Leubner is an Assistant Professor in Language Education at the University of Wisconsin – Whitewater, USA. Her research focuses on community-engaged practices and justice-oriented approaches to language education and teacher education. She works closely with teachers, youth, and community members in designing (and researching the impacts of) Spanish and Hmong heritage/native language education programs. These efforts use participatory design and action research to create curricula and pedagogy that teaches language through intra-ethnic studies, community-based learning, critical project-based instruction, and natural use of translanguaging and multilingual literacies.

Chatwara Suwannamai Duran is Associate Professor of Applied Linguistics at University of Houston. Her research explores contested language ideologies, multilingual repertoires, and multiple literacies among refugees and immigrants predominantly from Myanmar and Thailand. Her work has implications for language and literacy pedagogy and has appeared in several journals such as *Linguistics and Education, Journal of Language, Identity and Education* and *International Multilingual Research Journal*, including a number of edited volumes. Duran has recently published her first book *Language and Literacy in Refugee Families* (2017) based on her multi-year ethnographic study in Karenni families in the United States.

Emily Feuerherm is an Assistant Professor of Linguistics in the English Department at the University of Michigan-Flint. She received her PhD in Linguistics from the University of California, Davis. Her research interests integrate community-based participatory research, language policy and practice, curriculum design, and ESL health literacy. Her publications include a co-edited volume with Vai Ramanathan called *Refugee Resettlement in the United States: Language, Policies, Pedagogies* (2016), chapters in other volumes such as *Language, Immigration and Naturalization: Legal and Linguistic Issues* (2016), and *Language Policies and (Dis)Citizenship* (2013). She also has a co-authored article with Jacob Blumner in *Across the Disciplines* 'Growing pains and course correction: Internationalizing a writing program' (2018).

Daisy E. Fredricks is an Assistant Professor at Grand Valley State University. She received her PhD in Applied Linguistics from Arizona State University. Her research focuses on English learner education, restrictive language education policy and practice, and pre-service teacher preparation. Dr Fredricks has publications in *Bilingual Research Journal*, *International Multilingual Research Journal*, *CATESOL Journal*, as well as in peer-reviewed book collections. She served as an elementary and middle school classroom teacher in Michigan, Texas and Arizona.

Ayfer Gokalp is an ethnographer, whose research focused on language ideologies, language policies, and minority language maintenance. She received her doctorate in Curriculum and Instruction from Arizona State University in 2015. Ayfer successfully employed diverse research methods by utilizing her multiple roles to understand language ideologies and policies in that linguistically complicated context in her dissertation, entitled 'Language and Literacy Practices of Kurdish Children Across Their Home and School Spaces in Turkey: An Ethnography of Language Policy.' This dissertation was awarded Outstanding Dissertation Fellowship by Graduate College of ASU. Ayfer continues conducting ethnographic research at HTC Creative Labs.

Mikow Hang is a founding member of the Somali, Latino and Hmong Partnership for Health and Wellness (SoLaHmo), a community-driven translational research program of West Side Community Health Services. In addition, Ms. Hang is the research program manager at the University of Minnesota Medical School Program in Health Disparities Research (PHDR). She completed her masters in Public Health degree from the University of Minnesota School of Public Health in 2018. Her interests include immigrant and refugee health, women's health, and community-based participatory action research.

Sarah Young Knowles is a Professorial Lecturer in the TESOL program at American University, where she specializes in language teaching methods, second language acquisition, and teacher mentoring. She earned her doctorate in applied linguistics at Georgetown University, focusing on metalinguistic awareness in adult English language learners with limited schooling. Previously, she worked at the Center for Applied Linguistics, as a professional development consultant, and as a course developer and teacher trainer in the US and Ecuador. Her earlier experiences teaching English in Cameroon and working with adult immigrant populations in the Washington DC area have influenced her research and practice in significant ways.

Rosalva Mojica Lagunas is an Indigenous scholar, with family roots in Guerrero, Mexico who earned her doctorate in Curriculum & Instruction with an emphasis in Language & Literacy at Arizona State University. Rosalva's research and teaching focus is on bilingualism and biliteracy, elementary education, indigenous languages and education, language revitalization, and language planning and policy. She has explored these interests in the context of urban public schools in the US and Nahuatl heritage-language communities in Mexico. Her studies contribute to the larger fields of language education and sociolinguistics/applied linguistics, and to policy and practice.

Katherine E. Morelli is a qualitative and interdisciplinary researcher who takes a rhetorical and sociocultural approach to community literacy. Her research focuses on communication and language and literacy development in healthcare contexts, particularly among refugee families. Her research also considers the implications of transnationalism for second language pedagogy. She has taught ESL and undergraduate courses in writing, rhetoric, literacy and technical communication. Morelli holds a doctorate in English with a concentration in Writing, Rhetoric and Literacies from Arizona State University and a masters in Applied Linguistics from UMass-Boston. From 2018–2019, she is Visiting Assistant Professor in the Department of English at Boise State University.

Luis Enrique Ortega is a founding member of the Somali, Latino and Hmong Partnership for Health and Wellness (SoLaHmo), a community driven translational research program of West Side Community Health Services. He has 30+ years in public education and transitioned his passion for working with underrepresented students and parents and brought it to the field of community based participatory action research. He currently is Co-PI of a 5 year NIH Grant (Project TRUST) that combines Youth and Parent Participatory Action Research and teacher professional development to address student connectedness.

Shannon Pergament is a founding member of the Somali, Latino and Hmong Partnership for Health and Wellness (SoLaHmo), a community driven translational research program of West Side Community Health Services, Inc. (West Side). Shannon is Co-Director of Community Based Research at West Side. She holds Master's degrees in Public Health (MPH) and Social Work (MSW) from the University of Minnesota. For over 20 years, Shannon has worked in the area of health equity, building collaborations with ethnically diverse communities to promote community and cultural assets and reduce health disparities through community based participatory action research (CBPAR), health education and policy.

Kristen H. Perry is an associate professor of literacy education in the Department of Curriculum & Instruction at the University of Kentucky. She researches literacy and culture in diverse communities, investigating everyday home/family and community literacy practices, particularly among immigrant and refugee communities. She also researches educational opportunities with respect to ESL, literacy, and higher education for adult refugees. As co-director of Project PLACE, she provides professional development to classroom teachers working with English learners. Perry received the 2012 Early Career Achievement award and the 2007 J. Michael Parker Award for research in adult literacy from the Literacy Research Association.

Nicole Pettitt is an Assistant Professor of TESOL at Youngstown State University in Ohio. Her ethnographic and community-based research centers on the language and literacy learning of refugee- and immigrant-background women and girls, as well as the historical, political, and local contexts that shape their educational experiences.

Amy Shanafelt is Research Project Manager in the Department of Family Medicine and Community Health at the University of Minnesota. She received her masters in Community Psychology from Metropolitan State University in 2010 and has been working in community engaged health research ever since. Amy has managed multiple research studies at the University of Minnesota, with topics including, high school breakfast and student health, childcare nutrition and physical activity environments, youth development and most recently, the Minneapolis minimum wage ordinance and its effect on the health of workers. Amy is involved with campus-wide public engagement committees and is dedicated to reciprocal and mutually beneficial engagement between the University and community.

Doris S. Warriner is Associate Professor in the Department of English at Arizona State University. Her research examines the relationship between communicative practices and the lived experiences, literacy development and learning trajectories of immigrant and refugee families. Drawing on theories and approaches from applied linguistics, literacy studies, educational anthropology and linguistic anthropology, she explores how social practices and learning trajectories are influenced by large-scale processes such as displacement, ethnic conflict, immigration and transnationalism. Recent publications appear in *Curriculum Inquiry, Anthropology and Education Quarterly,* the *Journal of Multilingual and Multicultural Development* and the *International Multilingual Research Journal.*

Introduction

Doris S. Warriner and Martha Bigelow

Research methods courses and introductory texts on designing and conducting qualitative inquiry aim to prepare researchers for executing a study and then writing about the 'findings' for a wider audience. Most of these books cover broad topics such as research design, data collection, data analysis and coding. Some of them consider challenges involved in negotiating access, securing informed consent, building relationships, establishing trust, reflecting on practice and engaging in reciprocity. Some of them address the benefits of qualitative approaches to inquiry and explore what qualitative approaches to knowledge production can offer. Some methods books describe standard practices frequently used to conduct qualitative research and offer ways to observe, write up field notes, transcribe, code and represent data from a multitude of sources. Sometimes researchers hear suggestions for how to manage some of the ethical issues that arise while embarking on the unpredictable intellectual journeys that tend to accompany ethnographic and qualitative approaches to inquiry. Indeed, a number of well-regarded books on qualitative research methods, interviewing or ethnography have sections or chapters that encourage the researcher to take seriously ethical issues, concerns and questions. For instance, there are discussions of the relationship between ethical considerations and the trustworthiness of qualitative research (Merriam & Tisdell, 2016); descriptions of standard policies and practices for seeking approval to conduct research that involves human subjects and minimizing risk or harm (Boellstorff *et al.*, 2012; Creswell, 2016; Mayan, 2016); reflections on 'the ethics of doing good work' as an interviewer and engaging in reciprocity (Seidman, 2013); and the importance of protecting the vulnerable during processes of recruitment and obtaining informed consent (Olson, 2011). While many such texts contain mentions, reminders, cautions and advice on what ethical researchers could or should do when out 'in the field', none explore the hidden dimensions of designing and carrying out a research study in ways that both plan for ethical practice and anticipate the unexpected quandaries and complexities that inevitably emerge while engaging in research with/for/on behalf of others – particularly when the participants have historically been left out of the research agenda driver's seat.

Often left underexplored and undertheorized are the challenges that emerge while designing or implementing a qualitative study and

the messier issues that arise during the research process. The unanticipated, complex and emotional dimensions of the process are often left
unarticulated, requiring researchers (new and experienced) to navigate
them on their own, often in the moment, even though there is collective
but unpublished wisdom among researchers on so many aspects of the
research process. With varying degrees of uncertainty and angst, qualitative researchers embark on each step – including introductions, obtaining
consent, observing, interviewing, analysis and representation. Because
each encounter, interaction and decision comes with specific circumstances and complications, it is typically difficult to prepare in advance
for some of the more challenging situations. Researchers often need
to decide what to do and how to do it in the moment and on the spot.
Sometimes they are satisfied with their choices, sometimes these choices
can derail or adversely influence the goals and priorities of the research.
These dilemmas have begun to be explored in the field of applied
linguistics in general (e.g. DeCosta, 2015) and in work with refugee-
background communities, in particular (e.g. Block et al., 2012; Block et al.,
2013; Hugman et al., 2011; Jacobsen & Landau, 2003; MacKenzie et al.,
2007; Ngo et al., 2014; Voutira & Dona, 2007). As we grow as researchers,
and train future researchers, we wish to create opportunities for researchers
to share stories about the more complicated dimensions of our experiences and to explore our encounters with the complexities of the research
process.

One of the strengths of this volume is that it gives voice to researchers
from minoritized communities; another strength is that it demonstrates
the power of reflecting on the challenging (and sometimes unpredictable)
process of carrying out research with underrepresented groups. In addition,
by questioning the linear presentation of research process that is typically
depicted in accounts of research processes, the contributors highlight its
non-linear, emergent, emotional, even messy nature. Finally, the volume as
a whole illustrates what a constant state of questioning might yield (e.g. in
terms of researcher disposition, study findings, and theoretical contribution). As the first volume to be published in the *Researching Multilingually*
series, this collection dramatically demonstrates the need for rethinking
our methods of inquiry, our processes of data collection, and our representation of findings – particularly 'where languages, and the people
speaking and using them, are vulnerable, and under pressure, pain, and
tension' (series call for proposals). The chapters reveal the various linguistic
complexities and possibilities that researchers face as they undertake their
research.

In this edited collection, we intentionally and deliberately carve out
a space for delving into and exploring the complicated procedural, relational, interactional, ethical and emotional aspects of the qualitative
researcher's lived experience. These are the narratives that are typically left

out of published dissertations, journals and books. In an effort to shed light on the dimensions of the research process that are often left unaddressed in these written accounts, we invited a handful of experienced and novice researchers to reflect on and share their experiences about some of the challenges they faced while trying to manage and respond to the unanticipated setbacks and messier moments of the research process. These authors share some of the challenges they encountered during their research and writing processes, alone or with their collaborators. They explore the challenges that emerge behind the scenes and consider how to best represent the experiences and views of the individuals and communities they work with, how to not misconstrue what participants have said, how to avoid offending community members or stakeholders, and how to fairly and accurately represent a situation or an event. They consider the difficulties of recruiting participants, obtaining informed consent, collecting data, analyzing data and (re)presenting findings. They also reflect on questions of access and representation with a focus on the role of relationships and communication. These experienced and new researchers explore questions about how to avoid misconstruing what participants have said, how to avoid alienating insiders, and how to best represent a situation, an event, or change in perspective. By examining the complicated relationships, dynamics and understandings that emerge while doing their research, they demonstrate the value of critically reflecting on one's research process, goals and aspirations.

In addition, the contributors to this volume theorize the power and limits of university-based research conducted on behalf of and sometimes in collaboration with members of local communities. Reflecting on research conducted across educational and community contexts, the authors share insights (and sometimes misgivings) on their research process, the ethical and emotional dimensions of participating in collaborative research, and the 'untold stories' of research design, data collection, data analysis, and representation of findings. For example, the research on the language, literacy and communication challenges that are involved in the (im)migrant and refugee experience have yielded important insights into processes of displacement, membership, exclusion, power and trauma. Yet, applied linguists, educational researchers and educational anthropologists continually struggle to find ways to make their research relevant to the academy as well as the students, families and (diaspora) communities with whom they work. Many of the chapters in this collection raise questions about how to design a study and create research questions that are appropriate to the context and relevant to participants. Many chapters examine how to use (or devise) research methodologies which resonate with their participants' ways of being, and when and how to explore ways of creating and sharing knowledge with participants and other stakeholders.

When we consider the conventions of typical research methods such as focus groups, interviews, or surveys, we discover that they don't always play out the way they are described in often-referenced handbooks, highly-recommended texts, or graduate-level research methods classes. For instance, there is little to no guidance on how to do research with communities unfamiliar with researchers, who may not be print literate, who understand the world through narrative and relational ways, or who, at the same time, are trying to bridge multiple social contexts of their own (e.g. religious, generational, linguistic). The chapters in this collection show us that, although we can predict bumps along the way, we may need to be flexible and improvise in situations that were not anticipated as we try to generate new understandings and knowledge in complex contexts in the absence of pre-approved standard protocols about how to proceed.

With such quandaries and complications in mind, contributors to this volume were invited to explore and reflect upon their most troubling research dilemmas including the relationships in their research site; the situated and dynamic ways that individuals position themselves within the context of a research interview or focus; and how approaches to data collection might be modified in ways that create a more transparent and humanizing approach to research. Some of the authors also explored how their own multilingualism and language brokering efforts facilitated communication, understanding, and trust or how the emotional or affective dimension of the research process shapes what can be learned and understood. Reflecting on the constraints, opportunities and situated practices that emerge in the research process, each chapter describes and analyzes how the researcher has managed (individually or in collaboration with others) the challenges and unanticipated aspects of conducting research on behalf of or alongside members of immigrant, refugee, and other minoritized communities. They explore the complexities of the qualitative research process – e.g. how a study came to be, how decisions made by researchers influenced the focus or scope of the project, how relationships between researchers and participants (or potential participants) evolved in and through interaction and over time (and with what consequences) and how relationships themselves help to shape one's focus, plans, questions or findings.

Authors also critically reflect on dynamics, developments and quandaries that have emerged behind the scenes in complex research situations, in the margins of what gets centered by the project or the researchers, or in the corners of our collaborative research endeavor. Taking into account the affordances and constraints of different approaches to inquiry, as well as the historical factors that help to shape various research agendas, the authors reflect on their experiences implementing practices that are generally considered to be more inclusive, democratic, critical or ethical; and they raise questions about how inclusive, democratic, critical or ethical certain practices ultimately are for their projects. Collectively, the autobiographical accounts provided here offer a range of new perspectives on often-asked questions about the when, where, how and why of ethnographic, interpretative and qualitative approaches to inquiry.

All of the authors were invited to respond (directly or indirectly) to one or more of the following focal questions:

(1) What are the possibilities (and limits) of our theories and methods for understanding and representing the views and experiences of those who have been the object of anthropological inquiry but seldom the producers of anthropological knowledge?

(2) What kinds of relationships, partnerships and collaborations are applied linguists and anthropologists equipped to build and foster? What are the possibilities, challenges, and limits of such work?

(3) What ethical dimensions are involved with collecting information, stories, and views of those often marginalized or excluded from the pursuits of social science?

(4) Are there other ways to discover, produce, represent or disseminate information and perspectives that have been produced by members of historically marginalized communities? What audiences should we try to reach, and how might we better reach them?

Even for experienced researchers, there are usually unanticipated challenges and unexpected complications when trying to access a new research site, when recruiting participants, when out 'in the field' conducting research, or when writing up one's analysis. While most of us have learned how to obtain informed consent from research participants, we have not necessarily learned how to discuss the challenges involved when consent-as-a-process approaches to research allow participants multiple opportunities to drop out of a study (Hugman *et al.*, 2011). As researchers, we sometimes face decisions about whether to use one's own students as research participants and the possibilities of using class time for research activities. In such situations, the decision to conduct research in our own classrooms or with our own students then requires a number of additional decisions to be made, including how to ensure students don't feel coerced and how our own multiple positionalities might influence what we focus on and pay attention to in the research context.

The primary goal of this collection is to showcase and disseminate first-hand reflective accounts of the untold stories of the research process – with a focus on the challenges of obtaining access, the messiness of data collection and data analysis (including that which did not go as planned or had to be innovated), roles, relationships, agendas and reciprocity. By giving priority to often-neglected dimensions of community-based collaborative work, this collection should be of interest and use to applied linguists, educational researchers and anthropologists of education. Examining language, literacy and culture in relation to processes of migration and transnationalism, the volume offers reflections on the power and limits of university-based research conducted on behalf of or in collaboration with members of local or under-represented communities. Some authors have decided to reflect on how researchers might more effectively reach 'the public', shape policy initiatives, and demonstrate the value of anthropological and linguistic approaches to discovery, relationship building, knowledge-production and dissemination of findings. Other contributors have considered the historically influenced ways that refugee youth and adults have experienced displacement, language learning, and disenfranchisement in the realms of education, employment, and health care. By exploring some of the more complicated relationships, dynamics and understandings that emerge, the chapters in this volume demonstrate the value of reflecting on the 'untold stories' of research design, data collection, data analysis and representation of findings.

The first section focuses on processes of social identification, positioning and participation with chapters that explore how researchers strive to position themselves in relation to the project or their participants, how they might be positioned by others and the role of their identities in such processes. Chatwara Duran, for instance, explores how her relationships with Karenni youth mediated not only the kinds of interactions and relationships she had with their parents but also her collaborative process of knowledge construction with the parents and the children. Ayfer Gokalp describes how she was positioned by the Kurdish children in her study; how this positioning influenced decisions she made in the research site about data collection, data analysis and representation; and the ways in which power relations (between speakers and between their languages) influence such phenomena. Chris Browder reflects on the dangers of using commonly understood labels as researchers (e.g. SLIFE) and offers alternatives that expand not only what we ask but how we know and how we represent what we learn. Emily Feuerherm considers some of the challenges involved in enacting a participatory action research agenda in a community based project and critically reflects on the extensive relationship-building process as well as the complications that emerge when languages, cultures and gendered identities intersect in both expected and unexpected ways.

In the second section of the volume, authors share their experiences with the complicated dynamics that emerge when researchers are neither insiders nor complete outsiders to the research context, how they manage often unexpected roles, and the ways that reciprocity can take many different forms. Rosalva Lagunas reflects on the challenges experienced while conducting ethnographic research in a village where many of her relatives live and work, how her insider-outsider status was shaped by shifts in her practices and beliefs, and the dynamic ways that her relationships influenced her research questions (and vice versa). Sarah Young Knowles' chapter explores the challenges and rewards involved in conducting research that crosses cultural and language borders, and examines how the insider-outsider dichotomy is useful when considering the influence of her non-native competency in Spanish, the language of her participants and interviews. This chapter reminds us of the importance of doing research multilingually and the serious limitations of knowledge produced through data gathered only in the researcher's strongest language. Nimo Abdi demonstrates the value of reflexivity in shaping her understanding of how her 'otherness' as a Somali-American influenced the decisions she made as a researcher, and she interrogates issues of representation and voice to argue for 'decolonizing methodologies that take into account community as a unit of analysis'. Daisy Fredricks considers the modifications she made while observing, interviewing, and analyzing data in order to understand more deeply the experiences of refugee youths; her account highlights the ways that humanizing research agendas can be both flexible and responsive.

The final section of the book contains chapters that consider questions about what constitutes knowledge production, the researcher's role in knowledge production, and how we might move from conventional understandings of qualitative research process to more innovative, engaged and responsive approaches. Katie Bernstein's chapter explores questions of reflexivity and reciprocity in relation to questions about the 'on-the-ground ethical challenges' she encountered while conducting ethnographic research with refugee children, their families and their teachers. She proposes that all researchers strive to engage in an ethics of practice and address the question 'To whom am I answerable now?' whenever working with vulnerable populations. Nicole Pettitt describes and theorizes some of the creative and sensitive ways that reciprocity can be woven into a research project collaboratively designed and conducted with immigrant and refugees, even as she questions what counts as reciprocity and what kinds of reciprocity count. Kristen Perry raises important and timely questions about the required use of pseudonyms, what happens when participants ask researchers to use their real names, and the long-term implications of such choices. Her ethno-methodological tale is one that might influence all researchers' efforts to obtain informed consent in challenging research contexts. Morelli and Warriner explore the emotional and interactional dimensions of a challenging multidimensional research project to show that researchers' decisions and understandings are often influenced by a wide range of affective and subjective factors – many of which cannot be anticipated. Finally, Bigelow and her co-authors provide a riveting account of the ways that power and equity might be enacted and interpreted differently in a community-based participatory action research project collaboratively designed and executed by a team of researchers from the university and the community. Looking at hierarchies, disciplines and roles, they argue that, even while actively striving for 'ethical, equitable, and productive collaborations', power-related challenges are endemic to this kind of work.

With this volume, we have explored questions about access, relationship-building, trust, ethics and reciprocity with a particular focus on what it means (and looks like) to carry out research on the experiences of (or in collaboration with) marginalized, under-represented, minoritized, or vulnerable participants. Each author has reflected on, engaged deeply with, or critiqued dimensions of ethnographic or participatory research endeavors in order to show how individual researchers might experience and respond to a wide range of practical, logistical or emotional issues. Theorizing their own autobiographical experiences, emerging scholars new to qualitative research as well as those who are more experienced offer innovative ideas and illustrative examples of practice that complement and/or challenge common understandings of what constitutes research design, ethics and positionality. By showcasing the experiences and reflections of emerging scholars alongside the accounts of more experienced researchers, this volume should serve as a useful resource for new and experienced researchers alike. This book offers an opportunity to dig deeply into some of the most challenging and confounding aspects of the work that qualitative researchers do.

As these accounts dramatically demonstrate, researchers (novice and experienced) need to be increasingly flexible in our roles as we discover how we are perceived or what we might do to collect data in different ways. Perhaps the meta-reflections in this book will even inspire researchers in other and white/mainstream/non-Western contexts to examine their standard practices. It is likely that we can all do better across various ethical-methodological dimensions of our research. Collectively, these accounts of learning or relearning to do research raise a number of timely questions that should give us all pause. Do we need to examine all of our training? Do we need new or parallel paths for engaging in ethical, humane, epistemologically rigorous work? We believe that the chapters in this collection offer a resounding 'yes' to these questions. One of the key issues at hand is that we are all trying to produce new knowledge and understandings through engaging with communities different from our own, or with communities in which we feel some sense of belonging but discover that we are positioned in ways that complicate both insiderness and outsiderness. Furthermore, many of the questions that were taken up by the contributors to this volume involve minoritized communities that may be unfamiliar with navigating a relationship with a researcher who also seems to be sort of like a teacher, sort of like a community member, or sort of like an elder, but is enacting a role that may be perplexing, awkward or even invasive. Their work demonstrates that who we are and who we become in a research setting (and how that all influences what we learn and how we learn) deserves close examination. In many cases, the perspective, positionality and personality of the researcher contributes to many possible intersecting challenges, limitations, and opportunities (Huisman, 2008).

Finally, the first-hand accounts of the research process included here represent the value of interdisciplinary approaches to inquiry. The scholarship showcased here crosses many boundaries within existing and evolving systems, hierarchies and institutions. Through exploring new ways of understanding the processes of research, relationship building and knowledge production – including how difference might be viewed, practiced or reconstituted within established sociocultural, historical, or political realities, we believe that this work provides examples of ways that researchers might begin to consider and delve into issues that they might not have contemplated as deeply or as regularly. By engaging in and stimulating further dialogue about research processes and practices, the chapters in this volume illustrate the need to find new ways to talk about the process of creating knowledge in contexts framed by difference and new ways to understand and respond to some of the unanticipated circumstances that emerge while engaged in such work. We look forward to continued conversations with others pursuing such work and encountering such challenges.

References

Block, K., Warr, D., Gibbs, L. and Riggs, E. (2012) Addressing ethical and methodological challenges in research with refugee-background young people: reflections from the field. *Journal of Refugee Studies* 26 (1), 69–87.

Block, K., Riggs, E. and Haslam, N. (eds) (2013) *Values and Vulnerabilities: The Ethics of Research with Refugees and Asylum Seekers*. Toowong QLD: Australian Academic Press.

Boellstorff, T., Nardi, B., Pearce, C. and Taylor, T.L. (2012) *Ethnography and Virtual Worlds: A Handbook of Method*. Princeton: Princeton University Press.

Creswell, (2016) *30 Essential Skills for the Qualitative Researcher*. Los Angeles: SAGE.

DeCosta, P. (ed.) (2015) *Ethics in Applied Linguistics Research: Language Researcher Narratives*. New York City: Routledge.

Hugman, R., Bartolomei, L. and Pittaway, E. (2011) Human agency and the meaning of informed consent: Reflections on research with refugees. *Journal of Refugee Studies* 24, 655–671.

Huisman, K. (2008) 'Does this mean you're not going to come visit me anymore?': An inquiry into an ethics of reciprocity and positionality in feminist ethnographic research. *Sociological Inquiry* 78 (3), 372–396.

Jacobsen, K. and Landau, L.B. (2003) The dual imperative in refugee research: Some methodological and ethical considerations in social science research on forced migration. *Disasters* 27 (3), 185–206.

MacKenzie, C., McDowell, C. and Pittaway, E. (2007) Beyond 'do no harm': the challenge of constructing ethical relationships in refugee research. *Journal of Refugee Studies* 20 (2), 299–319.

Mayan, M.J. (2016) *Essentials of Qualitative Inquiry* (2nd edn). New York: Routledge.

Merriam, S.B. and Tisdell, E.J. (2016) *Qualitative Research: A Guide to Design and Implementation* (4th edn). Hoboken, NJ: Jossey Bass/ Wiley.

Ngo, B., Bigelow, M. and Lee, S. (eds) (2014) Introduction: What does it mean to do ethical and engaged research with immigrant communities? Special issue: Research with immigrant communities. *Diaspora, Indigenous and Migrant Education* 8 (1), 1–6.

Olson, K. (2011/2016) *Essentials of Qualitative Interviewing*. New York: Routledge.

Saldaña, J. (2016) *The Coding Manual for Qualitative Researchers* (3rd edn). Los Angeles: Sage.

Seidman, I. (2013) *Interviewing as Qualitative Research: A Guide for Researchers in Education and the Social Sciences* (4th edn). New York: Teachers College Press.

Voutira, E. and Dona, G. (2007) Refugee research methodologies: Consolidation and transformation of a field. *Journal of Refugee Studies* 20 (2), 163–171.

Part 1: Language, Culture and Identity

1 'I have so many things to tell you, but I don't know English': Linguistic Challenges and Language Brokering

Chatwara Suwannamai Duran

In 2009, I received a forwarded email, originally written by a volunteer, who worked with a Phoenix-based refugee resettlement agency. She wrote that she taught English to newly-arrived refugee families, predominantly from Burma,[1] and 'help them get started in Arizona.' She hoped to recruit more volunteers to work with the families at the refugees' homes. I was excited about being a volunteer and emailed her for more details. She promptly replied:

> 'These refugees speak a variety of tribal languages, but also some Burmese, Lao and Thai.' (E-mail conversation, 16 September 2009)

After a few more email exchanges with her, I learned that many refugees are very homesick and in need of friends. The volunteer added, 'Just having someone to talk to them in their native language and encourage them would be a big help' and 'Some of the teenagers – they speak Thai very well but they are having difficulty learning English.' She expressed that she knew some Thai words and that 'there is a lot lost in translation' during communication with these newcomers. She believed that native Thai or Burmese speakers would be better able to help these refugees in some way.

Being a native speaker of Thai, who has had first-hand experiences of acculturation in the USA, and being a graduate student in the field of language and literacy education at the time, I enthusiastically offered my assistance without hesitation. Through the volunteer work, I was introduced to many Karenni families in town, whose multiple languages, literacy practices, and skills not only intrigued me but also augmented my understanding of the linguistic complexity of refugees from Burma. I enjoyed weekly visits and hangouts, teaching English at their homes, helping with the children's homework, accompanying the parents on errands, and giving them rides. Eventually, my volunteer work evolved into a dissertation research project. The primary goal of the project was to document and analyze the Karenni refugees' out-of-school multilingual resources (Canagarajah, 2009; Kramsch, 2009) through the lens of language socialization in bilingual and multilingual communities (Bayley & Schecter, 2003; Duff, 2011; Fogle, 2012).

In this chapter, I examine and reflect on my experiences as a researcher working in this context, the methods and approaches I used, and the challenges I encountered while working with recently-arrived Karenni families who were originally from Burma but who had lived in Thailand's fenced refugee camp for at least fifteen years prior to coming to Phoenix, Arizona. The Karenni families I worked with spoke, read and wrote languages that are considered (by applied linguists) to be Less Commonly Taught Languages (LCTLs) in the USA. These families are underserved because of their unrecognized languages in their host nation. Lack of linguistic knowledge to communicate with marginalized populations has become an issue of linguistic inequality, and for my part, I was eager to learn from the families. In my multiple roles (e.g. as a tutor, family mentor and friend to the families), I drew on a range of linguistic resources to communicate on a regular basis. Working to negotiate meaning with each other, the participants and I relied on our multilingual repertoires and a variety of strategic communication such as translating and interpreting (converting one language to another involving a dictionary or a bi/multilingual person) and code-switching (using two or more linguistic codes). Some participants and I also communicated in English, a language that had come, over time, to serve as a lingua franca. With some of the participants' family members, I spoke Thai because they had learned Thai as an additional language when they lived in the refugee camps in Thailand. (Participants' detailed linguistic inventories are discussed below.) All of these communicative techniques and languages were used contingently among the Karenni families and me.

While working to establish relationships I began to question my role as a university-based researcher that was distant from the refugee participants in addition to my previous roles as a volunteer tutor and a friend. I had been trying to find and use transparent and culturally-sensitive approaches to understand the lived experiences and views of the multilingual participants who had been minoritized and underrepresented throughout their life trajectories. I knew that language was a key in both *data* and *process* (Green & Thorogood, 2004) and that attempting to complete the project involved unlocking multiple communicative languages. I was afraid that things wouldn't work. Therefore, I tried to recall what worked in my previous communication with the participant families so that I could use those approaches and methods in the research setting. My worries included how to present what I learned from the participants to a wider audience, who were not there with me during the data collection period.

In the literature on conducting research in/with/for minoritized and marginalized communities, researchers sometimes mention the fact that they encounter cross-cultural differences that present challenges similar to mine when dealing with linguistic diversity. In many cases, employing translators/interpreters is recommended as a way to solve communication difficulties. Knowing this, I first looked for translators/interpreters for my project because the participants and I did not share the same native language. However, as the scholarship shows (Edwards, 1998; Liamputtong, 2010; Temple, 1997), there are drawbacks even with this approach. For example, researchers have to depend on translators/interpreters' 'certain extent for perspective' and that might not be the research participant's perspective (Temple, 1997: 608). This is because translators/interpreters' views are influenced by 'their own lived experiences' (Liamputtong, 2010: 150–151). *Professional* translators/interpreters in particular appear to be strangers to the research participants, who may not wish an outsider to know about or be an interpreter for them when they express their important yet sensitive issues (Edwards, 1998). In addition, professional translators/interpreters tend to select word choice that is more formal than what the participants really say or what they intend to convey (Tsai *et al.*, 2004). Other difficulties include the translators/interpreters' focus on verbal language without non-verbal signal and cultural meaning (Liamputtong, 2010).

During my fieldwork, I came across the term Language/Linguistic Brokering (LB), meant to capture the practices used for translating and interpreting both in formal communication (e.g. at a doctor's clinic) and informal conversation but with linguistically and culturally sensitive and comprehensible approaches. That is, in addition to translating and interpreting words similar to translators and interpreters, language brokers also serve as linguistic, cultural, and knowledge mediators (Tse, 1996a). They are also known as 'cultural brokers' who provide culturally-contextualized explanation. American Speech-Hearing-Language Association (ASHA) has defined a language broker as a person who knows the client's speech community, environment, sociolinguistic norms, and community-related information (ASHA, 2016). In this way, as Liamputtong (2010) emphasized, the involvement of a language-cultural broker helps researchers understand the participants' local culture, 'avoid social errors, and sustain good relationships' (2010: 67) with the participants. Within this framework, LB is a social, cultural, methodological, and professional practice and technique rather than a theory.

In educational research, Wenger (1998) defined 'brokering' as 'connecting' people and creating continuities across boundaries (1998: 103). Brokers are members of multiple communities and therefore can be agents of these communities. As I considered my ethnographic study to be a collaborative venture with deep roots in a community of practice where my participants – both children and adults – and I learned from one another, I adopted this concept and technique of brokering and connecting, with my goal being to unlock the participants' linguistic and cultural meaning as well as creating interpersonal relationship and learning opportunities between the broker and brokee (Lee *et al.*, 2011).

However, the pathway to incorporating LB was not as easy as it seemed. At first, based on the definition of LB above, combined with the communicative techniques that the participants and I had been using, and the amicable relationship that the participants and I had established, I believed that I could recruit language brokers from the participants' very own community. In fact, it took me some time to figure out how to manage to use LB at the research site. In the remainder of this chapter, I focus on the processes, complications, and outcomes of employing LB in my research. In the first section 'So close but yet so far', I reflect on insider/outsider issues that drove me to find a solution for cross-linguistic data collection. I include dilemmas from the research process that remain unaddressed even to this day. Second, I discuss demands and complexities of the linguistic diversity and conflicting logistics that emerged when I tried to employ LB. I highlight 'linguistic inventory' that I used both to resolve the linguistic puzzle and to match an interviewee with the right language broker due to each participant and language broker's unique multilingual repertoires. Third, I discuss what I gained from these multi-layered processes. Apart from a better understanding of the participants' socio-historical and cultural backgrounds, LB particularly had a significant role in building relationships between the participants and me on the research site. Altogether, this chapter highlights the value of multilingual practices in general, and language brokering in particular, that might be used to create rapport and understanding between researchers and researched.

So Close But Yet So Far

My research was a collaborative undertaking involving researchers and research participants, who shared similar backgrounds yet pertaining insider/outsider issues (Liamputtong, 2010). I felt that I was an insider of the participants' community considering my own immigrant status in the USA and my use of English as a second language (Kusow, 2003). The Karenni families seemed delighted to interact with me, perhaps because they had lived in Thailand for many years before arriving in the USA, and they communicated with me using Thai, English, Karenni, and code-switching of all the languages they knew. We also shared several Southeast-Asian cultural practices and beliefs (e.g. taking off shoes before entering one's house, sitting on the floor comfortably, welcoming both invited and unexpected guests by offering food no matter what time it is, eating rice as the main carbohydrate source, celebrating social and cultural events in accordance with the lunar calendar). At the same time, there were also differences in our historical and educational backgrounds and immigration experiences that made me an outsider (Kusow, 2003). Most participants had lived a rural lifestyle with agricultural backgrounds and limited formal schooling. They had experienced war, persecution, and lived in a remote refugee camp. After arriving in the USA, they lived in a socio-economically disadvantaged neighborhood, where there was a high crime rate. All of the Karenni families I worked with lived below the poverty line and were eligible for food stamps. My background, conversely, was described as 'educated' and 'having no problems' by the participants. I had had more than 20 years of formal schooling; earned a college degree, came to the USA as an international graduate student, and have benefited from an American middle-class lifestyle.

Despite the differences, both the participants and I worked hard to get to know each other and build rapport. I adjusted how I presented myself (e.g. I dressed down when visiting their home and neighborhood) and timed my visits so that they would work with their schedules. I communicated my availability and demonstrated my sincerity by helping the refugee parents when they needed help with translating documents that came in the mail, obtaining services they needed (e.g. auto insurance, truck rental, doctor's clinic, drugstore) and assisting their children with their homework. In return, the Karenni families offered me food and company. After many months of regular visits, it seemed that I had gained their trust and respect, and there was a level of comfort between us. Over time, these families (and even their neighbors) began to affectionately call me 'saramo'[2] (teacher), allowed me to take their children to stores, events, churches, and restaurants; and invited me to their community meetings and social gatherings.

Although a rapport had been established, the participants and I did not share the same native language. Hesitation to talk about complicated issues that needed lexical knowledge in a second language sometimes prevented the participants from speaking up (Kosny *et al.*, 2014). Sometimes, during a conversation, when the participants couldn't find a word in the language that I understood, we skipped the unsolved part, avoided certain topics, or even changed the subject. During one of my visits to their apartment units, Sherry, a 45-year-old mother, said to me, 'When you come to my house, I have many things to tell you. But, I don't know English.' All of these experiences made me realize that many stories might go untold as a result of our language differences, even though they wanted to catch up with me as much as I wanted to learn more about them and their families. The participants blamed their limited English proficiency while I blamed the fact that I did not speak Karenni or Burmese.

I enjoyed socializing with the participants, collecting artifacts during my visits and observations (e.g. documents and photos) and taking field notes, but I became pre-occupied with the linguistic challenges facing us. As a result, planning to conduct interviews with three families (16 individuals) living in the same apartment complex was delicate, particularly because each participant had a unique linguistic repertoire. Attempting to find a way to manage the linguistic challenges, I asked myself many questions, including: How can data collection be done in multiple languages? What language should I use as a medium of communication? Should I work with interpreters? Professional ones? Where can I find them? Can I ask the participants to be my interpreter? Surprisingly, participant children responded well with my weekly presence and appeared to be natural interpreters, helping their parents and neighbors and bridging the linguistic gap in countless conversations. I saw some solutions, but more questions emerged. For instance, I wondered whether it was okay to ask the children to act as interpreters. What kind of ethical issues might come up if I did? To work through these questions and identify which methodological approaches to consider, I reviewed scholarship on research methods and cross-cultural communication with a focus on how to work effectively and respectfully with minoritized and marginalized populations. I also reflected on how my relationship with the participants seemed to be influenced by my insider/outsider status – i.e. by the fact that I was not an outsider but I was also not a complete insider to the community (Kusow, 2003). Taking all of this into consideration, I decided to try out a few different approaches.

Linguistic Inventory and the Path from Interpreting to Language Brokering

One of the challenges that came up early on during my work with the Karenni refugees was that each family seemed to speak a different variety of a language associated with their ethnic group. Burma, the refugees' country of origin, has at least 130 subgroups and 117 living languages. Under the term Karenni, which is an eastern state of Burma, individuals and families from different villages and regions of the Karenni State may speak different dialects or even languages. For example, the participants claimed that 'Kayah or Karenni' and 'Kayan,' which linguists considered as 'various Kayan clusters' (Dudley, 2010: 12), were not mutually intelligible. The participants explained that Kayan was learned and spoken particularly by the long-neck group (those with brass neck rings) in Lai-Go village. Despite the linguistic diversity, the participants called themselves Karenni because of their shared pride and geographical origin of the Karenni State. They also do so to distinguish themselves from those from Chin, Mon, Kachin, Karen, Rakhine and Shan states of Burma.

Even more complicated, because many Karenni participants spoke what they called 'a small language', they have had to learn other languages to communicate with other ethnic groups, and such interethnic communications had been a vital part of their lives since they lived in Burma and Thailand. Some also said they could speak Karen, which is a big umbrella term that covers many different Karenic languages such as Gekho, Pa-o,

Sgaw, among others. In addition, members from the same family might have different levels of proficiency in different languages. For example, in one family of four, the parents spoke Kayan to one another but spoke Burmese and Karenni to their children because their children could not communicate in Kayan. In addition to managing the linguistic differences between us, interpreters helped with logistics (e.g. scheduling the participants for formal interviews) and this was especially useful when interviewees felt ambivalent to speaking English as a lingua franca. In all, most of my participants speak LCTLs and it was difficult to find professional interpreters for these languages in the Phoenix area where I collected data at the time of data collection. I, therefore, aimed to identify people from the community who might serve as an interpreter even if untrained.

Documenting the participants' multilingual repertoires, which was the goal of my research, required a linguistic inventory. In turn, this inventory helped me identify potential interpreters. Because I had known the participants for over a year before the formal interviews, I was able to draw linguistic profiles of each individual based on several informal conversations, my observations of their daily practices, and my examination of artifacts collected from the participants' homes. This allowed me to map the family background with the large part of each member's linguistic inventory, especially their oral communication in each language during the data collection period (see Table 1.1). Their proficiency level in each language was based on my observation of their daily language and literacy practices. It may not be applicable to proficiency levels assessed by any formal institution.

Table 1.1 shows the overlapping linguistic repertoires among the participants. I could identify those who could speak intermediate to advanced Thai or English in addition to their native languages. Some were adults, and some were children. In the field of behavioral sciences and education, language brokers are defined as children assisting their immigrant parents linguistically in 'adult-like' communication such as in teacher-parent conference at school, in the hospital, or at a financial institution (DeMent & Buriel, 1999; Morales & Hanson, 2005; McQuillan & Tse, 1995). Scholars have found that LB influences the cognitive, social, and academic development of multilingual children and adolescents who habitually practice LB for their families (Morales & Hanson, 2005; Orellana, 2009). Others add that individuals (regardless of age) draw on their multilingual repertoires to understand and articulate both linguistic and complex cultural components within the local communities they are in as language brokers (McQuillan & Tse, 1995). These scholarly perspectives have informed my own practices as well as how I socialized with the participants. Through weekly visits, I have found that some of my multilingual Karenni participants, both adults and children, were spontaneous interpreters on the research site. They explained the meaning of words with a nuanced understanding of the cultural and historical dimensions of those words. I saw their talents emerge as they became language brokers and offered insights based on their own

Table 1.1 Linguistic inventory of participants

Family	Name	Place of Birth	Age*	Primary Language(s)**	Other Language(s) Learned and Proficiency Level***
Teh Reh's Family	Teh Reh (M)****	Karenni State, Burma	33	Karenni	advanced Burmese, intermediate Thai, intermediate Shan, intermediate to upper intermediate English
	Loh Meh (F)		36	Karenni	advanced Burmese functional English
	See Meh (F)	Ban Mai Nai Soi Refugee Camp, Thailand	15	Karenni	advanced Thai, intermediate Karen, upper intermediate English
	Gu-Gu (M)		7	Karenni	functional to intermediate English
	Ngee-Ngee (M)		7	Karenni	
Ka Paw's Family	Ka Paw (M)	Lai-go Village, Karenni State, Burma	43	Kayan***** Burmese	functional Karenni functional English
	Sherry (F)		46	Kayan	advanced Burmese advanced Karenni functional English
	Daw (F)	Ban Mai Nai Soi Refugee Camp, Thailand	14	Burmese	advanced Karenni intermediate English
	Je Ru (M)		9	Burmese	advanced Karenni functional to intermediate English

Nway Meh's Family	Nway Meh (F)	Karenni State, Burma	45	Karenni	–
	Boe Meh (F)		70	Karenni	–
	Hla Meh (F)		18	Karenni	advanced Burmese intermediate English
	Saw Reh (M)	Ban Mai Nai Soi Refugee Camp, Thailand	15	Karenni	intermediate Burmese intermediate English functional Karen
	Sha Reh (M)		12	Karenni	intermediate Burmese intermediate English
	Toh Reh (M)		9	Karenni	intermediate English
	Eh Reh (M)		5	Karenni	functional English

*The participants' age during my formal data collection period.
**Primary Language is the language one speaks and knows best in both depth and breadth.
***Proficiency levels: **functional** = sufficient to communicate but in a very limited way, or only the situation one is familiar with, **intermediate** = handle many speaking, listening, reading and writing tasks, especially for their routine work and for educational purposes, **upper intermediate** = have all speaking, listening, reading and writing skills in both work and personal contexts, **advanced** = have all skills for both basic and complex content/subject matter and communicative situation, comfortable to communicate in a demanding setting that may require to learn challenging terms so quickly (adapted from Berlitz's Proficiency Level, 2016).
**** (M) = male, (F) = female
*****Kayan (pronounced /kajaŋ/) is a distinct language. On the other hand, Karenni, Kaya, and Kayah are referred to Karenni.

speech community, sociolinguistic norms, and cultural knowledge. Without being asked, they willingly served as interpreters, especially for their family members, neighbors, and close friends. For example, See Meh, a 14-year-old female participant, who spoke, read, and wrote Thai very well, happily helped me and her Karenni-speaking mother, Loh Meh.

In one of the interviews with Loh Meh, when we had difficulty communicating about Loh Meh's childhood and life trajectories, See Meh assisted me by adding more information to her mother's answers for me to understand the sociocultural and historical backgrounds. For example, when asked about educational background, Loh Meh said that she went to school and passed 'Poh Paed'. I understood that Paed means 'eight' in Thai and thought it was equivalent to 8th grade. However, See Meh clarified, 'เป็นครูได้' [can be a teacher] which means that her mother received enough education to be qualified as a teacher. She explained that the educational system in the Karenni state and in the refugee camp was different from others, namely the Thai and American systems that I am familiar with. In fact, Loh Meh had worked as a teacher of Karenni and Burmese in the refugee camp for more than five years. The insights from See Meh underlined Loh Meh's life trajectories for my understanding. I became more comfortable and certain with having language brokers from the participants' community, who could fill the gap between my insider and outsider statuses. Although language brokers from the participants' community were not professionally trained, they have close ties and they share linguistic and cultural backgrounds with the participants (ASHA, 2016). In addition, See Meh also told me that she hoped to maintain Thai and she wanted to practice multiple languages to establish community of support among refugees, who spoke LCTLs, because 'เพื่อพวกเขาต้องการความช่วยเหลือ [it is for them (refugees), when they need help].' As a result, See Meh happily became my regular language broker during our cross-language interviews.Her availability allowed me to schedule interviews with different participants based on the overlapping linguistic repertoires between See Meh, participant(s), and me.

When See Meh was not present, her father Teh Reh,who had oral skills in Burmese, English, Shan, Thai and Karenni, became another language broker. He was comfortable with the LB practices partly because his neighbors, mostly refugees from Burma speaking a variety of languages, often asked him for help with documents (e.g. auto insurance papers, benefit application forms and job application forms). Frequently, I participated in those exchanges because all of us wanted to make sure we understood the documents correctly and that they were responded to appropriately. As a result of these interactions, I realized that See Meh and Teh Reh had had refugee experiences, camp life and struggles in the resettlement processes, similar to other recently-arrived refugees. Therefore, they were acquainted with their refugee neighbors' needs, and wider problems in the community.

LB practices facilitated and strengthened the refugees' co-ethnic and interethnic friendships and linguistic support networks in the apartment complex where LCTL speakers resided. Apart from children-parents interdependent relationships found in language brokering studies (Dorner *et al.*, 2018; Morales & Hanson, 2005; Orellana, 2009), I have found that the web of relationships created among the participants, their co-ethnic friends, neighbors, and their family members provided a mechanism for responding to and managing the challenges involved with using multiple codes in the encounter. Community-based linguistic funds of knowledge were founded, called upon, practiced and valued during the data collection process, especially when Teh Reh or See Meh were unavailable and my interviewee and I did not share a lingua franca. For instance, on the day that I interviewed Nway Meh, who spoke only Karenni, I had to look for neighbors and other participants to assist me. The solution was surprisingly interesting. Our interview was carried out with multiple language brokers. I had recruited Loh Meh, who was Nway Meh's close friend and was available on that day. Loh Meh spoke Karenni, Burmese and English but she was not comfortable with using English as she was afraid that she could not deliver the right message from Karenni to English. Mu Yo, a friend of one of the participants who was fluent in dialects of Karen including Burmese, and English, became a language broker.

In this particular setting, Burmese served as a lingua franca between Loh Meh and Mu Yo, my spur-of-the-moment language brokers. Unlike Loh Meh, Mu Yo was confident in using English. She went to high school in the USA and had been in Phoenix, AZ longer than Loh Meh. Although I started the interview by asking questions in English, Mu Yo often switched to Burmese. When this happened, the message in Burmese was translated into Karenni by Loh Meh. When Nway Meh responded, the message was delivered in Karenni, translated to Burmese by Loh Meh, and translated again from Burmese to English by Mu Yo (see Figure 1.1).

Although I could find multiple language brokers on my research site, my own role was to understand and transcribe the English message when presenting data in the English-based academic arena. The remaining issue that played at the back of my mind was to complete back translation, as I was worried about the multiple translations to gain data and their accuracy in the process. Despite my concern, I did not complete back translations at the time because of my tight schedule and culture-related concern. Readers might say that I could ask my participants and language brokers for more and might even offer them monetary compensation. However, I learned that generosity is a shared value in Karenni and Thai cultures. Giving back to generosity in such cultures is not about offering payment but 'to be considerate' and 'to show concern for their feeling and welfare.'

Researcher	English ⇨	Mu Yo	Burmese ⇨	Loh Meh	Karenni ⇨	Nway Meh
Researcher	⇦ English	Mu Yo	⇦ Burmese	Loh Meh	⇦ Karenni	Nway Meh

Figure 1.1 Multiple language brokers

Because I had been their friend, not an employer, in the first place, giving them a payment could be interpreted as an insult to their genuine generosity and help. On the other hand, asking them to do additional work could be misinterpreted as being inconsiderate.

With these sensitive elements in mind, I did not do any back translation of data, unless the data were Thai and English, which I checked for accuracy myself. I later realised, after consulting literature on research methods in education, that back translation is in fact more common and most relevant when the research method, not the data part, involves written materials such as test development, surveys and questionnaires (Chapman & Carter, 1979; Peña, 2007).

Another feature of LB practices in my project was its applicability in and across all age groups. As I planned to collect data from young children, I learned that formal interviews did not work because of young children's short attention span and the generation gap between an adult researcher and young children (Orellana, 2009). Therefore, apart from observations, I played and talked with them as a group on topics they showed an interest in, such as about hobbies and video games. We used English as a lingua franca and they responded well to these approaches as they had known me as their English tutor. However, the youngest participant, Eh Reh (5), who had just started kindergarten, spoke entirely in Karenni. I conversed with him by using English, hand gestures, and vocabulary cards. But, to have a longer conversation with Eh Reh, his oldest sister Hla Meh, and his closest brother, Toh Reh, were language brokers, who not only helped me connect with Eh Reh, but also provided more information about him, such as his favorite activities and games.

It could be viewed as an ethical issue when children become language brokers for their friends, family members, and their researcher (me). Much research has reported that child language brokers feel frustration and pressure when language brokering for their parents (McQuillan & Tse, 1995; Rumbaut, 1994; Weisskirch & Alva, 2002). Apart from using consent and assent forms to inform parents and children that the children would be observed and asked questions, I had to be assured that the children were willing to participate on their own terms when I was at the research site. An example of children's voluntary language brokering was when 9-year old Toh Reh heard the conversation between me and his family members, and when he abruptly jumped into the discussion, I let him participate. Because my research explored multilingual repertoires among the refugee families, children's voluntary language-brokering practices are not only a part of the research methods but also the research findings, and provided theoretical contributions to multilingual children's agency as the research went along (see also Duran, 2014).

Another concern may be raised as to the reliability and validity of information gained from children (Tse, 1996b). This issue is debatable as there are two camps of thought in the studies of child language brokers. Those who are against the practice of child language brokers found that young age and proficiency levels have a negative effect on accuracy (Coleman, 2003). On the contrary, much research argues that child language brokers have developed sophisticated lexicons for different contexts and situations. They become more mature through these linguistic tasks (Diaz-Lazaro, 2002; Halgunseth, 2003; Orellana, 2009; Shannon, 1990). I was not aware of this controversy during the time of my data collection. In retrospect, as my ethnographic study that emphasizes 'thick-description' not numbers by nature (Geertz, 1994: 213–232) and involved multiple qualitative methods, I employed and triangulated data from multiple sources to increase credibility and accuracy. The methods included observation, document collection, and informal conversation with teachers, parents, friends, and siblings in addition to collecting data from children and multiple interviews (Denzin, 1978; Patton, 1999). I mentioned in the introduction that there are some unresolved issues to this day. Many sets of data from multiple methods that are not translatable or not sortable to be included for answering my original dissertation research questions are still there to be further studied if my future research questions guide me back to them.

What I Have Learned and Gained

Working with multi-layered data collection with linguistic diversity is inevitable when working with minoritized populations who come from linguistic backgrounds different from those of researchers. In the following, I discuss and reflect on the complexity of what I learned, how I learned it, and what I have gained from incorporating LB in a principled way in my research.

Learning and clarifying cultural knowledge and sensitive issues

Collaborating with participants who served as language brokers, I gained insights into the participants' historical and cultural backgrounds. For example, when I asked my adult participants for their date of birth, which was common in interviewing about life history, Teh Reh explained that it was difficult for most Karenni adults to answer this question because they rarely know their exact date of birth. He said that those who were born in the Karenni state usually did not have any record of this because their place of birth was so remote and mountainous that hospitals and officials were scarcely available. For legal purposes, many Karenni adults had 1 January followed by Christian year (A.D.) as their date of birth on their ID card. This date and year were officially determined by the refugee resettlement agents/officials, who helped them process an application for a refugee ID card, or what many refugees call a 'UN' card. Consequently, adult refugees' real age may be different from their *legal* age. Having this understanding in mind, I carefully asked this question to other participants and listened for more explanation from them. For instance, in an interview with Nway Meh, See Meh served as a language broker. I asked Nway Meh for her age instead of her date of birth. Nway Meh told me in Karenni that she was 35. Because we had See Meh with us, I told her that she could tell me her real age. Nway Meh explained in Karenni to See Meh, 'Actually, I am not thirty five. I am forty-five but my UN card says 35.' Unlike the problematic situation mentioned earlier that participants might avoid or skip a complicated subject because they did not know how to explain a certain matter in English, an available language broker on site allowed them to communicate insights in their native language.

Another interesting session was in an interview with Ka Paw. See Meh was our language broker, Thai and Karenni. When asked about his parents, Ka Paw said that his father died when he was young and he was separated from his mother during the war in Burma. It got emotional when he added, 'I don't know if she is still alive.' Without really thinking things through, I asked him, 'ติดต่อไม่ได้เหรอ' [Can't you try to contact her?]. See Meh, who understood the circumstances of refugees from Burma said, 'ติดต่อไม่ได้ค่ะพม่ากับเมืองไทย' [Between the borders, Burma and Thailand, it's impossible to communicate there]. As See Meh was there to help him explain such a sensitive issue, Ka Paw said that he had been safe because he was outside Burma but if his mother was still alive, contacting her risked her life. I, then, understood much more than the literal meaning of the words he used; I came to see that the political issues had affected an individual at a personal level and the refugees' perspectives here were invaluable for the understanding of their experiences. From the examples, language brokers encompass linguistic, cultural, and historical knowledge that is necessary, yet infrequently known, for university-based researchers, educators, service providers, and policy makers to understand refugees' backgrounds. In my project, although the participants and I are from similar Southeast Asian cultural backgrounds, our life trajectories are compellingly different. What I have learned from LB practices is added to both my personal and professional growth as a researcher, becoming more culturally sensitive and detail-oriented.

Relationship building

Research on the use of interpreters or translators with refugee families shows that they can also serve as gatekeepers to participants' information and adopt an authoritative role in (re)presenting the data and interpretation (Liamputtong, 2010). However, my experience working with language brokers demonstrated to me how valuable it is to build relationships, understanding, and trust. When I was at my research site, I demonstrated my understanding that I was less aware of their cultural practices than the language brokers might be. In addition, when there was a language broker at hand, I encouraged all of my participants to ask me about anything, even my personal life. This active nurturing of the relationship and trust assisted us in the process of self-disclosure and mutual reciprocity, i.e. the 'personal' information was exchanged both ways. Some participants, for instance, asked me about my childhood in Thailand, experiences of dating in American culture, problems I had in the USA, and educational experiences in an American college. Often, interviews became an engaging group-based protocol rather than a one-on-one basis because of the language brokers' involvement. The participants were comfortable to share information with the language broker, who was from the participants' community and whom they were familiar with. I see this as an opportunity, not only in developing our relationship as researcher and researched, but also in maintaining multiple roles as friend and mentor in both work and play arenas.

Remaining Challenges and Conclusion

Insights from my work with the recently-arrived Karenni families in Phoenix, Arizona showed that challenges in collecting data started during the very beginning, in large part because of the participants' unique multilingual repertoires and because the participants and I did not share a native language. Through experimenting with different approaches, reflecting on how things went, and reading scholarships on the challenges of conducting research with marginalized and vulnerable populations (e.g. Liamputtong, 2007; Pitts & Smith, 2007), I came to understand that different approaches might be used at different times and for different purposes. I discovered that utilizing LB practices enabled me to communicate with the participants, including their transnational network, and illuminated their historical and cultural backgrounds. Despite the increasing number of refugees worldwide, there are still very few professional interpreters who can directly translate/interpret a dominant language of the host community to 'a small language', which is a native language of many displaced groups, and vice versa. Recruiting, training, and supporting potential language brokers from the refugee participants' own community will benefit service providers and newly-arrived refugees, who need to access many unfamiliar resources and services during their transition.

It is important to note that a number of important questions and challenges remain unsolved. For example, I continue to wrestle with decisions about how to present the data that I have – should I present all of the languages involved in the transcription of the data? How so? What is important in the presentation of data, the direct answer from the interviewee or the translated version of the data from the language brokers? Other issues include: should we or how do we introduce our language brokers, who work backstage and are rarely mentioned in published research, to readers and audience? I may not have the best answers. But, for my dissertation and publications, my linguistic choice depends on my research questions, the emphasized content, the messages being conveyed, and what strengthens my argument in each piece. Other researchers may have different solutions to these issues depending on their goals in conducting a study, and approaches to analyze their data. Nevertheless, I believe researchers' genuine interest, cultural and linguistic awareness and sensitivity, and responsibility to participants' well-being will induce the most realistic and thoughtful methods in a given research context.

Notes

(1) I use Burma, officially known as Myanmar, in this chapter based on how my refugee participants use and understand it.
(2) The word 'saramo' [teacher] contains the meaning of respect, rapport, connection and trust.

References

ASHA (2016) Collaborating with interpreters. See http://www.asha.org/PRPSpecificTopic.aspx?folderid=8589935334&section=Overview#Role_of_Cultural_and_Linguistic_Brokers (accessed 25 February 2016).

Bayley, R. and Schecter, S. (2003) *Language Socialization in Bilingual and Multilingual Societies*. Clevedon: Multilingual Matters.

Berlitz Languages, Inc. (2016) Proficiency Levels. See http://www.berlitz.us/language-proficiency-testing-assessment/ (accessed 25 February 2016).

Canagarajah, S. (2009) The plurilingual tradition and the English language in South Asia. *AILA Review*, 22, 5–22.

Chapman, D.W. and Carter, J.F. (1979) Translation procedures for the cross cultural use of measurement instruments. *Educational Evaluation and Policy Analysis* 1 (3), 71–76.

DeMent, T. and Buriel, R. (1999, August). Children as cultural brokers: Recollections of college students. Paper presented at the SPSSI Conference on Immigrants and Immigration, Toronto, Canada.

Denzin, N.K. (1978) *Sociological Methods*. New York: McGraw-Hill.

Diaz-Lazaro, C.M. (2002) The effects of language brokering on perceptions of family authority structure, problem solving abilities, and parental locus of control in Latino adolescents and their parents. Unpublished doctoral dissertation, State University of New York at Buffalo.

Dorner, L., Orellana, M.F. and Jimenez, R. (2018) 'It's one of those things that you do to help the family': Language brokering and the development of immigrant adolescents. *Journal of Adolescents Research* 23 (5), 515–543.

Dudley, S.H. (2010) *Materialising Exile: Material Culture and Embodied Experience among Karenni Refugees in Thailand*. New York: Berghahn Books.

Duff, P. (2011) Second language socialization. In A. Duranti, E. Ochs and B. Schieffelin (eds) *Handbook of Language Socialization*. New York: Blackwell.

Duran, C.S. (2014) Theorizing agency among young language learners through the lens of multilingual reportoires: A socio-cultural perspective. In P. Deters, E.R. Miller and G. Vitanova (eds) *Theorizing and Analyzing Agency in Second Language Learning: Interdisciplinary Approaches* (pp. 73–90). Bristol: Multilingual Matters.

Edwards, R. (1998) Connecting method and epistemology: A white woman interviewing black women. *Women's Studies International Forum* 13 (5), 477–490.

Fogle, L.W. (2012) *Second Language Socialization and Learner Agency*. Bristol: Multilingual Matters.

Geertz, C. (1994) Thick description: Toward an interpretive theory of culture. In M. Martin and L.C. McIntyre (eds.) *Reading in the Philosophy of Social Science* (pp. 213–232). Cambridge, MA: MIT.

Green, J. and Thorogood, N. (2004) *Qualitative Methods for Health Research*. London: Sage.

Halgunseth, L. (2003) Language brokering: Positive developmental outcomes. In M. Coleman and L. Ganong (eds) *Points and Counterpoints: Controversial Relationship and Family Issues in the 21st Century: An Anthology* (pp. 154–157). Los Angeles, CA: Roxbury.

Hennink, M.M. (2008) Language and communication in cross-cultural qualitative research. In P. Liamputthong (ed.) *Doing Cross-Cultural Research: Ethical and Methodological Perspectives* (pp. 21–33). Netherlands: Springer.

Kosny, A., MacEachen, E., Lifshen, M. and Smith, P. (2014) Another person in the room: Using interpreters during interviews with immigrant workers. *Qualitative Health Research* 24 (6), 837–845. doi: 10.1177/1049732314535666.

Kramsch, C. (2009) *The Multilingual Subject*. Oxford: Oxford University Press.

Kusow, A. (2003) Beyond indigenous authenticity: Reflections on the insider/outsider debate in immigration research. *Symbolic Interaction* 26 (4), 591–599.

Lee, J.S., Hill-Bonnet, L. and Raley, J. (2011) Examining the effects of language brokering on student identities and learning opportunities in dual immersion classrooms. *Journal of Language, Identity, and Education,* 10 (5), 306–326.

Liamputtong, P. (2007) *Researching the Vulnerable: A Guide to Sensitive Research Methods*. London: Sage Publications.

Liamputtong, P. (2010) *Performing Qualitative Cross-Cultural Research*. Cambridge: Cambridge University Press.

McQuillan, J. and Tse, L. (1995) Child language brokering in linguistic minority communities: Effects on cultural interaction, cognition, and literacy. *Language and Education* 9 (3), 195–215. doi: 10.1080/09500789509541413.

Morales, A. and Hanson, W.E. (2005) Language brokering: An integrative review of the literature. *Hispanic Journal of Behavioral Sciences* 27 (4), 471–503. doi: 10.1177/0739986305281333.

Moyer, M. (2013) Language as a resource: Migrant agency, positioning and resistance in a health care clinic. In A. Duchêne, M. Moyer and C. Roberts (eds) *Language, Migration and Social Inequalities: A Critical Sociolinguistic Perspective on Institutions and Work* (pp. 196–224). Bristol: Multilingual Matters.

Orellana, M.F. (2009) *Translating Childhood: Immigrant Youth, Language, and Culture*. New Brunswick, NJ: Rutgers University Press.

Patton, M.Q. (1999) Enhancing the quality and credibility of qualitative analysis. *Health Services Research* 34 (5) 1189–1208.

Peña, E.D. (2007) Lost in translation: Methodological considerations in cross-cultural research. *Society for Research in Child Development* 78 (4), 1255–1264.

Pitts, M. and Smith, A. (2007) *Researching the Margins: Strategies for Ethical and Rigorous Research with Marginalized Communities*. New York, NY: Palgrave Macmillian.

Rumbaut, R.G. (1994) The crucible within: Ethnic identity, self-esteem, and segmented assimilation among children of immigrants. *International Migration Review* 28, 748–795.

Shannon, S.M. (1990) English in the barrio: The quality of contact among immigrant children. *Hispanic Journal of Behavioral Sciences* 12 (3), 256–276.

Taylor, D. and Dorsey-Gaines, C. (1988) *Growing Up Literate*. Portsmouth, NH: Heinemann.

Temple, B. (1997) Issues in translation and cross-cultural research. *Sociology* 31 (3), 607–618.

Tsai, J.H, Choe, J.H., Lim, J.M.C., Acorda, E., Chan, N.L., Taylor, V. and Tu, S. (2004) Developing culturally competent health knowledge: Issues of data analysis of cross-cultural, cross-language qualitative research. *International Journal of Qualitative Methods* 3 (4), 16–27. doi: 10.1177/160940690400300402.

Tse, L. (1996a) Language brokering in linguistic minority communities: The case of Chinese- and Vietnamese-American students. *The Bilingual Research Journal* 20 (3&4), 485–498. doi: 10.1080/15235882.1996.10668640.

Tse, L. (1996b) Who decides? The effects of language brokering on home-school communication. *Journal of Educational Issues of Language Minority Students* 16, 225–234.

Weisskirch, R.S. and Alva, S.A. (2002) Language brokering and the acculturation of Latino children. *Hispanic Journal of Behavioral Sciences* 24 (3), 369–378.

Wenger, E. (1998) *Communities of Practice: Learning, Meaning, and Identity* (1st edn). Cambridge: Cambridge University Press.

2 Revisiting Our Understandings in Ethnographic Research

Ayfer Gokalp

Ethnographic research in minority communities provides social science researchers with the opportunity to be involved in the world of the participants in order to build a deep understanding of their social and daily life practices. However, this method naturally comes with many challenges and limitations. In this chapter, I argue that these challenges could become resources for ethnographic research by inspiring methodological modifications and enriching the strategies used during the research process. I present my reflections on an ethnographic research project I conducted in a Kurdish community near the Syrian border in Turkey along with the implications of these practices to rethink our understanding of ethnographic research methods. After introducing the background of the study and the methods I employed, I discuss how I responded to the challenges I encountered and the complexities of the situation largely due to the multiplicity of my positions as a researcher. For instance, I describe and analyze the opportunities and constraints I faced while conducting research with young children. As an outsider to the native language of my participants, I reflect on the strategies I used to understand the complex and multilingual structure of my research field as a resource in my data gathering process. I conclude with sharing recommendations and unanswered questions for researchers who wish to conduct ethnographic research in a minority community and also for researchers who wish to include young children in their research.

Research Context

This study mainly evolved from the goals I had to bring the real life experiences and voices of Kurdish children, an understudied group, into academic conversations about language learning, language maintenance, cultural identity, and bi/multilingualism. I became particularly interested in Kurdish children's experiences because all discussions, even ones on the educational needs of Kurdish children, were heavily politicized and influenced by the larger social context in Turkey. The children's native language, Kurdish, and their identities as speakers of that language were important because of the way language practices and policies were applied in Turkey. I investigated the linguistic practices of Kurdish children at grass roots levels to develop an understanding of the daily language practices of children at home and school. My research in a Kurdish community documented that challenges, limitations, and contradictions of ethnographic research were an organic part of the process and resources for research rather than barriers. These challenges inspired methodological modifications and enriched strategies I used throughout my research process.

My role as a researcher varied for teachers, families, and children because of my multiple ways and spaces of data collection: i.e. home, school, classroom and playground. I conducted this research in an elementary school and in the participants' homes in Guzelyurdu,[1] a Syrian border village located in southeastern Turkey, where the vast majority of the population was Kurdish and where limited job opportunities appeared to significantly influence parents' views of languages and their language practices for their children. I was a participant observer at school, in classrooms, on the playground, and in the homes of Kurdish children. I am Turkish, a member of the mainstream group and I do not speak Kurdish, the native language of children and parent participants in my study. Hence, I was an outsider to the group that I studied even though I was familiar with Kurdish culture because of my regular contact with Kurds as I grew up.

In the original study, I analyzed Kurdish children's language, literacy, and learning experiences to understand the influence of language policies and ideologies in everyday real-life practices. I utilized ethnographic research methods such as participant observation, interviews, document/ artifact collection and analysis, field notes, focus groups and qualitative data analysis to glean insights into the experiences of Kurdish children across their home and school spaces. I also studied the beliefs, experiences, and practices of their parents, siblings and teachers to understand the layers of context that were heavily influenced by policies and mainstream ideologies. After one month of participant observation in the classroom setting, I visited families' homes to observe and document their daily routines for a holistic understanding of children's household practices and roles (Moll *et al.*, 1992). I conducted three individual interviews with 12 children. I also conducted three in-depth interviews (Seidman, 2006) with their parents, two first grade teachers and three administrators to understand their practices and lived experiences. I conducted interviews and all personal conversations with Kurdish people in Turkish, their second language. I also conducted three focus groups with the four teachers at the end of my data collection process. During focus group interviews,

I asked follow-up questions and presented my preliminary findings to them. Throughout the data collection process, I collected documents and other artifacts from students, teachers, and parents such as handouts, letters, and drawings (Pahl & Rowsell, 2010).

The major findings from my research challenged ideologies that ignore minority groups' diverse practices in the language and learning experiences of Kurdish children. These findings also contributed to the debates about education in mother tongue in Turkey at the same time it shed light on the learning experiences of Kurdish children.

Although I considered myself an insider to the diverse environment of my research and Kurdish culture in general, I was an outsider to the children's village, community, and their native language. My goal was to describe the social and daily life practices of the children, their families and teachers for a fuller understanding of Kurdish children's language and literacy experiences in the complicated context of mainstream policies and ideologies. To achieve these goals, I utilized my roles as a researcher as a part of the complicated and situated processes of relationship and trust building. I also needed to draw upon innovative procedures and approaches while doing research with children which was a big and challenging part of this research in their linguistically and politically complex, local context.

Researcher's Multiple Roles

Qualitative research is a 'situated activity and locates the observer in the world of the participants. It consists of a set of interpretive, material practices that make the world visible' (Denzin & Lincoln, 1994: 3). My role as a researcher in this study varied for teachers, families, and children because of my multiple data collection ways and spaces (i.e. home, school and playground). I was a researcher in the eye of the teachers; I was a teacher with a different (more respected) position for the parents; and to the children I was a teacher but an unfamiliar one. These roles were based on situation, context and interaction.

Children viewed me as a 'teacher' and I was initially afraid that I would be restricted to the teacher role because children, culturally, are not always comfortable sharing their ideas and feelings with their teachers as a figure of respect. This was especially true during my initial conversations with the children; however, this changed over time as a result of our interactions together. The children observed me very carefully. In a short time, I became a 'teacher who takes notes and sits at the very back of the class'. When the children realized I was interested in their drawings and handcrafts, they added another dimension to my role, 'picture lover'. They were well aware that I was interested in their experiences even before I started my interviews and group activities with them. The challenge I had during 'official' interviews with children was that it took a long time for the children to answer my questions because they were generally reluctant to talk.

I believe this was because they perceived me as a teacher and culturally the children did not always freely talk to their teachers. Because I could not change the children's perception of me as a teacher, I started tutoring students in the first-grade class I observed because it allowed both children and me to know each other better. After a few weeks, the children felt more comfortable and started to ask questions about different issues such as their course material, social life, and future. The questions they asked gave me the opportunity to learn more about the world of the Kurds, and it also showed me they were aware that my role as a teacher was different from the role of their regular teacher, who I call Cengiz.

The power issues that came up in different ways and settings because of the linguistically and socially stratified structure (Fishman, 2001) of my research field inevitably affected my positionality (Rose, 1997). The teachers were nervous about being observed and recorded at the beginning of my field research, and they continued to ask questions even though I had explained my research purpose several times. Both their questions and practices during my presence made their feelings towards me obvious. For example, they stopped their conversation or changed the topic when I entered the teachers' lounge. At first, Cengiz was nervous to have me in his class-room because he assumed I could report my observations to an authority from the Ministry of Education in Turkey. Teachers could get in trouble and even lose their jobs if they were reported to the Ministry of Education because of their teaching strategies and practices, and they were especially nervous because my research focused on the experiences of Kurds, a stig-matized, politicized community. To build good relations with teachers, I looked for practices to share with them and joined them to rent a bus to travel between the village and the city center. Because I used to be a teacher in a similar context before, I knew what teachers would need and appreciate most. So, I helped teachers with their duties and substituted when needed. This helped to convince them I was genuinely interested in building a good relationship and that I was not there to judge or evaluate them. I became 'a researcher who used to be a teacher like them' and this allowed me to learn more about their beliefs and practices in personal conversations.

I was transparent with parents about the research process just as I was with teachers. It was important to understand parents' perception of my role in their village throughout the entire research process. I was intro-duced to parents by Cengiz as 'Ayfer Hoca [teacher]' – what all parents also called me after that introduction – in the first parent meeting of the semester. During this meeting with parents, I explained why I was in their village and the focus of my research. After this meeting, parents approached me and told me that they would be very happy to talk with me and have me in their homes. Their excitement was obvious. I was a teacher researcher to parents and all the villagers. During a home visit, one parent introduced me to her neighbor who stopped by during my home visit as '… a teacher but different. She is asking questions about children and

Kurdish [language]. She will take these [what she learns] to her university in America.' It was opportunity to learn my position as a researcher from a 'researched' perspective that enriched my understanding of what parents told to me because what people say reflects the context of the talk, including the audience and audience's position in the world of speaker (Gee, 2011). Parents defined me as different because I was teaching like other teachers but I also visited homes and talked to parents about their experiences and listened to stories that teachers would not typically be told.

I was able to gain trust with parents in a shorter time than I did with teachers even though I was an outsider. Parents welcomed, respected, and shared their experiences with me because, as they told, they were happy to be 'listened' to and 'researched' on. I showed my interest in the families' real life experiences and challenges they had raising their children. I did not want to be viewed as someone who asked questions only for answers because I was genuinely interested in having authentic conversations. I answered all their questions about my study and the significance of it. Parents were comfortable sharing their experiences and beliefs with me; however, I needed to work hard on correcting their misunderstanding that I had a higher position than the teachers. Parents opened their homes and welcomed me as if we had known each other for years. Even so, I was still an outsider because I was not ethnically a Kurd and I was 'a researcher coming from America'. These two positions kept me as an outsider in their lives.

My roles for parents, teachers, and children were mostly co-constructed. Because I was interested in the experiences and beliefs of my participants, I considered this co-constructed role building as a resource to utilize an interactional learning process for my participants and me. My main goal was bringing the educational and social experiences of Kurdish minority children to the attention of policy makers and academia. Each of my multiple roles in this socially and linguistically complex research field provided me with perspectives on the different layers of the society that eventually helped to make a better sense of the complexity. For instance, I was able to observe an impact of this research on the participants. During the last focus group conversation with teachers, Kemal shared in a self-critical way that the gap between school and parents was most probably in part because he and other teachers did not visit students' families at home. Later in the conversation, he said:

I am telling it here in front of my teacher friends. You observed us in school and visited families. Even if I don't say so, you already know. We are not close with families enough. For example, you know families better. We see them only if they come to school. In such a village where students need more support, we should be visiting their homes often to be able to explain to them what they need to do for their children. If we get closer with the families, their children would feel more affiliated and comfortable in school. Circumstances don't allow us to do that but we can find a way.

As a result of my research procedures that included both school and house-holds, Kemal reflected on his relationship with families in the community and the way this facilitated or limited what he was able to accomplish as a teacher. My influence on the teacher participants' beliefs and practices was an unexpected outcome and it assured me that my research was a two-way learning experience.

Research with Young Children

This two-way learning dynamic was also evident in children's observations of their teacher. During a conversation between Cengiz and a parent who came to visit his class, Filiz, who sat behind her classmates, looked at me and asked:

Filiz: Aren't you writing this down?
Me: Why do you think I should write this down?
Filiz: I think it is important. A parent is asking something about her child, I think you find this important. You need to write this down to not forget.

This conversation with a first grader was one of many that showed me how good young children are at analyzing the social dynamics around them. I also witnessed young children navigate their practices according to contexts and their audiences that would exemplify Bourdieu's (1986) discussion of 'legitimacy' (1986: 5) in their linguistically diverse community. As a set of accumulated social practices that are developed in particular contexts (Au, 2006; Street, 2003), children's literacy practices included their high awareness of the appropriate practices in each of their diverse contexts (i.e. school and home) to become a full member of those contexts (Bourdieu, 1977). MacNaughton et al. (2007) discuss 'young children as social actors who shape their identities, create and communicate valid views about the social world and have a right to participate' (2007: 460). Similar to this discussion, Kurdish children created and communicated important views as social actors and research participants and they presented me with a treasure of data.

Even so, it was not always easy. The biggest challenges I often had in my research with young children were their preference to be silent, their short attention spans and the schedule of classroom activities. Swadener and Polakow (2011) point out that young children may not have enough vocabulary to express their feelings, but they are able to use non-verbal ways of communication to express their perspectives. This is significant especially for interpreting what children mean when they use other modalities of communication. I naturally did not have a chance to change the children's preference for silence and their short attention spans, as these are normal for their age. So, rather than working on trying to decrease the length of silence, I found myself frequently modifying conventional interview strategies by using the 'Mosaic approach' (Clark & Moss, 2011). Clark and Moss (2011: 5) define their framework as multi-method, participatory, reflexive, adaptable, focused on children's lived experiences, and embedded into practice. Following this framework, I employed multiple ways of gathering data from young children including drawing pictures to represent their thoughts, play times, and conducting conversations with parents, in addition to inviting children to talk in response to the interview questions. For example, I organized 30 to 40 minute group activities for the children during which I let them choose from among the activities I had brought materials for, such as drawing, playing with a toy or play dough and puzzles. I carefully chose materials that encouraged children to interact with each other as they played as well as ones that were based on children's interests.

Most students chose to draw. I talked and did activities with the children as they worked during these group times. I had conversations with each about the meaning of the figures in their drawings and I collected the drawings as research artifacts. These group activities allowed children to have fun while interacting with each other by doing their favorite activities comfortably. I was therefore able to gather large amounts of multimodal and conversational data about children's language choice among each other and the ways they position themselves and their friends within their social environment. I was able to learn more from even the most silent and shy students. For instance, a student named Kareem was silent almost all the time during the day. However, he shared numerous drawings with me. I was able to have a conversation with him only when he brought me a picture he had drawn. For example, I had the chance of having a conversation with Kareem about his home practices when he gave me the picture below, which depicts me, my son and my home as defined by him (Figure 2.1).

Another outcome of these group times for this research was that I got to know children and their interests better because it was a comfortable, shared space where everyone was busy with activities while also talking. Knowing children better, I was able to ask the right questions to each child

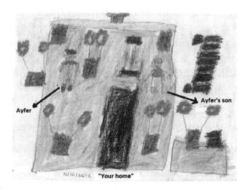

Figure 2.1 A picture drawn by Kareem

in future interviews in addition to the rich amount of data I gathered in these activity groups.

Orellana (2009) discusses how often immigrant children serve as language and culture brokers for their families and the ways they have more responsibilities than their peers. The children who participated in my research also had language and culture broker responsibilities because of the linguistically and culturally diverse structure of their environment. The children did not talk about these experiences during my conversations with them probably because they did not even consider those as noteworthy experiences since it was part of their life. I observed them serve as language and culture brokers during parent-teacher meetings. While language broking, children draw on their knowledge of the school system and teachers' expectations to interpret for their parents. They were positioned as an arbiter by their teachers and parents and trusted by both sides. Because these meetings were the only times I could observe these practices of children, I tried to prioritize them in my schedule. Most of these parent-teacher meetings were random. That's why, I was prepared to change my plans in the middle of the day when I learned that a parent was coming to the school otherwise I would not be able to learn about how Kurdish children successfully utilized their language and academic repertoire for language broking. Yet they were labeled as 'late learners or students who are behind' in their academic spaces because of their diverse home language and cultural practices that is similar to what youth from other minority communities experience (Orellana, 2009).

Children explicitly expressed their excitement for talking with me. However, they also had other things to do like play with their friends or sometimes they were not in the mood to talk with me even if they had decided on the time of our meeting. For instance, I was able to conduct an interview with a child after rescheduling it ten times because she simply did not want to talk at that time.

Although I saw children every day and interacted with them many times throughout the study, I ended up holding fewer structured individual interviews with young children than I had planned. Despite all these challenges, conducting research with children in the school field enriched my understanding of their social and linguistic practices. I consider the challenges and limitations of this research as organic part of children's experiences in their linguistically complicated context. I could not have learned what I learned from the children from anyone else.

Research in a Multilingual Minoritized Community

I used the Turkish language during my communications in Guzelyurdu village because I do not speak Kurdish. I also used a Turkish-Kurdish interpreter even though the parents spoke Turkish, my native language. I had aimed to conduct a discourse analysis by comparing participants' talk in Kurdish and Turkish even before going to the field. I hoped to find out if participants said different stories and if they said things differently. I also wanted to understand the reasons behind any potential differences between their two languages one of which is socially and historically stigmatized (Polat, 2007). However, this was not possible because of various limitations including the fact that I could not find an interpreter who could write in Kurdish and translate the text in Kurdish to Turkish with different meanings and use of words. Discourse analysis was not possible, but I hired the interpreter to minimize any potential misunderstandings between me, as a researcher and a person who is a member of the mainstream society in my research context, and my participants. I did not want to miss the opportunity to provide my participants with a meaningful conversation in their native language, and this provided me with the opportunity to have more data right at the point where the two languages cross each other. Through the end of the data collection process, after I was done with conducting all the interviews with parents, the Turkish-Kurdish bilingual interpreter conducted interviews in Kurdish with the parents and then translated audio data into Turkish. The goal of doing this was to explore whether parents said anything different than what they had said to me in Turkish. Relying on Bourdieu's (1986) discussion of 'legitimacy', I worked on providing a context in which Kurdish language would be 'legitimate'. In doing so, I wanted to investigate whether parents positioned themselves differently in their talk while answering the questions in Kurdish, their native language, which is linguistically minoritized (Fishman, 1991) to a Kurd who is from their own community.

Although the interpreter was born and raised in Guzelyurdu village and although Kurdish was her mother tongue, I worked with her for several hours to clarify how to conduct an interview, and I made sure she asked the same questions I was asking but in Kurdish. We also worked on the basics of conducting interviews such as how to start, and transitioning between questions. Another area we worked on was how to ask questions if she wanted to hear more or needed clarification. We focused on ways to elicit more detailed answers from parents when they gave short answers. I created the interview protocols she used to interview parents about raising Kurdish children in a Turkish dominant world. The interpreter transcribed these interviews into Turkish for me to analyze.

I cannot know exactly how my Turkish background affected my interactions with the parents from their perspective. However, I believe how I negotiated my identity as a researcher who was both an insider and outsider has significant implications for other researchers who examine the social and linguistic experiences of a minoritized community. I modified my methods and research process to make sure my participants were comfortable and confident during their participation in this research, although it is not clear whether conducting interviews in Kurdish completely addressed that limitation. I was able to compare the interview transcriptions conducted in Turkish to the ones in Kurdish. I hoped that conducting interviews in Kurdish would show that one language was not superior to another language in my research. I also hoped I was able to show the respect and value I had for the parents and their linguistic practices. Triangulating data in qualitative research is suggested especially in research about complex contexts such as this one (Denzin & Lincoln, 1994). Interviews in Kurdish served for me to triangulate the data from language perspective in this research's linguistically stratified context to investigate if parent participants did not feel comfortable enough to say particular things in Turkish which they later communicated in Kurdish. I was able to compare the interview transcriptions conducted in Turkish to the ones in Kurdish. This design allowed the parents to express themselves in multiple ways, and they did so in both their native and second languages. Also I was able to see if there was anything they did not share with me because they did not feel confident in Turkish as their second language.

Implications

The findings of this research contribute to the heavily politicized debates about Kurds in Turkey with insights into the real-life practices and experiences of Kurds at grassroots level. The study contributes to academic discussions about Kurds in Turkey, which is an understudied group (Polat, 2007; Skutnabb-Kangas & McCarty, 2006), with its deeper understanding of Kurds' experiences at grass roots that was developed by using ethnographic methods of participant observation, interviewing, document collection and analysis. This study suggests that the inclusion of young children in qualitative research broadens the understanding of the researcher at the same time that it expands the research perspective of minority communities' social and linguistic experiences. My research suggests utilizing methods such as the Mosaic Approach (Clark & Moss, 2011) to overcome the commonly-faced challenges of conducting research with young children. This study recommends that researchers planning to conduct similar research apply on-going modifications of both methods and practices in the field according to children's needs and desires. Through the methods and modifications used in this study, I was also able to learn more about children's experiences within and across home and school spaces in order to carry a holistic picture of their experiences to the academic spaces. I would like to emphasize that these challenges are a natural element of research with children and they contribute to the learning experience of the researcher whether the researcher was able to overcome the challenges or if s/he left them as 'unanswered'.

The close examination of my participants' lived experiences, language ideologies, and literacy practices through participant observations and interviews showed that children, their parents, and even teachers valued

Turkish and English at the same time they devalued Kurdish because of the stigmatization and oppression they experienced both at the individual and social level. With these findings, this study adds to the understanding of linguistic complexity in countries such as Turkey, where English is taught as a foreign language but not used in daily life, an underestimated topic in academic discussions (Bruthiaux, 2003).

My reflections on the process of conducting research in this setting and with these participants demonstrate that challenges and experiencing constraints is to be expected in ethnographic research. They also suggest it is our responsibility as researchers to modify our methods in ways that allow us to be responsive to our participants, and to think of these modifications and adjustments as part of our research as we describe the voices and grass roots experiences of minority communities to the larger settings of education, politics, and academia.

Note

(1) All names of places and people are pseudonyms.

References

Au, K.H. (2006) *Multicultural issues and literacy achievement*. London: Lawrence Erlbaum Associates.

Bourdieu, P. (1977) The economics of linguistic exchanges. *Social Science Information* 16, 645–668.

Bourdieu, P. (1986) The forms of capital. In J.G. Richardson (ed.) *Handbook of Theory and Research for the Sociology of Education*. New York: Greenwood Press.

Bruthiaux, P. (2003) Squaring the circles: Issues in modeling English worldwide. *International Journal of Applied Linguistics* 13 (2), 159–178.

Clark, A. and Moss, P. (2011) *Listening to Young Children: Mosaic Approach*. London: NCB.

Denzin, N.K. and Lincoln, Y.S. (1994) Introduction: Entering the field of qualitative research. In N.K. Denzin and Y.S. Lincoln (eds) *Handbook of Qualitative Research*. Thousand Oaks, CA: Sage.

Fishman, J. (1991) *Reversing Language Shift: Theoretical and Empirical Foundations of Assistance to Threatened Languages*. Clevedon: Multilingual Matters.

Fishman, J.A. (ed.) (2001) *Can Threatened Languages Be Saved? Reversing Language Shift, Revisited: A 21st Century Perspective*. Clevedon: Multilingual Matters.

Gee, J.P. (2011) *Social Linguistics and Literacies: Ideology in Discourses*. New York: Routledge.

MacNaughton, G.M., Smith, K. and Davis, K. (2007) Researching with children: The challenges and possibilities for building 'child friendly' research. In J.A. Hatch (ed.) *Early Childhood Qualitative Research* (pp. 167–205). New York: Routledge.

Moll, L., Amanti, C., Neff, D. and González, N. (1992) Funds of knowledge for teaching: A qualitative approach to developing strategic connections between homes and classrooms. *Theory into Practice* 31, 132–141.

Orellana, M.F. (2009) *Translating Childhoods*. New Brunswick, New Jersey, and London: Rutgers University Press.

Pahl, K. and Rowsell, J. (2010) *Artifactual Literacies Every Object Tells a Story*. New York: Teachers College Press.

Polat, N. (2007) Socio-psychological factors in the attainment of L2 native-like accent of Kurdish origin young people learning Turkish in Turkey. Unpublished thesis, University of Texas at Austin.

Rose, G. (1997) Situating knowledges: Positionality, reflexivities and other tactics. In *Progress in Human Geography* 21 (3), 305–320.

Seidman, I.E. (2006) *Interviewing as a Qualitative Research* (3rd edn). New York: Teachers College Press.

Skutnabb-Kangas, T. and McCarty, T. (2006) Key concepts in bilingual education: Ideological historical, epistemological, and empirical foundations. In J. Cummins and N. Hornberger (eds) *Encyclopedia of Language and Education* (2nd edn, pp. 3–17). New York: Springer.

Street, B. (2003) What's 'new' in New Literacy Studies? Critical approaches to literacy in theory and practice. *Current Issues in Comparative Education* 5 (2), 77–91.

Swadener, B.B. and Polakow, V. (2011) Special Issue: Children's Rights and Voices in Research: Cross-National Perspectives (eds) *Early Education and Development*.

3 The Trouble with Operationalizing People: My Research with Students with Limited or Interrupted Formal Education (SLIFE)

Christopher Browder

Introduction

The acronym 'SLIFE' stands for Students with Limited or Interrupted Formal Education and was coined by DeCapua and Marshal (2010). An examination of educational research (Browder, 2015) as well as literature from professional organizations (MATESOL, 2015) and educational consortiums (WIDA Consortium, 2015) shows that this is currently the term most commonly used when discussing recent-arrival adolescent English learner (EL) students who '[l]ack basic academic skills and concepts, content knowledge, and critical thinking skills and may not be literate in their native language' (DeCapua *et al.*, 2009: 4). Checklists for identifying SLIFE suggest that this subgroup can include students with a wide range of first language and educational levels (see Mace-Matluck *et al.*, 1998; New York State Department of Education, 1997). Depending on the method of identification, SLIFE may be literate, low-literate, or non-literate. Likewise, SLIFE may be missing no years of schooling, two years of schooling, six years of schooling, or may be entirely unschooled. Limited or interrupted education may be the result of cultural norms, under-resourced schools, poverty, prejudice, oppression, geographic isolation, migration, natural disaster, or even violence.

Researchers agree that SLIFE 'struggle with coursework', 'do not score well on standardized tests' (Freeman *et al.*, 2002: 5), and 'drop out at alarming rates' (DeCapua *et al.*, 2009: 3), but research supporting these generalizations is rare (Browder, 2015; Zehr, 2009). For this reason, in 2012, I set out to conduct one of the first quantitative studies on SLIFE aimed at understanding how their previous literacy and schooling affect their educational outcomes in the US (Browder, 2014, 2015).

This chapter is a methodological reflection on conducting research on the educational outcomes of SLIFE. This chapter challenges common practices in quantitative research and school system data collection on marginalized groups. Specifically, I will focus on the issues involved with operationalizing the construct of SLIFE for research purposes.

My Study

I am both a high school teacher and an educational researcher. I teach high school EL students and also conduct research to understand them better. For years I had read accounts of the academic challenges SLIFE face, but in my own school I was seeing some inspiring examples of SLIFE being academically successful. I wanted to understand these incredible counter-examples of academic success. For my research, I decided to see whether SLIFE really had significantly lower educational outcomes than non-SLIFE EL students. Did they learn English slower? Were they still doing more poorly on standardized tests of academic achievement years after arrival? More importantly, when educational resilience happened for SLIFE, why did it happen?

Reviewing the Research on Identifying Students as SLIFE

Before conducting any research on SLIFE, 'one of the first tasks is to operationalize or consider the meaning of educational level' (Bigelow & Watson, 2011: 467). In other words, it was necessary to operationalize the concept of limited or interrupted formal education so I could identify the students who were SLIFE and compare them with those who were not.

I assumed that I would easily be able to find an operationalization of SLIFE in the existing research. Instead, I found that research on SLIFE was very rare at the time (Freeman *et al.*, 2002; DeCapua *et al.*, 2007) and clear operationalizations were even rarer. The literature generally featured examples and descriptions of this type of student instead of clear guidelines that could be used to identify students as SLIFE for research and distinguish them from other students.

Furthermore, when I did find guidelines, they were often not consistent with the guidelines provided by other institutions or researchers. For example, I found that the New York State Department of Education (1997) identified students with two or more documented missing years of schooling relative to their age as 'students with interrupted formal education', while the Maryland Department of Education (2012) identified students with documented interruptions of only six months or more as having 'interrupted schooling'. Thus, a student who might be considered a SLIFE by one person or institution might not be considered one by another.

Moreover, I saw that definitions tended to confound education, schooling, and literacy in a manner that is very problematic. For example, New York State expects EL students to have two or more documented years of missing schooling *and* be at least two years below grade level in reading or math *and* have very limited literacy in their first language to be identified by their term 'students with interrupted formal education', or SIFE (New York State Department of Education, 2011). Thus, New York expects students with interrupted or missing schooling to also have both lower education (i.e. math ability) and lower first language literacy. This might not seem problematic at first, but it is for various reasons. Firstly, research tells us that schooling, education, and literacy are three very different constructs. Cultural anthropologists have been distinguishing schooling from education for decades (Lave & Wenger, 1991). They define schooling as time spent in school and define education as the learning we expect students to gain from school.

Secondly, a year of schooling in one context is not necessarily equivalent to a year in another. Schooling varies by nation (Flaitz, 2006; UNICEF, 2014). In some nations, schools are well-resourced, but in other nations, schools may lack essential materials and qualified teachers. Similarly, the quality of schooling within a nation may vary by region or even by neighborhood. Students in some contexts might never experience schooling with computers, libraries, textbooks, or, in some cases, even pens and pencils (DeCapua *et al.*, 2009). They never experience schooling with qualified teachers, in fact, some schools have no teacher, or just have teachers who rely completely on rote learning. Therefore, students in some places could attend school consistently but never enjoy the quality of education students in other places do.

Thirdly, students do not all benefit equally from seemingly equal schooling (Bigelow & Watson, 2011). For a wide range of reasons, some students will learn more than others even if provided with the same experiences. This may help explain how some people can become very educated without much formal schooling while others who are well-schooled can remain undereducated.

Similar to education, research shows that first language literacy also does not correspond well with schooling (Tarone *et al.*, 2009; Tarone, 2010). This is largely because literacy can be acquired without schooling (Scribner & Cole, 1978) and vice versa (Robson, 1982). Some contexts have schools but do not have strong traditions of literacy. This can also vary from family to family within a society.

It is also important to consider that there are many different types literacy that need to be taken into account when considering the impact

L1 literacy has on learning written English (Burt *et al.*, 2003). For instance, some learners such as the Somali Bantu, come from cultures in which the language is rarely ever used in written form and may have only recently been codified. They are referred to as 'preliterate' and are expected to have special disadvantages when learning written English because literacy itself may seem very strange and foreign to them. They can be contrasted with other learners, like people from rural El Salvador, who come from cultures that have traditions of literacy but have not learned to read well because of a lack of opportunity. They are referred to as 'non-literate' or 'semi-literate' depending on how well they read. They have advantages because they have seen text everywhere and know its many uses. Once we know that a learner is somewhat literate, however, we then need to ask whether they are 'Roman-alphabetic literate', 'non-Roman-alphabetic literate', or 'non-alphabetic literate'. Students whose first languages use the Roman alphabet, such as Spanish or French, are not learning an entirely new writing system but merely a new way of using it. Students whose first languages use a non-Roman alphabet, such as Thai or Hindi, are learning a new system but have experience with phonics and letters. Students whose first languages do not use alphabetic systems, such as Chinese, have to learn an entirely new way of writing that has fewer similarities.

To complicate matters further, some educational advocates warn us that documented interruptions in schooling are unreliable indicators of limited formal education because students who are new to the US educational system may not be forthcoming about problems in their schooling history, and the schooling records they bring with them are often incomplete or inaccurate (Advocates for Children of New York, 2010). For these reasons, advocates have requested that education agencies consider multiple indicators for determining which students are SLIFE and not expect all SLIFE to have documented interruptions in their formal schooling.

Even just for documented interrupted schooling, operationalization can be complicated because interruptions can be measured in many ways. As a researcher measuring interruptions, I could measure time spent since last attendance, or I could measure total time spent out of school. After all, there are surely differences between an 18-year-old boy who spent six years in school to complete grade five but has not attended in over six years, and an 18-year-old boy who did not receive any early childhood education, but has been in school for the past six years since age 12. For the sake of parsimony, I could just count the total years of schooling in the homeland or use the last grade completed in the homeland as my measure of schooling, but this would not account for the time spent out of school. After all, a 12-year-old boy who recently completed grade six is surely different from an 18-year-old boy who completed grade six but has received no schooling since. This difference is especially serious considering that the two boys will be placed in different grades based on their age when they enroll in US schools, so the 12-year-old will be functioning on grade-level when he is placed in grade seven, but the 18-year-old will be placed in grade nine even though he only has a sixth grade education (Gahungo *et al.*, 2011).

How I Chose to Identify Students as SLIFE for My Study

To operationalize SLIFE as a construct, I chose to create a compound measure by combining four indicators based on information collected on students' arrival in the US and using the definitions used in educational policies. Those four indicators were (a) one year or more of missing schooling relative to grade placement, (b) below-grade-level math skills, (c) beginner-level English, and (d) low first language literacy. I chose to use dichotomized indicators instead of continuous variables because this is how data were usually encoded in public education. Unfortunately, I found that I had to discard the math indicator because too many students had not been given the math placement test. In the end, I determined that students with two of the three SLIFE indicators would be classified as SLIFE and included in the SLIFE subgroup. I was not satisfied with this. In fact, I preferred some sort of continuous variable, but I needed to create a measure that was similar to the way SLIFE were described in the literature and educational policy.

The Findings Using My Construct of SLIFE

The findings of my study showed that some of the common beliefs about SLIFE may lack empirical support.

Firstly, my attempt to create some sort of compound variable to identify students for a SLIFE subgroup raised doubts about the SLIFE construct. Normally, when combining multiple variables into one compound variable used as a scale, a researcher expects those multiple variables to be correlated. After all, if the different variables are actually indicators of one common variable, then they should all be correlated (George & Mallery, 2003). The SLIFE indicators in my study, however, lacked the correlation (i.e. Cronbach's Alpha) necessary to show they could be used to form a reliable scale for measuring a common concept (Browder, 2014, 2015). In other words, if there is no evidence that the components are measuring a common variable, then we have not empirically demonstrated that the common variable even exists. I was trying to study SLIFE, but I had no evidence that there really was a specific group of EL students who could be logically distinguished from their peers as SLIFE. If such a group existed, they certainly lacked the uniformity expected of people one might group together.

I tried very hard to form a compound variable that matched the descriptions in the educational literature and policy to the point at which I was really almost forcing the data to fit something they did not fit. For instance, I tried changing the cut points used to form the indicator variables, using two years of missing schooling instead of one, or increasing or decreasing the range included as low-level first language literacy, but it did not help. I tried operationalizing the indicator variables as continuous variables instead of dichotomous variables, but it made no difference. I even tried converting the variables to Z-scores based on the standard deviations in the sample, but that did not help either. I also tried adding and removing variables from the scale, but it did not help; it only reduced the scale to whatever two variables happened to be significantly correlated making it no longer match the concept of SLIFE portrayed in the educational literature and policy. I found that nothing I could do to the indicators would improve the reliability of the compound measure as a scale. Measures of education such as math and English were correlated with one another, but not with first language literacy. English was correlated with measures of missing or interrupted schooling, but first language literacy was not. Of course, I considered that the data used to form the SLIFE indicators might be inaccurate, but the fact that they individually had significant relationships to the dependent variables in my study suggested otherwise.

The lack of correlation between the SLIFE indicators made me doubt the validity of the very concept of SLIFE. I was becoming aware that, depending on how it is operationalized, the concept was bound to either be too inclusive, lumping together students with very different risk-factors, or too exclusive, not including many of the students educators think of as SLIFE. For instance, depending on how the SLIFE construct is operationalized, SLIFE might or might not include a student who has grade level math and first language reading skills, but has been out of school for a while. Similarly, SLIFE might or might not include a student who has received uninterrupted yet very inadequate previous schooling, and as a result, has very low math and first language reading skills.

Just as the preliminary analyses of my study challenged the generalizations commonly made about SLIFE, so too did the eventual findings. My findings showed that the SLIFE compound variable was associated with lower scores on tests of academic achievement and slower English learning, but the differences were not statistically significant with the alpha set at 0.05 because their outcomes were so variable. The popular concept of SLIFE in educational literature and policy depicts them as being far more at risk for academic failure than other EL students (Freeman *et al.*, 2002; DeCapua & Marshall, 2010), but my findings suggested that their educational outcomes might be more variable than assumed. In fact, based on my findings, one might even conclude that many SLIFE are educationally resilient. Admittedly, the SLIFE in my study were generally supported by appropriate educational interventions, such as newcomer programs, sheltered ESOL classes, summer school ESOL classes, and after school support, but even with such support, it is still very impressive that some could make up for years of missing or inadequate schooling in such a short time.

Moreover, the associations between the SLIFE variable and the educational outcomes were better explained by examining the individual SLIFE indicators used to form the SLIFE variable. For instance, the slower rate of English learning for SLIFE appeared to be almost completely explained by differences in first language literacy. SLIFE with low first language literacy learned English slower, but SLIFE with higher first language literacy progressed quickly. This begs the question, why not just focus on students' first language literacy instead of their schooling background? Likewise, SLIFE had lower scores on tests of academic achievement, but further analyses showed that the differences were almost completely explained by differences in students' English proficiency. If the educational outcomes are mostly determined by English proficiency and first language literacy, then why pay so much attention to students' previous formal schooling measured in years or grade levels completed?

SLIFE: Do We Need This Construct?

My research has taught me that we must ask what purpose it serves to have the construct, SLIFE. What consequences or benefits are there for the students who are labeled and categorized in this way and then 'placed' or 'accommodated' accordingly? Some educational researchers have been expressing concerns about the way educational linguistics constantly creates new categories for language learners in order to facilitate homogenous grouping, design new curricula and materials, or collect data (Kibler & Valdes, 2016). Does the concept exist to justify creating new interventions for EL students with special needs? Does it identify the students who are best served by newcomer programs? Does the label help stigmatize students? Does it lower our expectations and lead to lower tracking? Does it scare schools and teachers, or does it evoke sympathy and justify accommodation? Would students fare better if they were known by their teachers as SLIFE after leaving the newcomer programs and entering grade-level classrooms, or would they fare worse?

Similarly, my research has taught me that we must ask whether it is necessary or helpful in education to create any dichotomous variable that places students into a group with a label. School systems and the federal government regularly place students into dichotomous groups such as those who receive free-or-reduced-priced meals (FARM), those who receive services from special education programs (SPED), those who are classified as English learners (EL), and those in certain racial or ethnic groups (e.g. Hispanics). Educational administrations use these labels to determine whether these at-risk groups of students are being adequately served and to identify students as eligible for certain services. This is arguably necessary, but it creates artificial distinctions. Family income, ability to learn in unaccommodated mainstream classrooms, English proficiency, and even ethnicity can all be operationalized as continuous variables for more precise data collection. In fact, there is no cut off point where we can be certain that students have or do not have these traits or where these traits clearly begin to affect educational outcomes or stop affecting them. The effects of these variables are certainly gradual and vary widely from student to student.

If SLIFE actually includes a very wide variety of students with very different needs and abilities, then school administrators and educators must re-examine some of their policies, procedures, assumptions, and expectations. I suspect that they will need a more nuanced understanding of what it means to have limited or interrupted formal education if they are to serve SLIFE well instead of lumping this diverse assortment of learners together to provide a one-size-fits-all remediation. There clearly seem to be many different types of SLIFE with very different needs. Simply identifying students as SLIFE or non-SLIFE might actually distract educators from seeing each student's unique needs and addressing them properly.

Conclusion

Readers should not misunderstand that I am arguing that SLIFE do not exist or that they do not deserve our support. The construct of SLIFE is problematic, but I am certain that there really are EL students who arrive in the US very academically underprepared for meaningful participation in grade-level instruction, and I am certain that some of these students will need a great deal of support so they can succeed in school.

Readers also should not misunderstand that I believe a student's prior schooling experience is not a variable worthy of research or useful for educational placement. Like other researchers, I desire that as much data be collected as possible, but I question the collection of data when it involves labeling students in a manner that is inaccurate or potentially harmful.

Researchers should also not misunderstand that I insist SLIFE be just one thing that everybody agree upon. It is simply that I find it worrisome that we could be having a discussion about SLIFE, and making generalizations about SLIFE that have implications for policy and practice, when we do not even agree on what SLIFE are. We researchers are writing about SLIFE based on our experiences with specific groups we consider to be SLIFE. Many of us, for instance, have worked with recently-resettled Hmong or Somali Bantu refugees. Others have worked with Haitian or Salvadoran immigrants. The people in any one of these SLIFEish groups, however, may be very different from the people in any other SLIFEish group. Likewise, a person in one of these groups might also be very different from the other people in their same group. Some teachers or researchers are working with traumatized people from geographically or politically isolated pre-literate, pre-scientific, and highly-collectivistic cultures. Others, however, may be working with people from countries like Guatemala, a country in which people are generally educated to at least a sixth grade level and Roman-alphabet literate. These people are all very different from one another.

The operationalization of the term SLIFE is more than just an issue for research. It is a public policy and social justice issue. How we define SLIFE determines who will receive certain types of ESOL services and who will not (Advocates for Children of New York, 2010). In fact, research on SLIFE has recently been used by expert witnesses for civil rights cases involving SLIFE who were denied services by their school system (*Issa v. the School District of Lancaster*, 2016). The generalizations we make about SLIFE determine how they will be treated and served. We make generalizations about SLIFE in the course of explaining how schools can serve them better, and we make generalizations to justify special services, but we must be careful that our generalizations do not portray this group through a patronizing or overly-simplistic deficit discourse.

References

Advocates for Children of New York (2010) *Students with interrupted formal education: A challenge for the New York City public schools.* See http://www.advocatesforchildren. org (accessed 20 July 2014).

Bigelow, M. and Watson, J. (2011) The role of education, literacy, and orality in L2 learning. In S. Gass and A. Mackey (eds) *The Routledge Handbook of Second Language Acquisition* (pp. 461–475). London and New York: Routledge (Taylor and Francis).

Browder, C. (2014) English learners with limited or interrupted formal education: Risk and resilience in educational outcomes. PhD dissertation, University of Maryland, Baltimore County.

Browder, C. (2015) The educational outcomes of English learner students with limited or interrupted formal education. In M. Santos and A. Whiteside (eds) *Proceedings of the Ninth LESLLA Symposium, 2013* (pp. 150–172). San Francisco, CA: Lulu Publishing Services.

Burt, M., Peyton, J., and Adams, R. (2003) *Reading and Adult English Language Learners: A Review of the Research.* Washington, DC: Center for Applied Linguistics.

DeCapua, A. and Marshall, H. (2010) Students with limited or interrupted formal education in US classrooms. *Urban Review* 42 (2), 159–173.

DeCapua, A., Smathers, W. and Tang, L. (2007) Schooling, interrupted. *Educational Leadership* 64 (6), 40–46.

DeCapua, A., Smathers, W. and Tang, L. (2009) *Meeting the Needs of Students with Limited or Interrupted Schooling.* Ann Arbor, MI: University of Michigan Press.

Flaitz, J. (2006) *Understanding Your Refugee and Immigrant Students: An Educational, Cultural, and Linguistic Guide.* Ann Arbor, MI: University of Michigan Press.

Freeman, Y., Freeman, D. and Mercuri, S. (2002) *Closing the Achievement Gap: How to Reach Limited-Formal-schooling and Long-term English Learners.* Portsmouth, NH: Heinemann.

Gahungo, A., Gahungo, O. and Luseno, F. (2011) Educating culturally displaced students with truncated formal education (CDS-TFE): The case of refugee students and challenges for administrators, teachers, and counselors. *International Journal of Educational Leadership Preparation* 6 (2).

George, D. and Mallery, P. (2003) *SPSS for Windows Step by Step: a Simple Guide and Reference* (4th edn). Boston: Allyn and Bacon.

Issa v. School District of Lancaster, 5-6-cv-03881-EGS (The United States District Court for the Eastern District of Pennsylvania, 26 August 2016).

Kibler, A. and Valdes, G. (2016) Conceptualizing language learners: Socio-institutional mechanisms and their consequences. *Modern Language Journal* 100 (S1), 96–116.

Lave, J. and Wenger, E. (1991) *Situated Learning. Legitimate Peripheral Participation.* Cambridge: University of Cambridge Press.

Mace-Matluck, B., Alexander-Kasparik, R. and Queen, R. (1998) *Through the Golden Door: Educational Approaches for Immigrant Students with Limited Formal Schooling.* Washington, DC: The Center for Applied Linguistics and Delta Systems.

Maryland State Department of Education (2012) *Maryland Accommodations Manual.* Maryland State Department of Education.

Massachusetts Association of Teachers of English to Speakers of Other Languages Inc. (2015) *Students with limited or interrupted formal education.* MATESOL: Massachusetts Educators of English Language Learners, See http://www.matsol.org (accessed 28 November 2015).

New York State Department of Education (1997) *Teaching Language Arts to Limited English Proficient/English Language Learners: A Resource Guide for All Teachers.* New York State Department of Education.

New York State Department of Education (2011) *Guidelines for Educating Limited English Proficient Students with Interruptted Formal Education.* NYSDOE.

Robson, B. (1982) Hmong literacy, formal education, and their effects on performance in an ESL class. In B.T. Downing and D.P. Olney (eds) *The Hmong in the West: Observations and Reports: Papers of the 1981 Hmong Research Conference, University of Minnesota* (pp. 201–225). Minneapolis, M: Southeast Asian Refugee Studies Project, Center for Urban and Regional Affairs, University of Minnesota.

Scribner, S. and Cole, M. (1978) Literacy without schooling. *Harvard Educational Review* 48 (4).

Tarone, E. (2010) Second language acquisition by low-literate learners: An under-studied population. *Language Teaching* 43 (1), 75–83.

Tarone, E., Bigelow, M. and Hansen, K. (2009) *Literacy and Second Language Oracy.* Oxford: Oxford University Press.

UNICEF (2014) *State of the World's Children 2015.* New York, NY: United Nations Childrens Fund.

WIDA Consortium (May 2015) *SLIFE: Students with limited or interrupted formal education.* WIDA Focus: http://www.wida.us (accesed 28 November 2015).

Zehr, M.A. (2009) Yes, students with interrupted formal education can catch up. *Education Week.*

4 A Researcher's Coming-of-Age through Participatory Action Research: The Intersections of Cultures, Identities and Institutions

Emily Feuerherm

As a novice researcher writing a dissertation based on a participatory action research (PAR) project, I ran into many of the critical dilemmas described by Kysa Nygreen (2009) in her first attempt at PAR. Like her, I was inspired by PAR 'as a model of engaged critical research for social change' (2009: 14) and a way to engage in research that rejected 'the oppressive and reproductive tendencies of traditional social science research' (2009: 14). At the heart of PAR is the belief that research should be conducted *with* the subjects/participants, rather than *on* them and that they are experts about their lives with the ability to critically reflect on their oppressed or marginalized positioning and take action to achieve change (Bradbury & Reason, 2003; Israel *et al.*, 2013; Reason 2006). Although PAR is well theorized, in practice it is complicated by the extensive relationship-building between diverse individuals and stakeholders, with sometimes conflicting stakes in the processes and products of the research and action (Mayan & Daum, 2016; Wilmsen, 2008). Further complications result through intersections of identities, languages, and cultures which can change the research trajectory and timeline (Caretta, 2014; Langhout, 2006; Muhammad *et al.*, 2015). For academic researchers attempting to meet deadlines for dissertations or tenure and promotion, these complications may impede engagement with PAR approaches.

In this chapter I will explore key turning points in a PAR project, which was the site of my dissertation, in order to highlight the importance of critical reflection on the multifaceted identities of all partners and stakeholders involved. My dissertation was based on the development of a community-based ESL course for Iraqi refugees: From 2009 to 2014 I worked with a refugee resettlement agency in California, which I anonymize by calling the Immigrant Resource Center (IRC), to develop the Refugee Health and Employment Attainment Program (RHEAP). The details about the program and its development are described in Feuerherm (2013a, 2016). In summary, the idea for the program was presented to me by IRC, I conducted initial interviews with Iraqi refugees to start the program, and through an iterative process collaboratively designed and then turned over total control of the program to the Iraqi refugees and community volunteers it was meant to serve. However, this smooth-sounding trajectory silences the contested nature of the process and the previously published accounts of this program are incomplete. Because PAR often requires collaboration and coordination between people from diverse backgrounds, critical reflections that foreground identity are useful in analyzing the trajectory of the research and are a first step in deconstructing institutionalized, privileged positions of power in traditional models of research (Muhammad *et al.*, 2015; Pascale, 2011). I am returning to this research several years later to engage in a more critical reflection on my roles as a researcher, program developer, and curriculum designer. The goal of this chapter is to balance the other, less critical accounts of this research with the hope that those entering into a participatory research project can prepare for the complex, challenging, and confounding aspects of the participatory process.

Any research that engages participants from a vulnerable population, such as resettled refugees, must hold up unparalleled ethical procedures and ensure that research brings about positive, reciprocal benefits for refugee participants and communities (Block *et al.*, 2012). Research on refugee resettlement has shown that refugees are often discursively constructed as victims by the press (Baker & McEnery, 2005; Loring, 2016) and the agencies that aid their resettlement (Tyeklar, 2016), while policies denying access to rights or jobs continue to recreate harmful, unjust practices in the lands of resettlement (Feuerherm, 2013b; Ricento, 2013). Thus, research with refugees should prevent harm and symbolic violence by including their voices and identifying actions that result in greater justice (Mackenzie *et al.*, 2007). These ideals are aligned with PAR approaches to research, particularly PAR's commitment to the redistribution of power, recognition of a community's knowledge and capacity, and the action component of the research. However, PAR principles alone are insufficient in building relationships, equitable partnerships, and transformational action, particularly when researchers are etic to the community with whom they work (de Leeuw *et al.*, 2012; Janes, 2016; Nygreen, 2009). As a novice researcher attempting PAR, I found that my identity as a white, middle-class female researcher and community volunteer positioned me in conflicting roles which I was underprepared to critically reflect upon and navigate.

By re-examining my data – the interviews, ethnographic field notes, and RHEAP's curriculum – that was the basis of my dissertation, I hope to problematize some of the key developments and turning points in my experience of practicing PAR. This chapter explores the contested spaces my previous articles on this project have left untouched in order to show how the research was shaped by my partners' and my identities. The story is organized chronologically with the following themes highlighting the role of identity in PAR: the difficulty of getting access to individuals initially and the process of informed consent; the conflicts that arose between my goals and those of the partnering institution; the building (and breaking) of relationships with research partners; and the conundrum of writing a single-authored dissertation from a participatory action research project. By critically returning to these key moments in my research, I show that theorization of PAR does not prepare (novice) researchers for the practice of PAR, especially when the researcher's lens is etic to the community with whom she works. Although these insights are specific to my experience developing a small, local program with a very specific immigrant group, they may be *theoretically* or *provocatively generalizable* for use in other PAR contexts (Fine, 2008). In other words, although my experiences with PAR are particular to this context and the identities of those involved in this research, I hope that this critical reflection may help others become better prepared to navigate and reflect on PAR in other contexts.

Consent Across Cultures

My community partnership began with the local resettlement agency, the Immigrant Resource Center (IRC), and not with the Iraqi refugees with whom I hoped to collaborate. On one hand, this alignment was important because it provided access to the Iraqi refugee community, but on the other hand, it structured the initial stages of the research and the curriculum in problematic ways: my relationship with IRC blinded me from identifying early biases and ethical problems in the research structure. IRC encouraged early intervention without offering sufficient cultural and linguistic support, and neither my institution's policies on ethical procedures nor my theoretical understanding of PAR were enough to counterbalance their influence.

The story begins in 2009, when I started volunteering as an ESL tutor with IRC. Because of my background in teaching English to speakers of other languages (I had earned an MA TESOL), IRC proposed a new program to me which they hoped I would develop: the Refugee Employment Attainment Program (REAP, and later, the Refugee Health and Employment Attainment Program, or RHEAP). IRC's concern was that many of the recently resettled refugees, especially those without dependents, were particularly vulnerable to running out of cash assistance before finding jobs. According to the case workers, several recent refugees, especially those from Iraq, were threatened by homelessness, and the difficulty of their job search was compounded by the recession. IRC was not alone in this concern, nor was it limited to a particular geographical region; it was also documented by Andorra Bruno (2011) in a report from the Congressional Research Service and by the Human Rights Institute at Georgetown Law (2009). IRC needed swift action to address this situation, but my role as outsider prevented me from gaining access to the refugees for nearly six months: I was neither part of the resettlement community, nor part of the refugee community. Because I was not a case worker at IRC I could not contact the refugees directly, and because I was an outsider to the community I relied on IRC to make the contact for me.

In spite of these obstacles, I was determined to follow participatory approaches to curriculum design – a context-specific curriculum involving students in the process (Auerbach, 1992) – where students would engage in problem posing to address their immediate needs (Wallerstein, 1983). I envisioned a program led by the Iraqi refugees it was meant to serve so that participants would feel ownership in the program as they directed their own learning. I saw this approach as a good alternative to an ends-means curriculum development approach where the curriculum was prescribed by me as the researcher/teacher. Additionally, I believed it could stand as a defense against deficit discourses found in theories of L2 acquisition and policies of refugee resettlement. Because participatory curriculum development foregrounds learners' capacities and skills rather than deficits of English fluency, it would frame the program through the strengths of the community, not the shortfalls. An example of the ends-means curriculum approach can be seen in the competency-based curriculum still popular in many adult ESL programs and similar to the pre-immigration centers for Indochinese refugees in the 1980s that Tollefson (1989) examined. As Tollefson (1989) argued, the policies and practices of such programs tend to be mired in ideologies of belonging that label and position refugees as lazy, dependent, lawbreaking, racist, subservient, backwards and skillless. Participatory curriculum design, like PAR, is situated in a community, renegotiates power in the classroom, and draws on a community's capacities to address inequalities in their daily lives. To begin conceptualizing a community-based ESL program with IRC, I needed to know more about the resettled refugees' experiences and perceived needs. IRC and I settled on needs-analysis interviews with their case-worker staff and clients (Iraqi refugees) to begin the curriculum development process.

Koirala-Azad and Fuentes (2009) recognize that the reliance on collaboration with people of varied backgrounds, engagement in a democratic process, and iterative relationship-building through dialogue and reflection can pose serious barriers in the process of PAR. Collaboration and relationship-building is time-consuming, and external pressures on the community or researcher may limit its effectiveness in taking action or maintaining participation throughout every step of the process. At this early stage in the research, I had not had time or opportunity to engage in the full relationship-building process with Iraqi refugees. Instead, I relied heavily on my relationship with IRC for PAR and curriculum building. The interviews with IRC staff were straightforward, but I was reliant upon them to connect me with future students – a task that was not easy or direct. The resettlement agency could not share their client's contact information with me directly, so they scheduled meetings with participants on my behalf. This was not only time-consuming, but there was at least one instance of miscommunication, where I arrived at a participant's house for an interview only to find that they were not expecting me. Because I did not speak Arabic, the interviewee's family member called a bilingual third-party and found out that the person I was supposed to interview was waiting for me at the local public library. Miscommunication had occurred before I even had the chance to begin my interview and the process felt unsatisfyingly non-participatory. Although I was eager to identify community partners to share in the process of program- and curriculum-building, as well as research, my only community partners at the time were the case workers and the volunteer coordinator at IRC.

To compound this situation, the fact that IRC was contacting the Iraqi refugees on my behalf could have resulted in further miscommunication. Did my interviewees fully comprehend that I was a graduate student conducting research, and not an employee or case worker from IRC? The interviews were also complicated by my outsider identity and lack of proficiency or literacy in Arabic. Because I had no funding to pay for translation services, and IRC could not spare their interpreters, I only had access to those refugees who could already speak English. I did not have access to those who may have been the most interested in additional ESL education and support. This is to say nothing of the potential conflicts that I may have been entirely unaware of regarding informed consent, and to what extent my position as a researcher from a university, a community volunteer from the resettlement agency, and a white woman born in the US to a middle-class family might have influenced the consent given before each interview.

As Block *et al.* (2012) discuss, it is difficult to create and implement a system of consent with refugee-background individuals, but it is important to make space for multiple and reflexive consent-giving to enhance the capacity for participants to be informed about the nature and content of the research, its purposes, and outcomes. Although I thought I had addressed all of the ethical issues involved in obtaining consent (specifically those demanded by my university's institutional review board), in hindsight I believe the relationships I built were not based on a full understanding of what informed consent or research are. I did not have Arabic translations of my informed consent form, nor did I have an interpreter or cultural guide with me. For researchers whose identity positions them as outsiders working with a vulnerable community, gathering informed consent from participants in the context of a single interview may not be possible without an interpreter and 'cultural guide' (Minkler, 2004). Perhaps as a consequence of such limitations on my part and of the programming initiative, it turned out that only one out of the five of my interviewees attended any of the resulting REAP classes. He was an Arabic-English interpreter in Iraq, employed at Wal-Mart at the time of the interview and the start of REAP. Upon further reflection, I wonder if he may have been more familiar with interviews and the process of consent than the other interviewees because of his English fluency and experience with American culture. I also wonder why I did not invite him to work with me early on as an interpreter and cultural guide. Looking back, I see that I missed an opportunity to be more critically reflective of my partnership with IRC. I should have been more focused on developing reciprocal partnerships with the Iraqi refugees in order to conduct better informed consent processes across linguistic and cultural boundaries.

With the start of REAP, I had the opportunity to improve the consent process. Although I used the same consent form as I had used for the initial needs-analysis interviews, in the context of the classroom setting I was able to lean on bilingual students to translate the forms and interpret our discussion of *research* and *consent* for those who were less fluent in English. Making the language accessible was the first step to reaching informed consent; the second step was to make the discussion an iterative process. Here again, the format of a classroom setting enabled me to address consent in ways I could not in a single interview. During our weekly meetings, I was able to discuss my research, my interest in PAR, answer questions, and offer concrete ways for students to contribute to the research process. Because gathering informed consent was now translated and iterative, it was more effective.

Curriculum and Self-Sufficiency

My initial interviews with Iraqi refugees and my process of gaining informed consent were not the only issues I am critical of in the first year of working on REAP; the emergent curriculum was also problematic. My relationship with IRC limited the extent to which I could implement a participatory curriculum because they wanted the program to focus on early employment and self-sufficiency. Early self-sufficiency is criticized by Tyeklar (2016) who argues that the US resettlement process – including resettlement agencies' discursive constructions of refugees – reproduces and perpetuates marginalization. She argues that resettlement agencies represent refugees as 'needy' and resettlement policies foreground early self-sufficiency at the cost of long-term self-sufficiency. While many of the refugees were keen to find employment in their previous careers, IRC's imperative (as dictated by federal policies of resettlement) was that refugees should accept the first available job. With IRC's influence, the first curriculum I developed for REAP was largely focused on finding a job, thus supporting the promotion of early self-sufficiency over language acquisition for social or other needs. The following two examples demonstrate the extent to which the ideology of early self-sufficiency is reflected in refugee resettlement policies, and the inadequacy of REAP in challenging this ideology.

In the needs-analysis interviews with Iraqi refugees, participants agreed that getting a job was important, but they did not feel that it should be the primary goal of REAP or that they would be satisfied with the first available job. For example, one woman I interviewed had been a professor in Iraq and was hoping to find a job working in an office; a job that would provide her with the salary and benefits to support her family. However, her resettlement agency pressured her to accept the job they had negotiated for her, working in a fast food chain. She was frustrated by this for two reasons: (1) there were no benefits and a low salary, making long-term self-sufficiency for her and her children unlikely; and (2) she felt that her identity as a highly educated woman was threatened. Hers is not an isolated case: Ricento (2013) describes a similar case study of a Colombian doctor, Fernando, who had been a doctor in his home country but was prevented from practicing medicine because his professional credentials were not recognized. In both of these cases, the refugees experienced dis-citizenship through the erasure of a part of their identity (Devlin & Pothier, 2006; Ramanathan, 2013a, 2013b). In REAP, I had hoped to address jobs and careers through a problem-posing and participatory curriculum. However, the first iteration of the curriculum was heavily influenced by IRC and focused on getting a job, not pursuing a career. Theories of PAR do not adequately account for systems of oppression that may be found in partnering community organizations, nor how to negotiate a balance between stakeholders. In this instance, my identity as volunteer program developer placed me at the crux of competing goals: IRC and early self-sufficiency, and the refugees' long-term self-sufficiency through career access. At this time, my relationship to IRC was stronger than my relationship to the refugees which limited my ability to take action for change. The 'action' in PAR focuses on policy changes, but my acceptance of IRC's policies around early self-sufficiency lacked critical reflection on structures of power and the processes of marginalizing refugees following US resettlement.

The second example where REAP and PAR were insufficient in challenging the ideology of early self-sufficiency began when a female participant intimated her interest in starting an Arabic-language day care. I was initially thrilled; I imagined the ways that this would benefit her family and her community, and I believed that it would be an opportunity to practice a more participatory curriculum. My co-teacher and

I investigated all of the requirements to start such a business, but found the certification requirements to be overwhelmingly complex, expensive, and time-consuming. Her excitement, like ours, soon faded into resignation as we discussed the extensive licensing procedure and the project was abandoned before it was started. PAR and attempts at a participatory curriculum were again insufficient in challenging these norms of practice.

These refugees' experiences point to the positionality of refugee-background identities socially placed into a powerful structure of dis-citizenship. Early self-sufficiency policies normalize the rejection of skills based on the country of origin. My deeply held belief in PAR ideals paired with my attempts at a participatory curriculum were insufficient to combat the social structures which marginalized these women by inhibiting their access to jobs of their choosing. My key partner in the research was still IRC, and this was evident through the IRC-influenced curriculum that did not challenge the marginalizing positioning of refugees through systematic employment pressures. What I needed was to establish a strong research partnership with the Iraqi refugees to balance the influence of IRC.

Cultural Miscommunication

Following the first six months of REAP, before the program received a Community Development Grant that added a health component (turning REAP into RHEAP), I held a focus group with the refugee participants and the community volunteer teachers and conversation partners. The purpose of the focus group was to reflect upon the structure and curriculum of the program in order to better align it with the interests and schedules of the community. Significant changes to the structure and curriculum were made as a result of this focus group (see Feuerherm, 2016, for a full account). One of the key changes was the identification of a community partner who was willing to take a leadership role in the program. Muhammad, one of the Iraqi refugees, was willing to commit his time and energy to REAP's improvement by becoming a bilingual volunteer teacher. He was a single, Iraqi male who had a Master's degree in English and had worked as an interpreter in Iraq before coming to the US as a refugee. Muhammad not only became a teacher in the following sessions of RHEAP, he helped with the childcare, he cooked delicious meals of traditional Iraqi food (and was not paid for this generosity), and, most importantly, he encouraged his friends and acquaintances to attend the program. His attention and effort grew the program by more than double the participation it had seen before, and students and volunteers alike enjoyed the food he prepared for every class. He also served as my informant of Iraqi culture and traditions. Through him, I was invited into families' homes to break the fast during Ramadan, I attended a barbeque hosted by a new, local Iraqi organization, and I was taken to local shops which sold Iraqi products. With his guidance, I learned more about Iraqi culture and my community at the same time. In return, I invited him to cultural events and a barbeque with my friends.

Participatory research processes require that relationships between academic and community researchers be built on friendliness, authenticity, care, open communication, empathy, honesty, and commitment (de Leeuw *et al.*, 2012; Mayan & Daum, 2016). Our relationship was mutually beneficial and bordering on friendship. However, it soon became clear that although I was secure in the platonic and professional nature of our relationship, he had developed feelings of a romantic nature. We had a pained conversation where he expressed his affection and I, deeply embarrassed, tried to stop him. As an unmarried woman, my interest in Iraqi culture coupled with our unaccompanied outings were interpreted not as a professional investigation of culture, food, and customs (as I had thought), but as romantic interest and availability. My naiveté was the result of very little prior exposure to Iraqi or Middle Eastern culture and my lack of critical reflection on conflicting cultural norms. Although I had made a point of talking to him about these outings, reflecting on their usefulness for my research and his role as an informant, I discounted his situated, cultural understanding and prioritized my own without critical reflection. Furthermore, the embarrassment and discomfort of the situation meant that we avoided each other, and now we have completely lost touch. There are a few studies that describe such complexity in the research process, particularly when the researcher is etic to the community and holds a privileged status. Caretta (2014) describes her experience of being an unmarried woman researcher in rural Kenya and Tanzania where she experienced the unwanted advances of men. She says that although she had a higher status than local women and access to both sexes, she was 'neither considered an 'honorary man' ... nor had [she] lost [her] sexual identity in the eyes of the locals' (2014: 495). Because I viewed my identity as a graduate student researcher eager to invest in my community through PAR, I had not adequately interrogated what it meant to be a privileged white woman engaging in collaborative community work with a vulnerable and marginalized population of majority-male refugees.

Langhout (2006) and Nygreen (2009) both describe their own critical dilemmas that evolved from their identities as white university researchers attempting PAR with historically oppressed communities. They separately conclude that PAR is insufficient in equalizing power between the university researcher and the community, and that critical, iterative reflexivity on intersectional identities and power is necessary (see also Muhammad *et al.*, 2015). The broken relationship between Muhammad and I is painful to recount and I continue to be troubled by its telling. For one, the telling is now one-sided. I have attempted to reach out to Muhammad since the incident – especially with the writing of this article – but all my contact information for him is outdated and worthless, and our mutual contacts have also lost touch with him. The breaking of our relationship means that Muhammad's voice is not included in the accounts of this research, which runs counter to PAR principles. And yet, I include this story as an example of how participatory research can 'muddle' relationships in ways that more traditional approaches do not. Research 'on subjects' leads to a clear, formal research relationship, whereas research 'with participants' can blur the lines between the formal relationship and friendship (or even be interpreted as something more). This can present the community partner with the risk of disappointment and abandonment, not only in extreme situations such as the one I experienced with Muhammad, but also any time a research project is completed and the research partner leaves (see Mayan & Daum, 2016, for additional examples). For these reasons, participatory researchers need to approach community partnerships armed with more than just theories of community-engaged research or admonishments to be critically reflexive: they must have mentoring and guidance through this process with examples of previous scholars' mistakes to learn from.

Principles of PAR outline the complexity of relationship-building, but they do not theorize what to do when things go wrong. Other accounts of my research omit the story altogether and the silence masks the complexity and challenges of doing participatory research. Through this telling, I acknowledge my failure to critically reflect upon the relationship building process, and the additional harm I caused to a valuable but vulnerable community member by abandoning an important relationship. I hope that my reflections on this event can open a more critical dialogue among participatory researchers that acknowledges successes *and failures* of partnership development so that participatory approaches to research are more reflexive on intersectional identities and power.

Funding, Power and PAR

It was at this point that REAP, through IRC, received a 3-year Community Development Grant from the Office of Refugee Resettlement. The grant specified that a health component be added to the program, changing the Refugee Employment Attainment Program (REAP) to the Refugee Health and Employment Attainment Program (RHEAP). Additionally, the grant enabled the program to hire a part-time program manager and pay for the Iraqi meals that until then had been generously prepared and donated by Muhammad. I assumed that he would be hired, having already invested nearly a year in the program and demonstrating his ability to encourage new students to attend. However, IRC felt that to better serve Iraqi refugee women and children, a woman would need to be hired. This was never explicitly stated, but Muhammad did not even get an interview for the position, although he applied. The grant specified that RHEAP should reach out more directly to families and children, and Muhammad was a single male. While some of his friends were married

with young children, most of the RHEAP participants that he had encouraged to attend were male. Those who did have wives and children generally did not bring them to RHEAP. Although I was surprised that he was
not offered the position, or even an interview, I had little control over the
process because the funding was distributed through IRC. The program
manager who was hired was a married woman with children, which gave
her access to the community of Iraqi refugee families that a single Iraqi
male did not have. In this case, nationality and visa status (Iraqi refugee)
intersected marital status and motherhood to provide access to a coveted
job. The effect of this was that several of the single men who had been
attending RHEAP no longer attended (including Muhammad), though
the married men began to bring their wives and children to the classes.

This balance of power through funding is different than that which
Nygreen (2009) experienced. As a graduate student PAR researcher,
she found that her multiple roles as project initiator *and* funder led to
her holding too much power, thus creating a 'false egalitarianism'. For
RHEAP, funding came through a partner agency, stripped me of power in
the hiring process, and balanced power between researcher and community. Despite the conflict I felt at the rejection of the community partner
who had furthered the program and my own experiential knowledge of
Iraqi culture, the woman hired by IRC to be the program manager, Mary,
was a clear asset to the program. Mary was a successful program manager
who, again, more than doubled the participation in the program and
increased the number of women and children served from a handful to
over 30 (about 15 women, 12 children and 5 teenagers). She organized and,
through the grant, paid the Iraqi women to make healthy meals for all the
students, teachers, and volunteers. She organized the health lessons, translating and interpreting English to Arabic whenever necessary. She moni-
tored the newly-developed children's program and organized events and
outreach to the community. Additionally, because of Mary's close relationship with the Iraqi refugee families, she informed me that they were in
need of instructional support for the citizenship test. Finally, RHEAP had
moved from being focused almost exclusively on finding a job and gaining
'self-sufficiency' to a comprehensive program that included social, health,
citizenship, and English instruction. With Mary's leadership, RHEAP was
able to gain the trust of the Iraqi women and children for whom this new
version of the program was intended while giving voice to their concerns.

Collaboration between Mary and I extended beyond the classroom:
we became research partners. Israel *et al.* (2005) state that *every* stage of
the research process should be participatory, including the dissemination
of findings. However, as a graduate student – like Nygreen (2009) – I was
compelled to write a single-authored dissertation. In order to balance the
institutional imperative to write a dissertation and the PAR imperative
to disseminate data collaboratively, Mary and I sought out other non-
academic means for sharing our findings: RHEAP volunteers, Iraqi

students, and I met with high school teachers to discuss differences in education-culture and college access; Mary presented our program at conferences and through Arabic television; and after I had a complete version of my dissertation submitted, Mary and I began a collaborative research agenda resulting in a book chapter. These efforts helped me balance the institutional obligation of writing a dissertation with the PAR principle that knowledge creation should be shared and disseminated by participants to broad audiences. This experience highlights the role a strong community partner can have on the research process. It also shows that the process of identifying a community partner requires time, critical reflection, and mutually agreed-upon roles and relationships between the partners.

Discussion

PAR is an approach to research that offers a social epistemology for social science that attempts to address privilege and act against oppression (Koirala-Azad & Fuentes, 2009; Pascale, 2011). Nevertheless, researchers attempting to adhere to the principles of PAR may find several impediments to their goals, for example: the large amount of time and critical reflexivity required to build equitable and trusting partnerships; the power-sharing process may be contested and driven by policies or funding; the action components and non-academic dissemination of research are not recognized (or valued) by researchers' institutions; and cultural misunderstandings based on interpretations of identities may disrupt the research process. As a novice researcher writing a dissertation, I was supported in theorizing the work for academic audiences but I lacked practical support for working with vulnerable and oppressed communities. My lack of experience and reflexivity early on led to a painful experience with a valued research partner. I hope that in sharing my own failure in this respect, I might demonstrate the need for independent support and mentorship for all who are involved in participatory research: academic institutions, public organizations, principal and co-investigators, and community researchers need a broad understanding of participatory research processes that address new relationship roles while broadening our understanding of accountability and ethics. Novice researchers should seek mentors who can provide practical guidance for conducting participatory research with minority populations. As Bromley et al. (2015) show through their interviews with community and academic research partners, the shift in research to more participatory models makes ethical priorities and roles more complex. In other words, PAR attempts to increase the ethics of the research process, but because of the blurred roles of research 'participants' (as opposed to research 'subjects'), the formal nature of the academic and community partner roles can be more easily misunderstood.

As participatory research becomes more common across disciplines, rigorous ethical principles need to address underlying shifts in process and product. Institutions should have a process for mentoring faculty and students conducting participatory research. Additionally, community ethics review boards are needed to oversee the ethical obligations of participatory research in local communities, giving the community an opportunity to evaluate the ethics of a proposed study. These systems could also provide a grievance procedure and mentorship opportunities. As I discovered through my first experience attempting participatory research, my institutional review board's policies and training regarding informed consent was not sufficient in attaining an adequate level of consent from my first participants. This was not only an issue of culture, but also of language. Academic institutions should support novice researchers with limited financial means by providing funding for interpreters or cultural mediators to aid in the process of gaining informed consent.

PAR principles alone are insufficient in preparing novice researchers for the complexities inherent in engaging with vulnerable minority populations, particularly when the researcher is etic to that community. Issues of consent, relationship-building (including trust and time), investment/ funding, and dissemination all require extensive critical reflection on the goals and identities of the participants. To not do so means risking exploitation, disappointment, abandonment, and/or rejection of the research process and product by the participants it is meant to support. At several points throughout my dissertation research, I lacked critical reflexivity on the role IRC played in the research trajectory, resulting in several instances where IRC's research needs and goals superseded those of the Iraqi refugee community. Then, my lack of critical reflexivity on intersections of culture and gender blinded me to the evolving situation with Muhammad. Critical reflection on the processes of participatory research also requires honest accounts of the flaws and failures in PAR. To only recount the ways that PAR has been successful in overcoming ethical issues reduces the push to be truly reflexive about the process. Research that highlights the messiness of a PAR approach to research, particularly regarding the multiple identities and positionings of the individuals and organizations involved, requires further critical analyses. The smooth-sounding research trajectories need to be complicated so that both failures and successes are shared in order to better meet the idealistic goals of PAR.

Acknowledgements

Many thanks to Doris Warriner and Martha Bigelow for the opportunity to share this story and for their many helpful comments on previous drafts. Thanks also to anonymous reviewers' invaluable feedback. And a special thanks to all those who participated in this research.

References

Auerbach, E. (1992) *Making Meaning, Making Change: Participatory Curriculum Development for Adult ESL Literacy*. United States: Center for Applied Linguistics. Retrieved from http://catalog.hathitrust.org/Record/007136627 (accessed 17 September 2018).

Baker, P. and McEnery, T. (2005) A corpus-based approach to discourses of refugees and asylum seekers in UN and newspaper texts. *Journal of Language and Politics* 4 (2), 197–226. doi: http://dx.doi.org/10.1075/jlp.4.2.04bak (accessed 17 September 2018).

Block, K., Warr, D., Gibbs, L. and Riggs, E. (2012) Addressing ethical and methodological challenges in research with refugee-background young people: Reflections from the field. *Journal of Refugee Studies* 26 (1), 69–87. doi: 10.1093/jrs/fes002.

Bradbury, H. and Reason, P. (2003) Action research. *Qualitative Social Work* 2 (2), 155–175. doi:10.1177/1473325003002002003.

Bromley, E., Mikesell, L., Jones, F. and Khodyakov, D. (2015) From subject to participant: Ethics and the evolving role of community in health research. *American Journal of Public Health* 105 (5) 900–908.

Bruno, A. (2011) *US Refugee Resettlement Assistance*. Library of Congress Congressional Research Service. Retrieved from http://digital.library.unt.edu/ark:/67531/metadc490999/ (accessed 17 September 2018).

Caretta, M.A. (2014) Situated knowledge in cross-cultural, cross-language research: A collaborative reflexive analysis of researcher, assistant and participant subjectivities. *Qualitative Research* 15 (4), 489–505. doi:10.1177/1468794114543404.

de Leeuw, S., Cameron, E.S. and Greenwood, M.L. (2012) Participatory and community-based research, Indigenous geographies, and the spaces of friendship. *The Canadian Geographer* 56 (2), 180–194.

Devlin, R. and Pothier, D. (2006) *Critical Disability Theory*. Vancouver: UBC Press.

Feuerherm, E. (2013a) Language Policies, Identities, and Education in Refugee Resettlement. PhD dissertation, University of California.

Feuerherm, E. (2013b) Keywords in refugee accounts: Implications for language policies. In V. Ramanathan (ed.) *Language Policies and (Dis)Citizenship: Rights, Access, Pedagogies* (pp. 52–72). Bristol: Multilingual Matters.

Feuerherm, E.M. (2016) Building a participatory program for Iraqi refugee women and families: Negotiating policies and pedagogies. In E.M. Feuerherm and V. Ramanathan (eds) *Refugee Resettlement in the United States: Language, Policy, Pedagogy* (pp. 75–95). Bristol: Multilingual Matters.

Fine, M. (2008) An epilogue, of sorts. In J. Cammarota and M. Fine (eds) *Revolutionizing Education: Youth Participatory Action Research in Motion* (pp. 213–232). New York, NY: Taylor and Francis.

Georgetown University Law Center, Human Rights Institute (2009) *Refugee Crisis in America: Iraqis and their Resettlement Experience*. Retrieved from http://scholarship. law.georgetown.edu/hri_papers/4 (accessed 17 September 2018).

Israel, B.A., Eng, E., Schulz, A.J. and Parker, E.A. (2013) *Methods in Community-based Participatory Research for Health*. San Francisco, CA: Jossey-Bass.

Janes, J.E. (2016) Democratic encounters? Epistemic privilege, power, and community-based participatory action research. *Action Research* 14 (1), 72–87. doi: 10.1177/1476750315579129.

Koirala-Azad, S. and Fuentes, E. (2009) Introduction: Activist scholarship possibilities and constraints of participatory action research. *Social Justice* 36 (4), 1–5. See https://www. socialjusticejournal.org/pdf_free/118Intro.pdf (accessed 17 September 2018).

Langhout, R. (2006) Where am I? Locating myself and its implications for collaborative research. *American Journal of Community Psychology* 37 (3), 267–274. doi:10.1007/s10464-006-9052-5.

Loring, A. (2016) Positionings of refugees, aliens and immigrants in the media. In E.M. Feuerherm and V. Ramanathan (eds) *Refugee Resettlement in the United States: Language, Policy, Pedagogy* (pp. 21–34). Bristol: Multilingual Matters.

Mackenzie, C., McDowell, C. and Pittaway, E. (2007) Beyond 'do no harm': The challenge of constructing ethical relationships in refugee research. *Journal of Refugee Studies* 20 (2), 299–319. doi:10.1093/jrs/fem008.

Mayan, M.J. and Daum, C.H. (2016) Worth the risk? Muddled relationships in community-based participatory research. *Qualitative Health Research* 26 (1), 69–76. doi: 10.1177/1049732315618660.

Minkler, M. (2004) Ethical challenges for the 'outside' researcher in community-based participatory research. *Health Education and Behavior* 31 (6), 684–697. doi:10.1177/1090198104269566.

Muhammad, M., Wallerstein, N., Sussman, A.L., Avila, M., Belone, L. and Duran, B. (2015) Reflections on researcher identity and power: The impact of positionality on community based participatory research (CBPR) processes and outcomes. *Critical Sociology* 41 (7-8), 1045–1063. doi: 10.1177/0896920513516025.

Nygreen, K. (2009) Critical dilemmas in PAR: Toward a new theory of engaged research for social change. *Social Justice* 36 4 (118), 14–35. See http://www.jstor.org/stable/29768559 (accesed 17 September 2018).

Pascale, C. (2011) Epistemology and the politics of knowledge. *The Sociological Review* 58, 154–165. doi:10.1111/j.1467-954X.2011.01967.x.

Ramanathan, V. (2013a) Language policies and (dis)citizenship: rights, access, pedagogies. In V. Ramanathan (ed.) *Language Policies and (Dis)Citizenship; Rights, Access, Pedagogies* (pp. 1–16). Bristol: Multilingual Matters.

Ramanathan, V. (2013b) Language policies and (dis)citizenship: who belongs? who is a guest? who is made to leave? *Language, Identity and Education* 12 (3), 162–166.

Reason, P. (2006) Choice and quality in action research practice. *Journal of Management Inquiry* 15 (2), 187–203. doi:10.1177/1056492606288074.

Ricento, T. (2013) Dis-citizenship for refugees in Canada: The case of Fernando. *Journal of Language, Identity, and Education* 12 (3), 184–188.

Tollefson, J.W. (1989) *Alien Winds*. New York, NY: Praeger.

Tyeklar, N. (2016) The US refugee resettlement process: A path to self-sufficiency or marginalization? In E.M. Feuerherm and V. Ramanathan (eds) *Refugee Resettlement in the United States: Language, Policy, Pedagogy* (pp. 152–171). Bristol: Multilingual Matters.

Wallerstein, N. (1983) *Language and Culture in Conflict: Problem-Posing in the ESL Classroom*. Reading, MA: Addison-Wesley Publishing Company.

Wilmsen, C. (2008) Participation, relationships and empowerment. In C. Wilmsen, W. Elmendorf, L. Fisher, J. Ross, B. Sarathy and G. Wells (eds) *Partnerships for Empowerment: Participatory Research for Community-Based Natural Resource Management* (pp. 1–22). Sterling, VA: Earthscan.

Part 2: Researcher Roles and Reciprocity

5 Doing Ethnographic Research as an Insider-Outsider: Reflections on Building Relationships and Doing Reciprocity

Rosalva Mojica Lagunas

Graduate students and future researchers are required to take methodology courses to prepare them to conduct research. However, there are often few or no methodological courses that are offered to students in order to prepare them to be in the field, especially when doing research in non-Western communities. This chapter examines the complexities and challenges that researchers may encounter when they are out in the field. I discuss the untold stories that these methodology courses may not cover. I specifically examine my experiences building relationships with and collecting 'data' from relatives and community members living in the village of Coatepec de los Costales, Guerrero, Mexico. As an ethnographic researcher and as a member of the community, I encountered a number of expected and unexpected obstacles and challenges while gaining access, while building trust and while conducting interviews and observations. Here, I describe first-hand reflexive accounts of the challenges involved in each of these processes and how my positionality was at the core of my study. I further explain why these untold stories need to be shared with others and how that process of sharing reflections might better prepare future researchers.

Research Context

The Nahuatl language, meaning 'clear intelligible speech', is a powerful and widely spoken imperial language that was, in fact, one of the many languages and varieties of Nahuatl that were spoken in Mexico before colonization. According to the census, (Archive of Indigenous Language of Latin America (AILLA), 2010; Baldauf & Kaplan, 2007; McCarty, 2011) there are over a million speakers of Nahuatl, an Uto-Aztecan language. There are varieties of Nahuatl across Mexico, all of which are disappearing from small communities. Despite the large number of speakers, the language is not being passed down to the younger generation and is at high risk of falling silent within the next one or two generations. Unfortunately, this phenomenon of language loss is common within Indigenous communities throughout the Americas.

These circumstances of language loss and layers of colonization have nearly killed my family's culture and language. Slowly, the language has been diminishing from our minds, bodies and hearts. Action is needed in order to stop the disappearance of the Nahuatl language from this land and from our family's heritage. With these priorities in mind, I decided to pursue a language reclamation project for my community, family, future family, and myself. In this chapter, I describe how building relationships was a key part of this project and the complexities and challenges involved.

Before I proceed, I would like to introduce myself as an Indigenous descendant would customarily do. My name is Rosalva, Mojica, Lagunas, first-generation Xicana woman with Indigenous roots in Coatepec, Guerrero, Mexico, a village located in the southwestern part of Mexico. My parents' names are Feliciano Altamirano Lagunas and Sofia Marciana Mojica Lagunas. Both are from Coatepec and are descendants of the Aztecs. Their native tongue is Nahuatl, often referred to as Mexicano. Although I was not born in Coatepec, I proudly acknowledge my ancestors from that place and my heart is there, so I consider myself from the village.

Coatepec de los Costales sits on a hill in Guerrero. Iguala is the closest city, and there are four villages that surround Coatepec. About 50 years ago, Nahuatl was the dominant language that was heard across the region. People would greet each other in Nahuatl and converse in the middle of the street. Over time, commerce and capitalism invaded Coatepec, and as social life changed, language shifted and the people began to speak more Spanish. Nahuatl was slowly disappearing from the community. Social dynamics also changed with back-and-forth migration to and from the United States and Mexico City. High mobility and new ideologies were brought into the village, resulting in changed linguistic practices.

Given the situation and the need for language reclamation within my community and family, I decided to conduct an ethnographic study in Coatepec de los Costales. During my stay, my uncle and aunt graciously offered their home, and I will always be grateful for their gesture. My six-month study explored language ideologies, practices, and management across generations (Spolsky, 2004, 2005, 2009). The following research questions (Seidman, 2013) guided the study:

(1) What are the language ideologies within and across generations in this setting?
(2) What are the observable language practices within and across generations in this setting?
  (2a) When and how is Mexicano[1] used within the domains of family homes, local schools and the community?
  (2b) When and how is Spanish used in these domains?
(3) What formal and informal language management strategies influence community members' language practices?
(4) In light of these findings, what are the implications for developing a community-based language revitalization plan?

Having these steering questions in mind and trying to uncover layers of passed-down ideologies, the focus of this chapter is not on the findings but rather on the process and journey, the untold stories that are forgotten but that are crucial to achieving some answers and to continuing these conversations. As I was preparing myself to do ethnographic work, there was little research written regarding the actual process of doing research in the kind of context I was about to enter. What would that look like? Was I going to be able to 'do research' the right way? Having an ethnographic perspective and applying ethnographic tools allowed me to deeply examine language policy in Coatepec, illuminating answers to my research questions. Possessing these tools and lenses allowed me to immerse myself in the village and partake of the villagers' ways of living and ways of being on this land. I became sensitive to the community's lifestyle and I became considerate to the way they viewed the world. I also made the commitment to live in the village for at least six months in order to develop relationships and gain the villagers' trust.

When I entered the village I was seen as a person who had roots in Coatepec, but at the same time I was an 'American', who did not know *their* culture, their way of being. My parents never taught me Nahuatl; I grew up speaking both Spanish and English. I was glad that my Spanish helped me to communicate with the residents of Coatepec, although it was difficult speaking to the elders, because I did not know Nahuatl. My origin in the United States created a barrier between them and me, which I had to break down. Many people assumed that I was a 'spoiled American', and perhaps thought I was judging their lifestyle. In my case, that was the biggest barrier that I needed to dismantle. Further I explore how I became a member of the Coatepec community. By the middle of my study, I had become a member of the community and was accepted as a member of Coatepec, because I lived the same daily lifestyle as them.

At the same time, I applied Critical Indigenous Research Methodologies (CIRM), in which respect, reciprocity, responsibility, and relationality constitute the '4 Rs' of research (Brayboy *et al.*, 2012). As both an insider and outsider, and through the use of Indigenous Knowledge Systems (IKS) and CIRM, I sought to capture the Indigenous knowledge within the community from a perspective that demonstrates the ancestral knowledges (Moreno Sandoval *et al.*, 2016), traditions, and the cultural values of Coatepec. During my time in the community, there was an exchange of knowledge between the people and me, although I was the one who gained so much from them. I hope to represent them in the best way to keep the sacred knowledge sacred and to share only that to which they agreed. I also hope to 'recognize self-determination and the inherent sovereignty of Indigenous people' through this work (Brayboy *et al.*, 2012: 423). I use the word sacred out of respect for my ancestors and participants. There are pieces of knowledge in the world which, if shared, can help others. I had the opportunity to learn from my people and asked their permission before sharing. I am devoted to our ancestors' gifts, and I do that with the utmost respect. I feel that what I have learned can help other emerging Indigenous scholars.

In the following sections, I describe the importance of CIRM and IKS. I also examine the complexities of doing research in an Indigenous community and describe the revelations throughout data collection and how my positionality was at the core of my research. The following questions led my focus: How can universities better prepare future researchers to do work in similar communities? What can we learn from sharing our data collection experiences with others? And, how will this benefit the field and researchers?

Living with Family Members

I spent six months in Coatepec de los Costales (January–June 2013). During my residency I lived with my uncle (my mother's brother), his wife and my grandmother, who live south of the zócalo (the center) in the town. I participated in everyday activities and responsibilities, such as cooking, cleaning, washing and tending to the house.

My uncle and aunt were both willing to accommodate my extended stay, as well as every trip I made prior to my long stay. They were happy to have another individual living in their home. Their four children had all married and started their own lives – three had moved to the United States and one remained in Coatepec. I explained to them the purpose of my stay, my role as a researcher, and how I wanted to integrate myself into their lifestyle. They agreed to help me and show me. At that particular time, my grandmother was very ill and my uncle was recovering from surgery, which left my aunt in charge of all the household duties as well as taking care of the fields.

It was difficult to balance my life as a researcher with that of a member of the family. First, I had to attend to my household chores such as sweeping the floors, helping my aunt make the food and washing clothes. I had also taken on the role of caring for my grandmother. Therefore, I was spending quite a bit of time with her and not enough time doing research. I did not realize that I was developing a deeper relationship with my grand-mother even though we could not communicate. Although I was not interviewing or taking field notes of the people, I was bonding with my grandmother and learning from her. Living in my research and family community felt like I was balancing on a tightrope. I was trying to stay on the rope without falling. I struggled with when to be a 'researcher' and when to just be the granddaughter, cousin, aunt or friend. I had a percep-tion of what a 'good' researcher needed to do and how it was important to take descriptive field notes. I felt as if my role as a researcher took a back seat as I spent time helping my ill grandmother. As I helped her, our relationship blossomed and I learned how to be, and how to belong. We never had a deep conversation because of our language barrier, as she was a monolingual Nahuatl speaker, but her actions and teachings through gestures showed me the deepest way of being a member of the community, and also passed down knowledge of ways of being that are slowly disappearing from our culture. These ways of being were taught indirectly during our sacred time together. This is a prime example of a case in which strengthening relationships demonstrates the power of ethnographic work. I later realized that I did not have to separate the two worlds, that I could do research in my family's community – I just needed to interweave both roles and to accept the ways my research was shaping and evolving (Lagunas, 2016).

Thus, relationships within the family are an important key when conducting research in these communities. Doing ethnography work is a prime example of one way of integrating into the community. When doing so, relationships are key factors in homes, schools and community. This work is sacred. In such cases, it was crucial to demonstrate that I was not only doing it for me or for the academic institution, but that I was also doing it for them. I was doing the work that they desired and needed in their community. I was there to illuminate answers to questions that could possibly lead to language revitalization.

In Coatepec, there is an unspoken relationship among all village members. Most of the members are united and are there to help each other in activities such as cooking and farming and in community events. Therefore, it is fundamental to foster these relationships with all members, in order to find participants to interview whom I might not have otherwise obtained. In addition, cultivating those relationships helped me to gain trust, giving them the confidence to share their honest experiences with me. I had created a safe space in which they were able to share their opin-ions without being criticized or critiqued. Most relationships developed organically through participation in everyday events such as hanging out at the schools, going to religious events, and helping in the kitchen during community events. I allowed myself to be seen and to be approachable by joining in light conversations.

Positionality

Prior to this study, I traveled to Coatepec to re-acquaint myself with the people and practices of the community. As noted previously, because my parents are from the village and I have family currently living there, I did have some experience with and knowledge of local customs and language practices. However, once I adopted a researcher's perspective, I came to see my prior connections to the place and the people as both an advantage and disadvantage. As I continued my work, I began to notice how my privilege played a role in my research and how others treated me. I wondered about how my positionality influenced my data and how I was received in the community. Although I had been to the village many times, I was born in the United States, and this meant I was still viewed as a (privileged) outsider. Although I live in the United States, where being white is a privilege, I am a brown Indigenous woman. Every day I deal with these issues in all contexts, including academia and in both my personal and work lives. As a conscious Indigenous female researcher, I am aware of the roles that I play and assume, as well as the impact these roles have on my research.

I consider it both an advantage and a disadvantage to be an 'insider/ outsider' to the community. Researchers may view me as an insider since my parents are native speakers and I have family members residing in the village. I have the advantage of knowing the community and some residents. On the other hand, community members viewed me as an outsider and referred to me as 'la Americana'. Although I have documented times when I felt like an insider, the residents' actions indicated that I still was not fully accepted into the community. As I feared that I might not be accepted, I was careful to prevent my biases and preconceptions from interfering with my work. I believe (looking back now) that keeping a reflection journal helped me stay focused.

Doing Research within Your Own Community and Indigenous Methodologies

When Indigenous people do Indigenous work in their own communities, they ask questions such as 'what does research look like?' and 'what counts as knowledge?' and 'how does this kind of research differ from that done in other communities?' In my own case, I struggled with collecting data while balancing the two roles of researcher and community member. At the beginning, I felt like a researcher 24/7, but later I negotiated those two worlds. For example, when I woke up I began by sweeping and helping my aunt prepare the breakfast. During our time together, I had my questions in mind, and although she was not one of my participants, I could not stop analyzing our conversations – for example, during our mealtimes, when our conversations were deeply complex, describing lives in Coatepec past and present. At times, I could not enjoy myself because I was thinking, 'This is really great for my research' and 'I'd better remember this, so I can write it in my journal'. It was tiring, because my brain was working nonstop, all the time. Research was not enjoyable. It was exhausting.

During my time there, my grandmother became very ill and I had to take a break from collecting research. I felt like a failure, that I was missing out on what I needed to be learning. During this experience, I realized that I was learning so much from my grandmother. Research was not one component of a binary life – I did not have to be in or out of that life mode. Research was fluid, and it was a dance in which I was both a researcher and a community member; I did not have to be one or the other. I wore both roles at all times and did not have to use all data, all conversations and all observations in my work. I learned through experience over time and soon realized it was acceptable to not be a researcher 24/7.

Indigenous research is a humbling experience (Smith, 2012); it is sacred, and research acts like ceremony (Brayboy & Deyhle, 2000; Wilson, 2008). Research has specific cultural protocols that are learned from being in the research community; these can be seen as ritual observances that are slowly being learned by the researcher. As the researcher continues in this ceremonious-like research, he or she is developing relationships by honoring the participants and deepening understanding of their way of being in this world, all while respecting this ritual of research. 'Reclaiming a voice … has also been about reclaiming, reconnecting and reordering those ways of knowing which were submerged, hidden or driven underground' (Smith, 2012: 72). During colonization, the Spanish forced our ancestors to stop speaking their native tongues, stop praying to their gods, and to reject other cultural traditions in order to assimilate into the Spanish culture. In these ways, the Spanish took knowledge away from our ancestors and colonized our bodies and minds. As an Indigenous woman, doing this kind of research helps me and my people to reclaim, reconnect with, and reorder our ancient ways and to awaken this suppressed knowledge.

The two most important ways of conducting research in an Indigenous community are to report back to the community and to 'share knowledge' – meaning it is a long-term commitment (Smith, 2012). We are not here to take knowledge, publish, and never go back to our communities. As we do this work, we make a sacred commitment to represent our communities in the best and most honest ways and to support them, because they are part of who we are. Thinking about Indigenous methodologies and reclaiming and reconnecting with the land of my ancestors helped me to do this sacred work. In the most humble state of being, I welcome the knowledge that I have gathered, and I write about it to the best of my ability to represent my people with the highest respect and honor.

Building Trust

There were times that my identity as the 'American' made it difficult for the Coatepeceños to accept me as one of them. Although both my parents were born in the village, this did not automatically translate into me being considered Coatepeceña. Before I conducted my six-month ethnographic research in my community, I visited the village at least once a year, but I stayed there for only a week. People knew that I was just visiting and that eventually I was going back home. But now when people asked me, 'How long are you staying?' and I responded, 'Five or six months', they just stared; some laughed, and some did not say much, but by their facial expressions I knew that they did not believe me. I knew that most people thought that an American could not survive that long in Coatepec, in large part because I was of a different social status and accustomed to a distinct lifestyle. I knew that I had to demonstrate to them that I was able to do so, that even though I would never be able to do all the things as well as they could, I was willing to learn.

The very first thing I did was to make sure I was seen in the community – that meant going to the stores, walking around the community, hanging out in the zócalo, attending community meetings and going to schools. I tried to be everywhere. I was present. But I made sure that I did not take my notebook or be seen recording data; I wanted them to see me as a participant in the community. First, I wanted to build trust. I knew that they were skeptical of what I was doing with the information I was gathering. I gained their trust by participating in a number of traditional events held in Coatepec. I made myself visible in the pueblo and befriended everyone. I tried and ate all the traditional cuisines, dressed similarly to them, and participated in many of the rituals of their daily lives (including work-related practices). As time went by, the members started noticing me. I was there for one week, then two weeks, then a month passed and they slowly began to trust me. They knew that I was staying and that I wanted to understand and learn from them.

One of the most important ways that I gained the trust of the people was to participate in the kitchen. My role as a woman in the community was to make the food. In many events, food plays an important role, and women are the primary providers of food and preparers of meals. I was invited to help the women cook, and I later realized that these shared experiences were crucial to my efforts to earn the trust of the women in the community. In the kitchen, we cooked at the same time. The women gave each other advice regarding health, families, and other household duties. Other times we gossiped. In all of these ways, we gradually built trust. I also spent time at the *parota*[2] washing clothes. Although I tried to get involved and live like the locals, washing clothes was not my strong point. I struggled in getting water from the well, and people noticed. I was still different. I believe people enjoyed seeing my struggle but at the same time they were glad that I was living like them. I wanted to live as closely as they did. They acknowledged my efforts. Although I could not do certain things as they did, I tried and they noticed. Sometimes the women would say, 'Estas lista para casarte' (You are ready to get married). Additionally, I bought bottled water as I tried to take care of my health during my stay. This was something that also stood out to the villagers.

After several months, it seemed as though I had gained their trust. I remember a specific day when I realized that I was accepted as one of the members of the community, and I recorded it in my journal. The following is an excerpt from my personal journal (Lagunas, 2016):

> It was a warm afternoon, and my aunt sent me to go grind the *nixtamal*, limed corn used for tortillas. I passed the outside vendor store and greeted the women with an 'adios'. They had always greeted me back, but this particular time was different. I took my pail of *nixtamal* to the Molino (mill) and the young women stared at me, amazed, and began asking, 'What is she doing? Is she going to make tortillas?' In Coatepec, a girl who is ready to make tortillas is considered to be a woman and is supposedly ready for marriage. It is a symbol of preparedness and a sign of knowing women's knowledge. The two young women stared at me, and I was able to feel their eyes watching my every move. At one point, they were unable to see me. I reached the Molino and asked to grind the *nixtamal*. The women there were surprised to see me all alone and had smiles on their faces. My hands were shaking and sweaty. I did not want to mess up and was under tremendous pressure. I slowly gathered the *masa* with my hands, moving it from one direction to the other until it was a big ball of dough. My hands were covered with *masa*. I paid and left. The *masa* quickly dried onto my fingers and hands. I passed the young women once again, and they said that I no longer had *nixtamal* but *masa*. This time as I said, 'Good-bye' they responded with a good-bye that was filled with happiness. It is hard to explain, but in their voice I heard the difference, and I felt that they continued to stare at me but with admiration and acceptance. (Field journal, May 21, 2013)

This moment describes the turning point at which I was seen not as a guest or visitor, but as someone from the community. I was able to make tortillas and that was essential for a woman in Coatepec. As mentioned earlier in my recorded journal, 'If you are able to make tortillas, then you are ready to get married', which means you are part of the community – and also exemplifies the role of a woman in our community. The people knew that I could make tortillas.

Interviews

While collecting data for my dissertation, I used a combination of informal and semi-structured interviews. 'Informal interviews are useful throughout an ethnographic study in discovering what people think and how one person's perception compares with another's' (Fetterman, 2010: 41). As the members of the community had never been interviewed, I first conducted informal interviews with them to build rapport in a natural situation. Informal interviewing is more like casual conversation. I believed that building trust was important, so they would feel comfortable when I began my semi-structured interviews, which I conducted after my first month of residing in the village.

With participants' permission, all interviews were audiotaped and some were videotaped, and later I transcribed and translated them. All interviewees were assigned a pseudonym. The interviews ranged in length, and younger students participated in informal interviews. Doing this helped me to develop trust, obtain authentic answers, and prevented interviewees from giving answers to please me. As I began my first interviews, I would notice my participants' facial expression waiting for my approval of their answers. I knew that I needed their trust and to make them feel comfortable, but knew it would take time to develop a relationship with them. As I have explained, I made myself visible in every aspect in order to gain their trust. I participated in community events, I helped the women with the cooking preparation, I was present at school every day, and I was seen in the community. In my later group interviews, some of the youth began joking around and began to talk freely with one another. There were no more silent pauses or nervous laughs.

The interviews did not go exactly as I had planned. I expected to do each individual interview with no other person present, but I soon realized that this was not possible for Coatepec. Members were rarely alone. There was always someone there listening or offering their input or comments. We had lots of interruptions as well. I cannot remember an interview I had with no interruptions; some were village announcements over the intercom, others were people walking by or kids needing their mother's attention.

Conducting Interviews in Coatepec: Challenges and Opportunities

The primary language spoken in Coatepec is Spanish, so all interviews in all age group categories, with the exception of the elders, were conducted in Spanish. Many of the elders were monolingual, speaking only Mexicano, and so in those cases I needed a translator. My aunt is a fluent speaker of Mexicano so she helped translate interviews. I audio-recorded the interviews (the elders' interviews constitute a source of language documentation as well as data for this study). Also, at that time, my grandmother became very ill and my mother came to the village to take care of her. My mother also served as a translator.

After my participants agreed to participate in the study, I scheduled times to interview them. At the scheduled time, I gathered my two audio-recorders, camera, and notebook and put it all in my colorful cloth bag. I had been carrying my bag everywhere I went so it had become part of my outfit. The few times that I did not have it with me, people asked, 'Where's your bag?' The bag represented that I was in my researcher role. The members knew that I was going to interview someone. The members knew that I carried my materials to do research, such as my audio-recorder, pen, notebook, and camera. Before going to my participants' homes, I asked my uncle or aunt where certain people resided, because I would often forget. They gave me directions on how to get there by saying, 'Go up to the zócalo, then make a left. Then you're going to pass the store, but it's before the church, right next to the second store…' I walked to the interviewees' homes and followed my uncle and aunt's directions. Once I got to the house, I knocked, but at the same time I yelled my participants' name or said *buenas tardes* (good afternoon)! I did this because it is difficult to hear a knock due to village announcements over the intercom, loud music playing or because they may have been in another room far away from the main door.

Through my experiences scheduling appointments, I learned about Coatepec time. When I went to an interview at the scheduled time, the interviewees were sometimes there, but sometimes not. If there was someone in the household, they would say that the participant I wanted to interview was still in the fields, washing clothes, or was busy doing a chore. I would thank them and then they would ask me to come back later, or the following day at the same time. Sometimes it was difficult to interview a participant due to their busy schedule. But I understood, as I too had responsibilities at home, and sometimes duties took longer than expected. I discovered this one day when I had an appointment at eleven in the morning but I also needed to wash clothes that same day. I woke up early and began washing at seven, but because there was little water, it took longer to wash the clothes than expected. By the time I had got home and helped my aunt to prepare lunch, it was one in the afternoon. That is when I learned about timing in Coatepec. Household duties are a priority, and occasionally they take longer than expected. In the beginning, the participants scheduled an interview by saying they would speak with me in the morning or the evening, but I always wanted a specific time, so they would give me a time. After my experience washing clothes and being late to my own interview, my view regarding time also changed. I understood that the interview would eventually be done but I needed to be patient. This experience helped me to connect with what it meant to be a researcher in Coatepec – it looked a little different than what I was taught.

Once I was ready to interview my participants, I conducted the interviews inside their homes or outside, wherever they preferred. My first interview was with Anita, a 14-year-old who was attending middle school. She let me into her home, gave me a chair, and offered me some water. I accepted and began my interview by asking her name and getting consent to audio-record and photograph. After the first question, her sister joined the interview. She sat to the right of me, just observing at first. This bothered me initially because I wanted Anita to express her ideas confidentially without anyone being present. I felt her sister's presence skewed her answers. Later, after a few more questions, Anita answered but her sister interrupted and chimed in. She voiced her opinion regarding the question I asked. I wanted to ask the sister to refrain from answering questions and also to perhaps leave the room, but I knew that I could not do that, because I was a guest and they were doing me a favor. I thanked her and left. As I walked back to my house, I felt disappointed that the interview did not go well. I thought, 'This is not what an interview is supposed to look like. I have been taught to have my questions semi-scripted and to be ready to audio-record, in a quiet place, with the researcher and the interviewee. I failed in every aspect.'

After feeling disappointed, I told myself that my future interviews would be different. I would be ready to steer the interviews the way I wanted them to be, the way I learned from my methods and methodologies courses. To my surprise, most of the interviews were the same as the first one. Another individual would always be present while I tried to talk to my interviewee. After some time, I learned that our village is not individualistic; people do things together, and they are often with someone as they walk to the store, work, cook, and so on. I realized the way we do research in Coatepec might look different from Western research methods. Every community is different, although there may be some similarities in ways of doing research.

Implications

Doing research in Indigenous communities or in non-Western settings looks different, and most of the time the methods courses offered at the university do not address these issues, nor prepare us for the challenges involved, or align with the priorities of the community itself. Indigenous scholars have written about Indigenous methodologies that are useful when in the field; however, these books are rarely used in general methods courses (Brayboy & Maughan, 2009; Smith, 2012). The discussion of how a researcher might alternate the methods they choose is necessary. The following are guidelines that I implemented when I was in the field. These guidelines are meant to be considered fluid and not linear.

(1) *Get to know your research setting and get involved as much as you can.* This will help you to discover how your participants live and do things. For example, in my case, at first I did not realize that most people were never alone, which led to frustration as I began interviewing. This is one way to gain your participants' trust. They will learn to respect you and be more willing to participate in the research.

(2) *Gain your participants' trust through grounding your positionality.* Recognize your biases and the way you see the world. How does this interfere with the kind of research you are doing and how does it benefit you? I needed to discover myself in order to connect with my participants.

(3) *Observe without a notebook.* It is acceptable not to record every moment; it is better to be present in the moment. That is how I gained my community's trust. Once I got home, I wrote as much as I could. Later, in my study, I began to take my notebook to write detailed notes.

(4) *Interview differently.* Realize and accept the way the community lives and breathes. We researchers are guests that people are allowing into their lives. Allow interruptions during the interview, allow stories and allow other participants to join in.

With this said, I am not saying to ignore all the methods that you were taught. I believe that training is the foundation for research practice, but our ideas of how to gain access or build relationships or collect data should be flexible; our preconceived notions will not necessarily fit all situations. As long as there is enough reason to discuss how and why we conduct research, both ways are valuable.

How do we align the methods that are taught in academia and better prepare our future researchers? And how do we include more methods courses that will benefit researchers working in these communities? These are questions that need further exploration. Moreover, there is a long overdue need to review and critique these issues. Anthropologists have been doing this type of work for many years and there has been some change, but not enough. Researchers such as Brayboy *et al.* (2012), Paris and Winn (2013) and Smith (2012), among others, have explored this field and have contributed to some of the changes in the way we do research, although it is just the beginning. Up-and-coming Indigenous researchers need to begin a dialogue regarding the challenges they encounter when conducting research in their communities so others can have a framework or guidelines on what to expect. Although these guidelines may not be appropriate for every community, they are a beginning. More discussion is needed regarding how Indigenous people conduct work in their own communities, and how we can learn to accept the struggles as part of the research. Every community is different, but stories like these need to be shared. Such episodes are similar to sharing *testimonies*, 'authentic narratives or journeys of oppressed groups' (Huber, 2009: 643), and one learns from them. It is important to share experiences of collecting data and to discuss issues such as what went well, what could have been done differently and so on. I know that it is a learning process and that research is supposed to be messy, but we can help each other by sharing and perhaps our research outcomes will be enhanced as a result.

As we continue to do this work, we need to remember that it is not for us but for everyone – it is a collaboration of knowledge. It is hard work, but it is a humbling experience in which one builds long-lasting relationships with his or her participants, their community, and themselves. Let us begin the discussion of research struggles and tell the untold stories.

Notes

(1) The community members often refer to their language as Mexicano.
(2) Parota is a large well. This is where members of the community go to wash clothes or to acquire drinking water, from the smaller well. This is a landmark in Coatepec.

References

Archive of Indigenous Languages of Latin America Collection, Benson Latin American Collection (2010) University of Texas Libraries, the University of Texas at Austin.

Baldauf, R.B. and Kaplan, R.B. (2007) *Language Planning and Policy in Latin America*. Clevedon: Multilingual Matters.

Brayboy, B., Gough, H., Leonard, B., Roehl, R., and Solyom, J. (2012) Reclaiming scholarship: Critical Indigenous research methodologies. In S. Lapan, M. Quartaroli, and F. Riemer (eds) *Qualitative Research: An Introduction to Methods and Designs* (pp. 423–450). San Francisco, CA: Jossey-Bass.

Brayboy, B. and Maughan, E. (2009) Indigenous knowledges and the story of the bean. *Harvard Educational Review* 7 (1), 1–21.

Brayboy, B.M. and Deyhle, D. (2000) Insider-outsider: Researchers in American Indian communities. *Theory into Practice* 39 (3), 163–169.

Fetterman, D. (2010) *Ethnography: Step-by-Step*. Thousand Oaks, CA: Sage.

Huber, L.P. (2009) Disrupting apartheid of knowledge: Testimonio as methodology in Latina/o critical race research in education. *International Journal of Qualitative Studies in Education* 22 (6), 639–654. doi:10.1080/09518390903333863.

Lagunas, R. (2016) Intergenerational language ideologies, practices, and management: An ethnographic study in a Nahuatl community. Unpublished thesis, Arizona State University.

McCarty, T.L. (2011) *Ethnography and Language Policy*. New York, NY: Routledge.

Moreno Sandoval, C.D., Lagunas, R.M., Montelongo, L., and Diaz, M. (2016) Ancestral knowledge systems: A conceptual framework for decolonizing research in social science. *AlterNative* 12 (1), 18–31.

Paris, D. and Winn, M. (2013) *Humanizing Research*. Thousand Oaks, CA: Sage.

Seidman, I. (2013) *Interviewing as Qualitative Research: A Guide for Researchers in Education and the Social Sciences*. New York, NY: Teachers College Press.

Smith, L. (2012) *Decolonizing Methodologies: Research and Indigenous Peoples*. London: Zed Books.

Spolsky, B. (2004) *Language Policy*. New York, NY: Cambridge University Press.

Spolsky, B. (2005) *Language Practices, Ideology and Beliefs, and Management and Planning*. New York, NY: Cambridge University Press.

Spolsky, B. (2009) *Language Management*. New York, NY: Cambridge University Press.

Wilson, S. (2008) *Research is Ceremony: Indigenous Research Methods*. Black Point, Canada: Fernwood.

6 Researcher-Participant Relationships in Cross-Language Research: Becoming Cultural and Linguistic Insiders

Sarah Young Knowles

On the researcher as an insider-outsider: 'This hyphen acts as a third space,
a space between, a space of paradox, ambiguity, and ambivalence,
as well as conjunction and disjunction.'
Dwyer and Buckle, 2009: 60.

Introduction

This chapter begins with a brief summary of my dissertation research, which was a qualitative case study examining metalinguistic awareness in four Central American women enrolled in a supplemental ESL class intended to develop their English literacy skills. My research design and questions about the nature of metalinguistic development and how it is facilitated (or not) by formal literacy instruction were supported by my case study approach that triangulated (1) teacher reports with (2) my classroom observations and (3) the participants' elicited interpretations of those classroom experiences in their native (L1) Spanish. This holistic approach highlighted the powerful if often hidden influences of pedagogical, personal, and environmental factors on the development and use of metalinguistic awareness in second language (L2) learning. The data collected through observations, teacher reports, and document reviews were essential in contextualizing the learning environment, but the L1 Spanish interviews provided the most meaningful data because they elicited the four participants' perspectives and experiences in their own words.

As I reflected on my data collection methods and the rich data that were elicited from the participant interviews in their L1 Spanish, I began to appreciate the nuances of conducting cross-cultural, cross-language research with this special learner population. I am a native English speaker, with intermediate-level skills in Spanish. In my study, I elicited the participants' words in Spanish, transcribed them, and translated them to the best of my ability. What impact did my L2 Spanish proficiency have on my status as a cultural and linguistic insider-outsider in my relationship with the participants? Is the insider-outsider dichotomy a useful one to consider in this type of research? In our Spanish-medium interviews, how did our roles change or balance out when the participants were positioned as linguistic insiders (as L1 Spanish speakers) and the researcher was positioned as a linguistic outsider (as the L2 Spanish speaker)? Finally, how do my abilities as a novice researcher-translator affect the presentation and interpretation of the data? After examining these questions in the context of my dissertation study, I conclude this chapter with a resolution to conduct cross-language research more intentionally and with greater reflexivity in the future.

Background on the Study

As Bigelow and Tarone (2004) noted over a decade ago, much of the research on adult instructed L2 acquisition to date has primarily been conducted on L2 learners with relatively high levels of L1 literacy, academic achievement and socio-economic status, and who learned an alphabetic system of writing as an L1 or L2. In the same vein, the notion of 'the good language learner' in second language acquisition (SLA) research has been explored from a variety of perspectives (e.g. Griffiths, 2008; Rubin, 1975), but without any mention of L2 learners with limited literacy skills in these formal instructed L2 learning environments.

My ESL teaching experiences with adult English language learners who had limited literacy skills helped shape my dissertation research. I was curious about the impact that language awareness, noticing, knowledge about language, knowledge about schooling and literacy practices, and use of print might have on L2 acquisition – particularly for those emergent L2 reader-writers who were enrolled in ESL classes that relied mainly on printed materials and literacy practices to guide L2 instruction. In my dissertation study, I focused on the concept of metalinguistic awareness, understood at the narrowest definitional level as the conscious and intentional ability to reflect on, analyze, and manipulate language (Jessner, 2006). I eventually began to formulate a research agenda that focuses in on the experiences, perspectives, and beliefs that this understudied learner population has in L2 learning. My goal has been to develop a more complete, empirically-supported understanding of the phenomenon of metalinguistic awareness, by heeding Ortega's (2012) call to broaden the scope of learner populations included in SLA research.

Collecting Case Study Data as an L2 Researcher and L2 User

There is a long history of case study research in SLA, but the most well-known cases have been conducted in the participants' L2 of English or with a focus on eliciting evidence of developmental language in the L2 (e.g. Lardiere, 2007; Norton, 2013; Schmidt, 1983). My case study followed four Central American women – Hana, Frida, Tina and Marta – during their attendance in an 11-week-long supplemental ESL literacy program in the suburbs of Washington DC. I met and recruited these women in the context of their supplemental ESL literacy class, which they attended for 30 minutes per day outside of their mainstream ESL class. Three of these four women had six or fewer years of formal schooling in their native countries. They ranged in age from early 20s to late 50s. Their length of residence in the United States ranged from 18 months to 25 years.

My long-term involvement with this adult ESL program as a classroom teacher, literacy class tutor, and teacher trainer (from 2003 to 2014) facilitated my access to the research process and my introduction to the participants. Before collecting any interview data, I received permission from the participants and their teachers to observe the supplemental literacy classes. Throughout the 11-week data collection period, I regularly sat in on the classes as an observer so that I became a familiar face to the participants. The frequent observations also allowed me to talk to the participants directly about what was happening in their classes, and to take extensive field notes on what was happening in the learning environment.

I conducted two or three L1 Spanish interviews with each of the participants individually, over a period of two months. The use of the participants' L1 Spanish for the interviews was of fundamental importance, and it provided an interesting contrast to my somewhat limited L2 Spanish proficiency. In Spanish, I can chat one-on-one about my personal life and some everyday topics, but I quickly get lost in lively conversations with multiple speakers, unexpected tangents, unfamiliar content, and colloquial language. In a formal setting, such as the data collection interviews, I can perform a prepared script and understand the majority of the responses. I can ask follow-up questions not included in the script, although I may need to make myself understood through circumlocution and other communication strategies. Knowing these limitations, I drafted my interview protocols in Spanish and had two native Spanish speakers from Central and South America review and correct them.

During the interviews, I read directly from the printed protocols, making a point to show that my L2 communicative ability was dependent to a great extent on a printed guide rather than automaticity in speech. I listened closely to the participants' responses and stopped them when

I struggled to understand something they said, asking them to repeat or clarify my misunderstanding. In sum, I adhered to what Winchatz (2006) has called 'ethical honesty about [one's] linguistic abilities during key interactional moments' (2006: 94). I did not hide my L2 limitations during data collection; I pointed them out when they were the cause of a communication breakdown. I positioned myself as someone who was eager to hear and learn from the participants, but who required their patience as I sometimes fumbled in my L2 communication.

The benefits of our collaborative use of their L1 Spanish and my L2 Spanish in the interviews were real and immediate. The interview protocols were designed to reflect and elicit key themes regarding language, L2 learning, and L2 instruction; beliefs and attitudes, experiences, strategies, struggles and successes and analysis of or reflection on language. These L2 learners are rarely, if ever, asked these questions in a systematic way in the adult ESL classroom – and even less so in the L1. The rich descriptions of language use and personal accounts given in the learners' L1 provided remarkable insights into my research questions about metalinguistic awareness. I captured details that provided much-needed insights into their metalinguistic abilities and beliefs. In the following example, Marta deftly explains a spelling rule in English that can be tricky for learners – the 'long /e/' – while simultaneously connecting it to the influence of intelligence on literacy development:

> En la escritura, hay veces que lleva dos letras y habla una, nada más. Hay que entender bien los sonidos de las letras porque a veces van dos, ¿verdad? Como 'keep.' Son dos letras, [i] [i]. [ki-i-i-pe]. Tengo que memorizarlas, porque al hablarla, keep, only es una. Por eso, escribirla tiene que ser bien inteligente para tener la escritura correcta, grabárselo bien en la mente.

> *In writing, sometimes there are two letters but you only say one. You have to understand the sounds of the letters very well, because sometimes there are two, right? For example, 'keep.' It's 2 letters: /e-e-/. /ki-e-e-pay/. I have to memorize those, because in speaking, keep, it's only one. You have to be very intelligent to remember the correct way to write it.*

Marta had completed two years of education in Mexico some 50 years previously. Her adroit explanation of the double /e-e-/ gave me a clear idea of what she had understood about English spelling from her ESL instruction, but it also brought to light a learner perspective that I had never before considered. Her reference to the need for 'intelligence' in mastering the rules of writing raises questions about the social, educational, and emotional barriers to learning that many of these learners may struggle with their entire lives. At the same time, she was demonstrating to me that she possessed the requisite intelligence and was positioning herself as having insider status when it came to knowledge about English.

The Insider/Outsider Debate in Cross-Cultural, Cross-Language Research

When I began my dissertation research, I didn't know that I was conducting 'cross-cultural' and 'cross-language research' (Liamputtong, 2008; Temple, 2002) and that there was a significant amount of literature, originating to a great extent from the field of health care research, written about the challenges of doing so (e.g. Choi *et al.*, 2012; Esposito, 2001; Squires, 2009; Temple, 2002). I simply saw the use of the participants' L1 Spanish in the study as both an advantage and a necessity to conduct this research, despite my limitations in my L2. Cross-language research has been defined as research in which 'a language barrier is present between researchers and their respondents' (Nurjannah *et al.*, 2014: 2), usually requiring the use of a translator or interpreter in collecting, transcribing, and translating the data (Temple, 2002). These perceived linguistic and cultural barriers are believed to pose unique threats to the validity of research findings (Esposito, 2001) and the trustworthiness of translated data (Squires, 2009).

Much of the concern about cross-cultural, cross-language research relates to the status of the researcher as an insider/outsider of the participants' culture. According to Liamputtong (2008) and Suwankhong and Liamputtong (2015), cultural insiders have a strong advantage over outsiders because of their commonalities with the research population, their tendency to be accepted as legitimate members of the community, and their clearer insights about the workings of the group they are studying. From this perspective, cultural outsiders are seen to have a distinct disadvantage in eliciting and interpreting data because they lack fundamental understanding of the research population.

I am different in many ways from Frida, Hana, Tina and Marta. For example, we differ in nationality, language, ethnicity, education, occupation, family, literacy practices, citizenship status, socioeconomic status, and life experiences. What, if anything, qualified me to be a culturally competent researcher, possessing the kind of appropriate cultural knowledge that 'provides a context for the phenomenon, research questions, results, and interpretations' (Choi *et al.*, 2012: 656)? Did my limited L2 Spanish proficiency and lack of shared culture further extend the insider/outsider barrier between me and my participants, or could my L2 status be seen as an advantage in this research context?

The debate about insider/outsider status in cross-cultural research has been discussed and problematized from a variety of perspectives (Dwyer & Buckle, 2009; Irvine *et al.*, 2008; Kusow, 2003). Researchers who are immigrants/border-crossers themselves and who conduct research with populations from their home culture and L1 have criticized the notion that being a cultural insider is an advantage, as cultural commonalities can lead to complacency, less informative data, and incorrect assumptions about shared knowledge. In her work with fellow Polish immigrants in the UK, Gawlewicz (2016: 35) described feeling disconnected from her participants as she struggled to elicit data: 'Some of my interviewees spared me certain context or culture specific explanations by simply saying: "We both know what I mean" and giving me a knowing look' (2016: 35).

These experiences have led so-called cultural insider researchers to question the validity of the insider/outsider dichotomy, and to propose that it is more of a continuum that emerges from the research experience itself. Duranti's (1997) seminal text on linguistic anthropology acknowledges the difficulty of linguistic outsiders to completely comprehend participants' emic perspectives, but reminds us that it is equally difficult for linguistic insiders to comprehend etic perspectives. After some less successful attempts at data collection with fellow Somali immigrants, Kusow (2003) concluded, 'The insider/outsider distinction lacks acknowledgment that insiders and outsiders, like all social roles and statuses, are frequently situational, depending on the prevailing social, political, and cultural values of a given social context' (2003: 592).

When I began data collection at the adult ESL program where I had held various roles for 11 years, I believed that I held a unique 'insider' position. I saw myself as competent to conduct Spanish interviews despite my L2 limitations, in part because of many years of classroom experience with the adult English language learner population. I believed that these experiences helped provide a needed amount of background knowledge for understanding and interpreting much of what the participants said in Spanish regarding their L2 experiences. From the program staff's perspective, my status as a long-time ESL teacher and a novice researcher who had read a great deal regarding the topic, likely positioned me as an insider. However, the question of how my participants would see me remained. Despite my limited L2 proficiency, could my status as an L2 learner/user myself make up for any lack of cultural knowledge or linguistic competence in the eyes of my participants?

Power, Vulnerability and Expertise in Cross-Language Research Relationships

The power dynamic between researcher and participant is a common one discussed in the interview context (Kvale, 2006; Vähäsantanen & Saarinen, 2012). Among vulnerable or marginalized research populations, this dynamic may require even further consideration – although Perry (2011) cautions against the labeling of such populations as disempowered or somehow incompetent. In cross-language research when the shared language is not the researcher's L1, an interesting twist on power and vulnerability may emerge. First, the ability of the researcher to serve as her own interpreter rather than using an outside source may be an advantage for interpretation and analysis. Esposito's (2001) experience in using transla-tors to access her data led her to conclude, 'Because of language barriers, I could not immerse myself in the actual words used by the women. Analysis and interpretation are accomplished *as one would analyze and interpret a silhouette* [my italics]' (2001: 576). According to Shklarov (2007), serving as one's own translator has potential benefits:

> Seeing two parallel cultural meanings or realities, and hearing two or more conceptual understandings might be challenging, but *if not obscured* [my italics], it might meaningfully enrich the in-depth perception of the context area and contribute tremendously to the ethical sensitivity and the quality of research. (Shklarov, 2007: 532)

Nurjannah *et al.* (2014) also acknowledged the potential challenges of being a bilingual researcher who is immersed in data that is not in one's first language.

Rather than viewing a less-than-fluent bilingual researcher as being a limitation of the methodology, I found support in the literature that it was an advantage by other researchers who had done the same. Chen (2011) found that being a non-native interviewer encouraged participants to share more, because 'the interviewer is obliged to let interviewees define their concepts, deferring to their position as a language authority and recognizing one aspect of the power relationship' (2011: 119). Winchatz (2006) explored the role that using the L2 has on cross-language ethno-graphic research, concluding that communicative misunderstandings due to language limitations on the part of the bilingual researcher can actually serve to 'problematize one's lack of lexical knowledge and ... to attain richer linguistic descriptions from participants' (2006: 89).

Although Winchatz (2006) reached the above conclusion after initially experiencing embarrassment and loss of face during communication break-downs in her L2 interviews, I actively sought linguistic corrections and insights from my participants. One benefit of seeking these explanations was that they provided key insights into my research questions about the partic-ipants' metalinguistic knowledge and awareness, as well as help in building my own L2 competence. However, I believe these explanations served an equalizing role not unlike what Muller and Gubrium (2016) describe:

> We suggest that language differences in the research interaction, commonly seen by both quantitative and qualitative researchers as detrimental and as weaknesses to be minimized in cross-cultural research, may in fact be used to empower marginalized participants. We suggest furthermore that a precursor to potential empowerment is a researcher's active decision to expose her linguistic vulnerability. (2016: 141)

I found that the intersection of the participants' L1 Spanish and my L2 Spanish contributed to a more equal playing field in the data collection experience. In many ways, our use of Spanish shifted the participants into the role of L1 expert in contrast to my role as L2 learner. My position as a L2 Spanish user-interviewer helped to (re)frame the participants' positions as linguistic experts and co-relationship builders. In addition, their use of their L1 allowed them to render their understanding of language (both Spanish and English) in explicit and clear ways, contributing to the underlying research questions driving the study itself. Using Spanish as the interview language allowed the tables to be flipped, as the participants became the 'language experts' who held the keys to the language and worked to help me access and produce it as the L2 Spanish speaker.

This linguistic expertise was evident when I asked for the meanings of words, another way to say something, the pronunciation of a word, or questioned the usage of a word. In this short exchange, Marta and I were discussing the meaning of the word 'upset', which she had recently encountered in one of her ESL literacy class stories, and how it can represent an emotional state or a physical problem (e.g. upset stomach). She understood the word quite well, but I was curious about how to say the word in Spanish – especially given its multiple interpretations in English:

Sarah: Como se dice en español 'upset'? Preocupada? [*How do you say 'upset' in Spanish? Preocupada?*]

Marta: Si pues preocupada. O muchas veces se dice 'Ay no … ¡ésta problema me tiene enferma!' Por el problema. No hay una enfermedad, pero te enferma. Tu *feel* es enfermo. Sick. Puede ser preocupada. [*Yes, preocupada. Or you can also say 'Oh no … This problem is making me sick!' Because of the problem. It's not a sickness, but it makes you sick. Your feeling is sick.*]

Our shared meaning-making in the above excerpt allowed Marta to give me an alternative and possibly more colloquial way of expressing 'upset' in Spanish, and she integrated both Spanish and English in her emphasis on the explanation, 'Tu feel es enfermo. Sick.' I view her occasional codeswitching to English in our conversations as her attempt as a linguistic insider to bridge the gaps in my own language proficiency. Moreover, Marta's frequent and rich descriptions of language and language use throughout our interviews allowed her to position herself as a knowledgeable insider, perhaps in direct contradiction to any stereotypes that might exist of a woman with only two years of formal schooling.

The participants certainly conformed to the expectation that this was a formal interview by following my turn-taking cues and answering my questions. However, our shared used of Spanish and my position as an endeavoring L2 Spanish user seemed to open the door to more personal talk, questions, and commentaries. The tables were again flipped when the participants took me up on my offer to ask me questions if they would like, or when I sought their reassurance about my Spanish proficiency. Through this growing personal relationship, we sought commonalities in our personal lives and our L2 learning experiences. My Spanish was complimented on several occasions by the participants, and they wanted to know how or where I had learned it. They asked me what I was studying, if I was married, if I had children, where I lived, and where I worked.

Within the L1-L2 Spanish interview setting, the participants and I positioned ourselves as L2 learners in various contexts, and we connected over those identities as we shared our beliefs and experiences about what had worked for us in our respective L2 learning attempts. Frida and I often found ourselves comparing struggles with our L2. When I pointed out that it is sometimes easier for me to understand what is said to me than to respond, Frida agreed: 'Igual con nosotros, que cuando nos hablan en inglés, entendemos. Pero el problema es expresarlo.' [*It's the same for us. When people talk to us in English, we understand, but the problem is how to communicate that.*] I gave the example of the double rolled – rr in Spanish; I can hear it, but I usually have a hard time producing it. Frida was quick to model for me how to produce it with the word 'carro', then empathized again, 'Eso sucede a nosotros. Entendemos a veces lo que nos dicen, pero no podemos decirlo.' [*This happens to us, too. Sometimes we understand what they say to us, but we can't express that*].

In one interview, I asked Marta about the L2 learning habits that she observed among her classmates in her mainstream ESL class. She talked about her classmates' use of smart phones in class to quickly look up an unfamiliar word or find an L1 translation when needed:

Marta: [...] Muy rápido escriben. Rápido encuentran, escriben y ya entienden. Mientras que yo [laughs] yo tengo que hacer preguntas para entender que es esa palabra. [*They write really quickly. They find it quickly, write it, and then they get it. In the meantime [laughter], I have to ask questions to understand what the word is.*]

Sarah: En mi opinión es mejor lo que está haciendo ... si no puede salir de la mente. [*In my opinion, what you do is better ... The word won't leave your head then.*]

Marta: No se la grabó bien. No trabajó para que se le quede la palabra. [*They didn't really get it. They didn't work so that the word would stick.*]

This brief consensus-building example, like many similar encounters during our interviews, helped shift our relationship from that of a clearly-bounded researcher-participant relationship to one of cooperative insiders sharing knowledge about L2 learning. An additional advantage of these types of discussions was that Marta could position herself as a linguistic insider through her gentle recasting of my awkward Spanish utterances ('no puede salir de la mente') in a more target-like manner ('No se la grabó bien'). I am grateful for Duranti's (1997) compassionate characterization of non-native researchers like me: 'However clumsy and inadequate ethnographers' attempts to speak the local language might sound, they symbolize a commitment, and show respect and appreciation for the cultural heritage of the people they study' (1997: 111).

The Perils and Potentials of Amateur Translating in Cross-Language Research: A Need for Critical Reflexivity

In my cross-language dissertation study, I fulfilled the roles of researcher, transcriber, and translator. The assumption that translation is a technical, neutral, and objective act has been strongly criticized by many qualitative researchers, and various calls have been made for more emphasis to be placed on the impact that translation (and translators) have on data and data interpretation in research reporting (Berman & Tyyskä, 2011; Choi et al., 2012; Gawlewicz, 2016; Hennink, 2008; Shklarov, 2007; Squires, 2009; Temple, 2002; Temple & Young, 2004). As Temple (2002) noted, 'Translators are active producers in research rather than neutral conveyors of messages' (2002: 846). Translating implies not only knowledge of language but cultural competence as well, with many criticizing the assumption that translators can automatically serve as cultural experts or informants simply because they share the same language as the participants (Berman & Tyyskä, 2011; Hennink, 2008; Shklarov, 2007; Temple, 2002).

An acknowledgement of the role of translation in the interpretation of data is absent in much of the cross-language research literature. My own research reporting in my dissertation fell into this category of simply providing English translations of the participants' elicited Spanish data, rather than reflecting on how the translation process unfolded, my qualifications as an admittedly amateur translator, and how my translation impacted my analysis. I accept and adhere to the notion of researcher reflexivity as an essential part of qualitative research (Saavides et al., 2014), but I somehow took that reflexivity for granted regarding my L2 Spanish. I now find myself needing to look for the 'methodological gems' (Winchatz, 2006: 89) that can emerge from the process of reflecting on my translation work. I can see the benefit of Temple and Young's (2004) advice to 'use the experience of translating to discuss points in the text where she has had to stop and think about meaning' (2004: 168). I appreciate Gawlewicz's (2016) admonition that '*conscious* [my italics] research translation should always be a priority while collecting data in a language different from the language of its subsequent report … For this reason, the role of a translator researcher is very distinct from the role of a researcher per se' (2016: 38).

In other words, my lack of reflexivity on the translation process in my dissertation write-up should be considered a limitation of the study overall, and one that I had not addressed until now. I must admit that being an amateur translator and bilingual researcher means that my translations are based on my best interpretation of the general gist of what my participants said; given my cultural and linguistic proficiency, there is little nuance in my background knowledge in my Spanish translations and interpretations. My transcribed and translated data included in the dissertation were reviewed and edited by my native Spanish-speaking advisor, but there is always the question that my choices for which data to include may have been impacted by my limitations in capturing the linguistic, pragmatic or cultural nuances of my participants' utterances. The level of rigor (Irvine *et al.*, 2008), reflexivity (Hennink, 2008; Berman & Tyyskä, 2011) and conceptual equivalence (Choi *et al.*, 2012; Nurjannah *et al.*, 2014; Squires, 2009) in my translations have gone unchecked until now, but will be addressed in my future work.

A Final Question and a Challenge to the Field

I undertook my dissertation research believing in the power and effectiveness of using the participants' L1 in the interview data, even though I would not be considered fully proficient in Spanish. I knew that some of my transcriptions would need work, that I would struggle to understand everything the participants said, and that I would have to be careful in drawing conclusions from my self-translated data. However, until I wrote the current chapter I did not truly consider the ramifications of cross-cultural research in this light. In writing my dissertation, I primarily wanted to focus on what I could learn from the participants regarding my very broadly defined notion of metalinguistic awareness. In writing this chapter, I have begun considering the benefits of being seen as an L2 user by my participants, as well as the need to reflect on the impact that my L2 use had on our relationship, the data and my interpretation and framing of the data.

How can cross-language research help us improve not only the quality and quantity of data we collect but also the relationships between researchers and participants? The L1 narratives provided by my participants gave me a much better idea about what L2 learning and use was like for these learners than anything that they could currently express in English. More important, perhaps, was the participants' experience of expressing their experiences, their perspectives, and their progress in L2 learning with the ease that comes with speaking in one's first language. Some cross-language researchers may have to rely on the use of bilingual research assistants to conduct L1 interviews and transcribe data, but that was not an option for me nor was it my preference. The opportunity to build relationships with my participants that shifted our positions as cultural and linguistic insiders-outsiders far outweighed my concerns about my L2 limitations.

Overall, the study challenged assumptions about the quality and type of linguistic awareness that emergent L2 reader-writers bring to their English learning experience, allowing us to reframe our notions of these learners as multicompetent (Cook, 2003) and good language learners (Griffiths, 2008). Existing SLA research has rarely elicited rich descriptions and perspectives on language and L2 learning from the very learners who may struggle the most to express themselves and who, consequently, most need to be asked. Our understanding of this understudied population will continue to be enriched by eliciting L1 data – and perhaps even by positioning ourselves as L2 learners/users as well. I encourage other researcher-practitioners to not only pursue cross-language research with marginalized L2 learner populations but to carefully examine the impact that doing so can have on both the quality of the data and the quality of the researcher-participant relationship. My acknowledged limitations in Spanish did not prevent me from engaging meaningfully with my participants. Rather, I believe that my L2 proficiency served as a way to bridge some of the gaps between insider-outsider status that my participants and I may have otherwise struggled with.

References

Berman, R.C. and Tyyskä, V. (2011) A critical reflection on the use of translators/interpreters in a qualitative cross-language research project. *International Journal of Qualitative Methods* 10 (2), 178–190.

Bigelow, M. and Tarone, E. (2004) The role of literacy level in second language acquisition: Doesn't who we study determine what we know? *TESOL Quarterly* 38 (4), 689–700.

Chen, S. H. (2011) Power relations between the researcher and the researched: An analysis of native and nonnative ethnographic interviews. *Field Methods* 23 (2), 119–135.

Choi, J., Kushner, K.E., Mill, J. and Lai, D.W. (2012) Understanding the language, the culture, and the experience: Translation in cross-cultural research. *International Journal of Qualitative Methods* 11 (5), 652–665.

Cook, V. (2003) The changing L1 in the L2 user's mind. In V. Cook (ed.) *Effects of the Second Language on the First*. Clevedon: Multilingual Matters.

Duranti, A. (1997) *Linguistic Anthropology*. Cambridge: Cambridge University Press.

Dwyer, S.C. and Buckle, J.L. (2009) The space between: On being an insider-outsider in qualitative research. *International Journal of Qualitative Methods* 8 (1), 54–63.

Esposito, N. (2001) From meaning to meaning: The influence of translation techniques on non-English focus group research. *Qualitative Health Research* 11 (4), 568–579.

Gawlewicz, A. (2016) Language and translation strategies in researching migrant experience of difference from the position of migrant researcher. *Qualitative Research* 16 (1) 27–42.

Griffiths, C. (2008) *Lessons from Good Language Learners*. Cambridge: Cambridge University Press.

Hennink, M. (2008) Language and communication in cross-cultural qualitative research. In P. Liamputtong (ed.) *Doing Cross-cultural Research: Ethical and Methodological Perspectives* (pp. 21–33). Dordrecht: Springer.

Irvine, F., Roberts, G. and Bradbury-Jones, C. (2008) The researcher as insider versus the researcher as outsider: Enhancing rigour through language and cultural sensitivity. In P. Liamputtong (ed.) *Doing Cross-cultural Research: Ethical and Methodological Perspectives* (pp. 35–48). Dordrecht: Springer.

Jessner, U. (2006) *Linguistic Awareness in Multilinguals: English as a Third Language*. Edinburgh: Edinburgh University Press.

Kusow, A.M. (2003) Beyond indigenous authenticity: Reflections on the insider/outsider debate in immigration research. *Symbolic Interaction* 26 (4), 591–599.

Kvale, S. (2006) Dominance through interviews and dialogues. *Qualitative Inquiry* 12 (3), 480–500.

Lardiere, D. (2007) *Ultimate Attainment in Second Language Acquisition: A Case Study*. Mahwah, NJ: Erlbaum.

Liamputtong, P. (2008) *Doing Cross-cultural Research: Ethical and Methodological Perspectives*. Dordrecht: Springer.

Muller, A. and Gubrium, E. (2016) Researcher linguistic vulnerability: A note on methodological implications. *Qualitative Health Research* 26 (1), 141–144.

Norton, B. (2013) *Identity and Language Learning: Extending the Conversation* (2nd edn). Bristol: Multilingual Matters.

Nurjannah, I., Mills, J., Park, T. and Usher, K. (2014) Conducting a grounded theory study in a language other than English. *Sage Open* 4 (1), 1–10.

Ortega, L. (2012) Epistemological diversity and moral ends of research in instructed SLA. *Language Teaching Research* 16, 206–226.

Perry, K.H. (2011) Ethics, vulnerability, and speakers of other languages: How university IRBs (do not) speak to research involving refugee participants. *Qualitative Inquiry* 17 (10), 899–912.

Rubin, J. (1975) What the 'good language learner' can teach us. *TESOL Quarterly* 9 (1), 41–51.

Savvides, N., Al-Youssef, J., Colin, M. and Garrido, C. (2014) Journeys into inner/ outer Space: Reflections on the methodological challenges of negotiating insider/ outsider status in international educational research. *Research in Comparative and International Education* 9 (4), 412–425.

Schmidt, R. (1983) Interaction, acculturation, and the acquisition of communicative competence: A case study of an adult. In N. Wolfson and E. Judd (eds) *Sociolinguistics and Second Language Acquisition* (pp. 137–174). Rowley, MA: Newbury House.

Shklarov, S. (2007) Double vision uncertainty: The bilingual researcher and the ethics of cross-language research. *Qualitative Health Research* 17 (4), 529–538.

Squires, A. (2009) Methodological challenges in cross-language qualitative research: A research review. *International Journal of Nursing Studies* 46 (2), 277–287.

Suwankhong, D. and Liamputtong, P. (2015) Cultural insiders and research fieldwork: Case examples from cross-cultural research with Thai people. *International Journal of Qualitative Methods* 14 (5), 1–7.

Temple, B. (2002) Crossed wires: Interpreters, translators, and bilingual workers in cross-language research. *Qualitative Health Research* 12 (6), 844–854.

Temple, B. and Young, A. (2004) Qualitative research and translation dilemmas. *Qualitative Research* 4 (2), 161–178.

Vähäsantanen, K. and Saarinen, J. (2012) The power dance in the research interview: Manifesting power and powerlessness. *Qualitative Research* 13 (5) 493–510.

Winchatz, M.R. (2006) Fieldworker or foreigner?: Ethnographic interviewing in nonnative languages. *Field Methods* 18 (1), 83–97.

7 Researching from the Margin: Challenges and Tensions of Doing Research within One's Own Refugee Community

Nimo M. Abdi

This chapter is a reflexive account of my experiences conducting research with Somali immigrant and refugee youth. Early in the research process, I was aware of my 'otherness', as a researcher who is also a Somali immigrant woman, seeking to study the school experiences of Somali immigrant and refugee youth in a large urban school district. My social position within my research was often influenced by race, ethnicity, religion, and immigrant status. For this reason, I start reflecting about how my 'otherness' situated me, as I struggled to gain access to institutional and community spaces. In order to situate my experiences as a black immigrant and Muslim researcher, I draw from works of researchers of color, and/or immigrant backgrounds, and from women of color, in particular. Second, I explore my own positionality vis-à-vis the youths in my research, the adults in their schools and their families. In this section, I employ critical lenses that interrogate issues of representation and voice as a backdrop for my own positionality. For instance, I pay close attention to the various identity positions I take up in my role as a researcher. And finally, I question how well my post-structural training not only situated me in the field but also complicated the process of analyzing my participants' experiences. In this section, I propose the notion of community as a source for identity work. In other words, I extend decolonizing methodologies that take into account community as a unit of analysis when writing about Somali communities, which have experienced colonialism in many forms – historically and into the present.

Addressing the role of researcher in the research process, Cousin (2010) explains 'the self is not some kind of virus which contaminates the research. On the contrary, the self is the research tool, and thus intimately connected to the methods we deploy' (2010: 10). To extend Cousin's (2010) point, our subjectivity guides not only the methodology we employ, but the research questions we pursue, and the theoretical lenses we utilize to interpret findings from our research (Carling *et al.*, 2013). Feminist and other researchers employing critical lenses laid the foundation for challenging positivist notions of 'truth' as something out there that needs to be captured (see Cousin, 2010: 9). Instead, feminist and various aspects of critical theory recognize truth to be multiple and subjective. Hence, the move to integrate the researcher self into the research process, has become an accepted practice within the interpretative research community (Labaree, 2002). This is relevant because reflexivity has become necessary to address and negotiate various aspects of the research project (Cousin, 2010).

The concept of reflexivity is important because it helps the researcher to understand the effect their research can have on the lives of those they study (Kirsch, 1999). For instance, reflexivity allows researchers to think about and review their research procedures throughout the process of the study, including research goals as well as analysis. Hence, as the researcher learns more about the researched, there may be a need to adapt the procedures of the study, as well as the goal of the study (Kirsch, 1999). For example, in my work with Somali youth, I had to re-evaluate some aspects of my research as the study progressed.

Meanwhile, researcher characteristics are often linked and understood in relation to positionality. As an immigrant Somali woman, who wears the Muslim headscarf or the hijab, conducting research in a US urban school district with participants ranging from school administrators, teachers and Somali youth, constantly highlighted tensions of identity and positionality. This tension is further implicated by the in/visibility of my race, religion and immigrant status in and beyond the research field. In other words, I am visible in my interaction with school and district staff, and invisible in my encounters with my participants (but this also changed as the research progressed). The interplay between researcher identity and positionality has been reported in general terms pertaining to issues of access (Kusow, 2003), data collection and analysis (Chavez, 2008; Srivastava, 2006). In order to understand how researcher identity is linked to the positions we negotiate in the research context, one has to consider the issue of insider-outsider status. I agree with Srivastava (2006) that the multiple identities and positionalities that we bring to the field are 'constantly in flux' and linked to our understanding of who we are, or what she called 'real life identities outside the field' (2006: 211). According to Srivastava (2006), 'These [multiple identities] were not dichotomous; rather, they drew on each other to facilitate exchange, alter power differentials, and access data' (2006: 211). Hence, my identity as a hijabi Somali immigrant woman researcher positioned me both as an outsider and insider in various times and contexts in my research. This view of the researcher position is more nuanced than the dichotomy of the insider-outsider first proposed by Merton (1972). According to Merton (1972) the insider-outsider divide is one that is rooted in issues of access with epistemological consequences. For example, the insider's association with the participants may give him/her access to exclusive and intimate knowledge that an outsider does not have access to (see also Labaree, 2002).

A more complex notion of insider status is one that considers the constant negotiations between 'the researcher's biography and the social relations of power and privilege in which the researcher is located' (Griffith, as cited in Labaree, 2002: 102). For this reason, insider-outsider status is not exclusive but rather is interdependent, where the researcher moves back and forth across insider-outsider boundaries. In my research, I found that my insider-outsider positionality shifted in various contexts and times throughout the research project as different aspects of my field identity such as race, gender, class, etc. became relevant. The assumption here is that the intersection of various social locations in which subjects are positioned and/or position themselves that call for epistemological consequences challenge the dichotomy of insider-outsider status.

While, these are important issues with regard to insider/outsider positionality, it is essential to examine the discursive field in which the research takes place, and how that impacts not only the analytical lenses that explain the participants' experiences, but how the discursive reality impacts the researcher. For instance, in qualitative research when we think of positionality, it is often about access to and interaction with informants. Many researchers choose not to write about the challenges of gaining institutional access to their respective informants or the ongoing relationship with the institution. For many of us, it is so pressing to disseminate work that prioritizes the voices and experiences of our informants that we shy away from dwelling on our personal journey in the research process. After all, the research is not about us but it is about our participants. Yet, it is difficult to ignore the discursive reality within which we conduct our research. For this reason, I would like to briefly explore the discursive field in which I emerged as a researcher.

On Accent, Hijab and Becoming a Researcher

For my dissertation, I conducted research in a large urban district in the Midwestern United States. The city has the second largest Somali immigrant and refugee populations in the US. This is relevant, because as a Somali woman who observes the Muslim headscarf, hijab, I am socially positioned as a black, immigrant and Muslim woman – as a member of the community. The visible nature of my multiple identities both facilitated and hindered my ability to interact and access institutions of school and community, at various stages of my research project. At the institutional level, the individual identity markers of being either black, immigrant, or Muslim would not have mattered as such in my attempt to access these institutions. Rather, it was the compounded effect of these markers and the fact that they mark a gendered Somali identity that was problematic in my experiences. In this particular context, being a Somali woman researcher did not fit into the assumptions and expectations people had about Somalis. My positionality challenged the preconceived notions of what it meant to be Somali (and a woman) among those in the Somali community as well as those in institutions of power such as public schools. At the same time, my position as a woman researcher of Somali descent demonstrated the blurred boundaries between an insider and outsider in the research field.

Abdi Kusow (2003) wrote about his experiences as a Somali researcher conducting research among Somali immigrants in Canada. Kusow (2003) encountered challenges gaining access to and building rapport among members of his Somali community. For instance, as soon as he revealed his identity as a researcher and shared his research questions, members of the Somali community were unwilling to participate in his research. People in the community declined to be interviewed or asked him to change his interview questions. Kusow (2003) explained that both gender and social identities influenced his status, which oscillated between insider-outsider. Kusow's (2003) account reflects an in-group conflict during times of civil strife; in my work with Somali youth and their families, the challenges I faced were different. My challenges were often related to the degree certain aspects of my identity were in/visible (Carling et al., 2013). Hence, the degree to which elements of race, ethnicity, religion, accent, and immigrant status, became visible or invisible influenced the shifting of my positionality within the insider-outsider spectrum (Carling et al., 2013).

At the outset of my research project, the visibility of accent, ethnicity, and immigrant status became an impediment. In the process of choosing a site for my study, I initially called five high schools that had large Somali student population. A pattern emerged; I would leave a message with the secretary, who often told me that the school principle would call me back in response to my request for conducting research in their school. Yet, none of the principles returned my calls. Hence, I expanded my list of schools to 15, this time includeing both middle and high schools. Some of the schools were in neighboring districts, but again I received no return calls. To experiment if my name and accent were the source of disinterest on behalf of the principles, I asked my husband, who is an African-American and a faculty member from a well-known university, to make the calls on my behalf. To my surprise, the principles of all five high schools returned our calls and explained to my husband that they would like to assist us before informing us of the policies for conducting research in the district. While difficulties with gaining access to schools is very common among researchers interested in educational issues, especially in large urban districts, I can't help but partially blame the challenges I was facing on my visible identity markers i.e. hijab, skin color and accent. Yet, it could also be that the difficulties I was facing were in part influenced by my student status, which may not wield enough power to inspire administrators to return my calls.

The next step was to gain district approval. At the time, I was living in a neighboring state and had to travel four hours to this particular district. Because cold-calling the schools was not very productive, I decided to show up at the superintendent's office with the hopes of making an appointment with the director for research. I was informed by her assistant that 'an appointment can only be made when she approves of the request' and that the assistant would call or email me. I was aware that I would not be able to meet this official without effort, so I made sure that I dressed appropriately to make the right impression with her assistant. I wore Western influenced attire together with my headscarf. Despite several attempts on my part, including several visits to the director of research's office, I was not successful in gaining access. Others have reported the importance of dress code when gaining access to communities or institutions. Srivastava (2006), who conducted research in schools in rural India, reported that she dressed according to the norms accepted among her participants. Srivastava (2006) alternated between Western attire and traditional Indian clothes depending on whom she was interacting with. Among the middle-class educational officials, she wore Western clothes, while among parents of the lower socio-economic class, she dressed in traditional Indian clothes (Srivastava, 2006).

Srivastava's (2006) observations resonate with my own experiences in conducting research within the Somali community. I have used clothes as a way of mediating cultural boundaries. However, as an observant Muslim woman, I did not remove my hijab. Instead, I have worn my hijab in culturally appropriate ways to gain access and negotiate power relations among youth participants and school officials. For instance, at the school, I wore abayas (a long and loose over-garment) and long skirts. Sometimes, I wore a big hijab that covers most of the upper body, while other times I would wear a smaller scarf. I was aware that the girls in my study and other females in the school were reading my hijab. Hence, in my veiling, I attempted to relate to the local communities. The hijab, or the Muslim headscarf, is perhaps the most politically charged garment in the western hemisphere, in which various meanings are produced and reproduced.

In my own work among Somali youth, I found that the hijab was used as a positioning tool among Somali girls and boys. Somali girls who chose to wear the scarf were considered good girls in the sense that they were not prone to the promiscuity of mainstream culture (Leet-Otley, 2012). The hijab was also used as a relational tool between genders and between generations. This was true both in public and charter school settings. In a study I carried out in a public school, it was easier for other hijabi girls of various nationalities to relate to me. They often shared stories of their struggle in observing the hijab. Conversely, Somali girls, who did not wear the hijab were unwilling to engage with me, despite many attempts on my part. It seemed that the non-hijabi girls may have struggled with their visible Muslim identity and so were not interested in talking with me. These girls did not socialize with other Somali and Muslim students during lunch breaks. I often wondered if non-hijabi Somali girls would have engaged me had I not worn the hijab. Hence, among Muslim youth, the hijab symbolized the disciplining gaze of their communities (Zine, 2012). While my hijab often helped me to gain access among Somali students, it was clear that it also limited me with students who were not as familiar or comfortable with it. This suggests that ways of dressing not only influences the position of the researcher within the field, but also shapes their relationship with institutions as well as participants. In other words, if we think about the implications of dress style in the research endeavor we can relate the hijab to bodily habitus (Bourdieu, 1991). In Bourdieuan sense, the hijabi body communicates more than a religio-cultural practice: Rather the hijab affects positionality, dispositions and attitudes of both researcher and participants. Hence, the type of veil and the degree it covered the body invoked nuanced meanings, which in turn influenced the type of relationships negotiated in the research. Moreover, the hijab as bodily practice also raised issues of power regarding the question of representation among hijabis vs non-hijabis. This was evident in my inability to access schools as well as some non-hijabi participants. The hijab as a signifier implicated both me as a researcher and my participants.

Like any socially ascribed identity, the hijabi identity was also a performative identity that changed in different contexts (Abdi, 2015). Thus, my experiences changed depending whether I was in a public versus a charter school. In the charter school context, the hijab placed me in a discursive reality that was quite different to the public school settings. In this context, the hijab also drew gender boundaries, and facilitated a distinctive gender relation among students, as well as among students and staff. Muslim teachers and school staff often chastised both female and male students for not being proper in their conduct with the opposite gender. There was an implicit understanding that often linked girls' degree of covering with behavior. For instance, those who wore the jilbab (scarf that covers most of the upper body) were expected to conduct themselves in a certain way, i.e. more conservative, in comparison to the ones wearing the khimar (smaller scarf that covers head and neck). To some, the hijab is more than a piece of cloth; rather the hijab is a religious signifier that encompasses both dress and behavior of the observer (Schmidt, 2004) as well as relations with the divine (Mahmood, 2001; Williams & Vashi, 2007). Because the hijab marks the body in a unique way, Muslim women and girls, who wear it are often under the gaze of Muslims and non-Muslims alike (Schmidt, 2004; Zine, 2012). However, this does not mean that only women are required to observe modesty in dress. In Islam, men are also expected to follow certain criteria in dress i.e. not wearing shorts that are above the knee. In Islam, dress style is an important component in mediating social conduct of community members. Hence, in the charter school context, girls and boys were not allowed to socialize during lunchtime or in the hallways. The hijab was not only an imposed identity on female students, but it was also used to regulate and discipline bodies (Abdi, 2015). On the one hand, my hijab identity was both welcomed and expected of me as a first-generation Somali immigrant. This helped me gain access and build rapport with students and school staff at the initial stages of my research (Carling et al., 2013). On the other hand, my hijab coupled with my accent challenged the perception of the traditional Somali woman among students and their teachers. This is so because several of the students and some school staff often mentioned that they had never met a Somali woman (read covered woman) pursuing an academic career. Hence, while my hijab allowed for a temporary insider status, it also positioned me as an outsider, because it was not the norm for Somali hijabi women to be enrolled in a doctoral program. My insider-outsider status constantly shifted as class, accent and age became more prevalent in certain research contexts.

Going into the field, it was not enough that I was a Somali and an immigrant who wore the hijab, I was also aware of my class status. Class, more than any other social positioning, is difficult to ascribe among immigrant and refugee communities like the Somalis. On the surface, Somalis seem to be socially monolithic. Yet, many of us carry with us bodies of cultural knowledge or what scholars call 'funds of knowledge' (Moll et al., 1992), where we continue to benefit from the nuances of accumulated cultural assets, despite our nominal financial resources as refugee-immigrant communities. Despite the similarity of our dress and other cultural practices, my participants and I were very different in more ways than we were similar. On the one hand, the young people that participated in my research were either 1.5 or second-generation Somali immigrants. Some did not have 'foreign' accents, while others spoke with hint of Black-stylized English. I on the other hand, as a first generation immigrant, who learned English outside of the US, speak English with a distinguishable Somali accent. And while I understood the colloquial uses of the students' English, I couldn't code switch like some of my participants. Furthermore, another factor that positioned me vis-à-vis my participants was age. Sometimes I did not understand the inside jokes that some of the young women shared. In their jokes, they often referenced popular music, celebrities and their youth subculture. I had to ask what certain phrases meant. All of these factors positioned me as an outsider, linguistically, generationally, and culturally, hence constantly reminding me of the work I needed to do as I negotiated field relationships with the youths in my study. Narayan (1993) reminds us to focus on relationships, despite all of the markers that divide or unite researchers with their participants:

> Instead, what we must focus our attention on is the quality of relations with the people we seek to represent in our texts: are they viewed as mere fodder for professionally self-serving statements about a generalized Other, or are they accepted as subjects with voices, views, and dilemmas – people to whom we are bonded through ties of reciprocity and who may ever be critical of our professional enterprise? (Narayan, 1993: 671–672)

The value of these field relationships is measured by the degree to which we as researchers are willing to engage and respect the field relations we negotiate. This is especially true when participants voice concern about voice and representation, i.e. our interpretations of their stories and experiences. It is often easier to frame these concerns as inevitable when engaging in postmodern theorizing of identity, especially among adolescents, where the focus is exploring how immigrant youth understand construction of self across time and place. However, I realized that in regard to ambiguity and uncertainty in relation to identity, Somali youths often were not happy with this understanding of their identity. Rather, they wanted to be represented as whole humans that were capable agents, who often overcame challenges, and whose identity remained firm in different contexts. This was in direct opposition to my representation of their identity as a negotiated domain within a complex web of power relations.

Some of the Somali youth participants in my research challenged me when I shared an earlier draft analysis of their stories. Here is a memo I shared with one female student:

> Torn between two cultures, Halima [a pseudonym] was rebelling against the culture of her home, by socializing with the neighborhood youth in ways not approved by her mother. She wanted to be accepted by her peers and did not want to be associated with her immigrant and Muslim background.

Halima said, 'This is not what I meant to say,' speaking of her experiences. She explained:

> I did everything teenagers do, the whole nine yards, having boyfriends and all, because everyone in my street was doing it, and I thought as a teenager that's what you're supposed to do. I never hid the fact that I was Muslim; many of these people knew I was Muslim, as I used to wear the hijab earlier in middle school. And I was not rebelling against my mom's culture, I just thought she didn't have clue what it meant to be in my shoes. When I used to sneak out in the middle of the night, I knew what I was doing was wrong.

Here, Halima corrected me such that she did not want to be portrayed as an immigrant youth with an identity crisis. Conversely, Halima expressed that she chose to engage in certain actions without shying away from her Islamic roots. She provided a much more complex and nuanced version of what it meant to be a Muslim youth in an urban context. She contested my portrayal of Muslim identity as a dichotomy of good/bad Muslim girl. However, Halima also wanted her story to be portrayed as a journey of finding one's self. She explained, 'I was confused then, now that I think back, I can't believe what I was doing.' Halima, who at the time of this interview, wore a headscarf and an abaya, made sure that I understood it was her decision to dress more modestly and change her circle of friends. Like many of the participants in my study, Halima related her newly found religiosity to a deep spiritual awakening that was partly due to involvement with her local mosques and partly to newly found connections with members of her community. Halima's analysis of her own experiences once again reminded me that the fragmented identity lenses I brought to my research were open to debate.

I was very surprised that many of the young people often referenced adults in their local mosques who had helped them rediscover their religio-cultural identity. I often wondered if I was hearing these stories only or partly because I was a hijabi myself. Regardless, it was clear that these young people wanted to be represented as whole human beings capable of making choices, not as chameleons, which was how I was seeing/theorizing them. Somali youth's resistance to the fragmented self can be understood as 'a need to decolonize our minds, to recover ourselves, to claim a space in which we develop a sense of authentic humanity' (Smith, 1999: 23). Writing about the impact of imperialism in the psyche of colonized people, Smith (1999) explains that 'fragmentation is not a phenomenon of postmodernism as many might claim. For indigenous peoples' fragmentation has been the consequence of imperialism' (1999: 28).

The question here is not whether Somali youth are immune from the contradictions inherent in the modern self. But rather, a more interesting point is to ask, why are Somali youth contesting fragmentation? Perhaps their opposition to a fragmented self may indicate that Somali youth as colonized people are critiquing postmodern ways of knowing and being in the world, or Western epistemology, even though many critical scholars understand and use postmodernism as a mechanism to disrupt the master narrative and hence allow for multiple truths to be recognized (Hall & Du Gay, 1996; Alcoff, 1991; Mohanty, 1989). The fragmented self in postmodern thought does not recognize the need of those colonized subjects to be a whole human again (Smith, 1999). This is particularly important for colonized communities, whose knowledge, histories and epistemologies have been denied or ignored (Smith, 1999; Meyer, 2008). For Somali immigrant youth, the disruption caused by displacement and the violence of civil strife is even more immediate than the colonial trauma of the past. Hence, Somali immigrant youth recognize that the post-structural lens, which I was drawing from in my analysis, negates an important component of their understanding of self, namely a communal self that is rooted in collective identity. According to Bulhan (2013) there are two aspects to Somali identity that are more important than others. These include an aspect of identity that is affirmed with certainty, and which is rooted in clan ethos. Here, genealogy or kinship are at the core of this collective identity. Hence, clan collective identity functions as a buffer and allows one to face the challenges of everyday life, not as an entity, but as a member of a community. The second aspect of identity among Somalis is identity at the individual level. This, argues Bulhan (2013), is replete with issues of uncertainty and ambiguity. However, what is more relevant here is the interplay between these two identity sources.

In educational research, others have discussed the role of community in decolonizing methodology. For instance, works by Delgado-Bernal (1998), Yosso (2005), Yosso and García (2007) among others speak to the importance of research frameworks that center the knowledge and epistemologies of communities of color, especially those coming from oral traditions. These researchers perceive community knowledge to be crucial not only in understanding colonized people's worldview, but also for community to be a space rich in resources that anchor the identities of its members. Hence, we can understand the needs of Somali immigrant youth to emphasize the communal aspect of their identity. This does not mean that Somalis do not struggle with issues of identity, rather it is through the process of constant negotiations between one's communal and individual identity where Somali youth identity work happens. This is significant because second generation Somali immigrant youth may not be able to access their clan-based identity to the same degree their elders can. Instead, for some Somali youth, the concept of community goes beyond membership in a particular clan, and is often extended to nationality and religion. For instance, for the youths I worked with, membership in Somali community organizations such as a mosque or sport club run by other Somalis provided resources and space for identification and belonging. Hence, the reconfiguration of Somali communal identity not only challenges clan identity ethos (Bulhan, 2013), but complicates one's construction of self, pertaining to questions of who one is, as well as questions about relating to the Other. But to return to the notion, conceptualizing one's subjectivity not as an independent entity but rather as a member of a community can be used to extend the concept of community as an important source for identity work.

Conclusion

In this chapter I have explored how the in/visibility of certain elements of my identity shaped my insider-outsider status with Somali youth. By providing a reflexive account of my experiences as a Somali female, immigrant and hijabi researcher, I have argued that reflexivity as a research tool allowed me to highlight the blurred boundaries of the insider-outsider position that I had to constantly negotiate as a researcher. As is evident in in the experiential accounts I shared throughout this chapter, I argue that reflexivity applies both to the theories that are brought to the field and the people in the field, such that not only are we interrogating the knowledge productions of what particular research questions mean, but also the people this knowledge represents and speaks of.

Furthermore, if reflexivity is concerned with the researcher's positionality and the various power relations negotiated throughout the research project. Then we can ascertain that reflexivity also to mean the degree to which one is willing to share power as it relates to issues of interpretation and representation. This is specifically true for those researchers who come to the research project with an emphasis of empowering the researched (Kirsch, 1999). As my notes in the above show, it was my commitment to preserving an authentic account of the lived experiences of the youth in my research i.e. reflexivity, combined with the process of member-checking, that lead me to consider alternative ways of thinking about understanding and analyzing identity work. Because the youths in my study challenged the ways I represented them, they helped me re-evaluate the values I brought to my work. After all, my intent was not to carry out the type of qualitative research Michelle Fine (1994) termed as 'contradiction-filled, a colonizing discourse of the 'Other' (1994: 70). Hence, reflexivity as a methodological tool can help us to imagine new ways to think about and theorize the social lives of our participants that we attempt to capture.

References

Abdi, N.M. (2015) Race and religion in the making of Somali youth identities. Unpublished doctoral dissertation, Michigan State University.

Alcoff, L. (1991) The problem of speaking for others. *Cultural Critique* 20, 5–32.

Bourdieu, P. (1991) *Language and Symbolic Power*. Cambridge, MA: Harvard University Press.

Bulhan, H.A. (2013) *In-between Three Civilizations. Archeology of Social Amnesia and Triple Heritage of Somalis* (Vol. 1). Bethesda, MD: Tayosan International Publishing.

Carling, J., Erdal, M.B., and Ezzati, R. (2013) Beyond the insider-outsider divide in migration research. *Migration Studies* 2 (1), 36–54.

Chavez, C. (2008) Conceptualizing from the inside: Advantages, complications, and demands on insider positionality. *The Qualitative Report* 13 (3), 474–494.

Cousin, G. (2010) Positioning positionality. The reflexive turn. In M. Savin-Baden and C.H. Major (eds) *New Approaches to Qualitative Research: Wisdom and Uncertainty* (pp. 9–18). New York, NY: Routledge.

Bernal, D.D. (1998) Using a Chicana feminist epistemology in educational research. *Harvard Educational Review* 68 (4), 555–583.

Fine, M. (1994) Working the hyphens: Reinventing self and other in qualitative research. In N.K. Denzin and Y.S. Lincoln (eds) *Handbook of Qualitative Research* (pp. 70–82). Thousand Oaks, CA: Sage.

Hall, S. and Du Gay, P. (eds) (1996) *Questions of Cultural Identity* (Vol. 126). London: Sage.

Kirsch, G.E. (1999) *Ethical Dilemmas in Feminist Research*. New York, NY: SUNY Press.

Kusow, A.M. (2003) Beyond indigenous authenticity: Reflections on the insider/outsider debate in immigration research. *Symbolic Interaction* 26 (4), 591–599.

Labaree, R.V. (2002) The risk of 'going observationalist': negotiating the hidden dilemmas of being an insider participant observer. *Qualitative Research* 2 (1), 97–122.

Leet-Otley, J.M. (2012) The spirit and strength of Somali youth in America. Unpublished doctoral dissertation, University of Minnesota.

Mahmood, S. (2001) Feminist theory, embodiment, and the docile agent: Some reflections on the Egyptian Islamic revival. *Cultural Anthropology* 16 (2), 202–236.

Merton, R.K. (1972) Insiders and outsiders: A chapter in the sociology of knowledge. *American Journal of Sociology* 78 (1), 9–47.

Meyer, M.A. (2008) Indigenous and authentic: Hawaiian epistemology and the triangulation of meaning. In N.K. Denzin, Y.S. Lincoln and L.T. Smith (eds) *Handbook of Critical and Indigenous Methodologies* (pp. 217–232). Thousand Oaks, CA: Sage.

Mohanty, C.T. (1989) On race and voice: Challenges for liberal education in the 1990s. *Cultural Critique* 14, 179–208.

Mohanty, C.T. (1988) Under Western eyes: Feminist scholarship and colonial discourses. *Feminist Review* 30, 61–88.

Moll, L.C., Amanti, C., Neff, D. and Gonzalez, N. (1992) Funds of knowledge for teaching: Using a qualitative approach to connect homes and classrooms. *Theory into Practice* 31 (2), 132–141.

Narayan, K. (1993) How native is the 'native' anthropologist? *American Anthropologist* 95 (3), 671–86.

Riessman, C.K. (1987) When gender is not enough: Women interviewing women. *Gender and Society* 1 (2), 172–207.

Schmidt, G. (2004) *Islam in Urban America: Sunni Muslims in Chicago*. Philadelphia, PA: Temple University Press.

Smith, L.T. (1999) *Decolonizing Methodologies: Research and Indigenous Peoples*. London: Zed Books.

Srivastava, P. (2006) Reconciling multiple researcher positionalities and languages in international research. *Research in Comparative and International Education* 1 (3), 210–222.

Williams, R.H. and Vashi, G. (2007) Hijab and American Muslim women: Creating the space for autonomous selves. *Sociology of Religion* 68 (3), 269–287.

Yosso, T.J. (2005) Whose culture has capital? A critical race theory discussion of community cultural wealth. *Race, Ethnicity and Education* 8 (1), 69–91.

Yosso, T. and García, D. (2007) This is no slum!: A critical race theory analysis of community cultural wealth in culture clash's Chavez Ravine. *Aztlan: A Journal of Chicano Studies* 32 (1), 145–179.

Zine, J. (ed.) (2012) *Islam in the Hinterlands: Muslim Cultural Politics in Canada*. Vancouver, Canada: UBC Press.

8 Working Toward a Humanizing Research Stance: Reflections on Modifying the Interview Process

Daisy E. Fredricks

Introduction

Recently, there has been a growing interest in humanizing research approaches, and many scholars from different disciplinary traditions have started to reflect deeply on the philosophies, methodologies, processes, and possibilities associated with such an approach on projects that are carried out with marginalized youth and communities using this perspective. Influenced by various humanizing approaches to research (e.g. Hones, 2002; Ibrahim, 2014; Kinloch & San Pedro, 2014; Paris, 2011; Paris & Winn, 2014), in this chapter I analyze the ways that I endeavored to humanize the interview process with the youth participants of a study that examined teacher and youth perspectives on restrictive language education in Arizona. I reflect on the challenges that I encountered during the youth interviews, how I responded to those challenges, and how the modified research methods contributed to the kinds of data that were collected and knowledge produced from humanizing research approaches. I also discuss important practices that contributed to humanizing the research process in this local context – i.e. being present at the school, building meaningful relationships, engaging in genuine dialogue and attempting to equalize the power balance between the youth and myself. I argue that humanizing approaches to research have much to offer researchers working with historically marginalized youth and researchers should maintain a critical perspective on how to implement or operationalize such perspectives. Researchers should also be prepared to adapt and modify their practices in response to what participants say and do in specific contexts of interaction and storytelling and invite participants to reflect and comment on what it means for outsiders to 'humanize' the research they conduct.

Humanizing Research

Paris (2011: 137) defines humanizing research as a 'methodological stance, which requires that our inquiries involve dialogic consciousness-raising and the building of relationships of dignity and care for both researchers and participants.' He argues that such an approach can 'increase the validity of the truths we gain through research' and is 'ethically necessary' – particularly when working with marginalized youth and communities – with intention to disrupt the long-standing ideologies, (language) policies and classroom practices that often position youth in deficit ways (Paris, 2011: 137). Hones (2002: xii) reminds us that 'refugee and immigrants carry with them intimate knowledge of [...] cross-national contexts and the effect on their lives.' Educational researchers (and classroom teachers) have much to learn from youth experiences – but space for youth to engage in dialogue with researchers about their experiences must first be created in order to extend such conversations into opportunities that promote change in teaching, community relations and policy.

To accomplish this, Hones (2002: xiii) draws from *dialogic teacher research*, which he describes as 'methods that are at once ethnographic, participatory, and narrative' that seek to 'engage researchers and participants in dialogues that shed light on economic, political, social, and cultural relationships' with a larger goal of promoting 'broader understanding and social justice in schools and communities'. Utilizing such an approach can serve to humanize the research process as participants can reflect on and share their experiences with an engaged listener. Moreover, this dialogic process can help some youth, particularly those coming from vulnerable backgrounds and traumatic experiences, to process – and in some cases, perhaps begin to recover from – such events, while researchers can learn more about the youths' individual and collective histories. In the same vein, Kinloch and San Pedro (2014: 26) argue that 'researchers have a responsibility to listen – closely and carefully – to *what* young people are saying, and *how* and *for what reasons* they are saying it.' One way to do this is to engage *with* youth through a 'dialogic spiral' – or a meaningful, co-constructed conversation – which can help to re-define our roles as researcher and participant and encourage projects that can help to humanize the research process (Kinloch & San Pedro, 2014: 30).

Ibrahim (2014: 14) states that research is 'not a simple intellectual and academic exercise'; rather, it is 'an act of love' that encourages developing profound relationships through genuine dialogue with the community. Thus, there is not a singular way to humanize the research process – nor should there be – as the methodologies associated with a humanizing approach are deeply dependent on a number of situated factors, including the larger political context, local landscapes and most importantly, the individual participants. In other words, a humanizing research approach must uniquely support the dynamic needs of the context and the relationships between the researcher and youth participants, which vary across people, time, and space.

Arizona's Restrictive and Dehumanizing Educational Language Policies and Practices

In 2000, voters in Arizona passed legislation to support restrictive educational language policy for the State's classified English learners (ELs). Such policies require classified EL students to be grouped according to English language proficiency per the Arizona English Language Learner Assessment (AZELLA) – the State's mandated language proficiency assessment. Students are segregated (Gándara & Orfield, 2010) from 'mainstream' students and then placed in a (controversial) Structured English Immersion (SEI) classroom that focuses on English language development (ELD) for four hours per school day. Known locally as 'the four-hour block', the stated goal of this policy is to provide an opportunity for teachers and learners to focus on the forms and functions of the English language through skills-based approaches to reading, writing, listening and speaking, with a strong focus on grammar and vocabulary. The purpose of this method of instruction is rapid proficiency in the English language so that EL students can be reclassified to 'Fluent English Proficient' (FEP) – per the AZELLA test – and transferred to a mainstream classroom to receive instruction in grade appropriate content areas such as math, science and social studies.

In recent years, research on Arizona's SEI model and the four-hour ELD block has yielded serious concerns about restrictive educational language policy (e.g. Fredricks & Warriner, 2016; Lillie & Moore, 2014; Wiley, 2012) and the accompanying classroom practices (e.g. Fredricks & Warriner, 2015; Grijalva & Jimenez-Silva, 2014) as scholars highlight the lack of theoretical and empirical evidence that support SEI in this context (Krashen *et al.*, 2012; Rumberger & Tran, 2010). For example, Long and Adamson (2012: 40) state that the 'lack of instruction in content areas, and the lack of opportunity it provides for students to acquire the specialized varieties of English they need for study in academic contexts, conflicts sharply with what we know about how school-age ELL students learn second languages and academic subject matter.' This demonstrates the disconnect between extant theories of second language acquisition (SLA) and effective language teaching, but also highlights a larger issue of access to the knowledge and language associated to a content-based curriculum. Lillie and Markos (2014: 138) warn:

> … the woefully inadequate access to core content instruction within the ELD classroom, in addition to limited resources to support students once they exit from the model (such as tutors, summer school opportunities or materials to support the continued language development of RC [reclassi-fied] students in mainstream classrooms) have drastic implications for ELs and RC [reclassified] students.

Collectively, this large and growing body of scholarship increasingly demonstrates that Arizona's SEI and the four-hour ELD block often do not adequately prepare EL students for the academic and linguistic demands of a mainstream classroom. Moreover, such restrictive educational language policy approaches create and sustain ineffective and dehumanizing learning spaces as the policy and prescribed classroom practices perpetu-ally position youths' home languages and cultures in deficit ways (Arias & Faltis, 2012; Ruíz, 1984).

Being Present at New Frontiers Elementary School

The reflections and questions that I share here emerged while con-ducting over two years of fieldwork (February 2011–June 2013) at New Frontiers Elementary School (all names are pseudonyms), a public school located in the Phoenix metropolitan area. At the time of this study (January 2012–June 2012), New Frontiers served K-6th grade youth who represented at least ten different countries and spoke a variety of differ-ent languages (i.e. Arabic, Dinka, English, French, Kirundi, Maay Maay, Somali, Spanish and Swahili). The majority of youth (over 90%) were either classified as an EL student, receiving ELD instruction via the four-hour block, or reclassified as 'proficient' in English and receiving main-stream, content-area instruction.

Initially, I served as a classroom volunteer with Mrs Williams, the fifth/sixth grade ELD teacher during 2010-2011. As a classroom volunteer, I went to New Frontiers Elementary School approximately three times per week (2–3 hours per visit) to work with the youth and to support Mrs Williams. This sustained, physical presence at the school – whether it be in classrooms, on the playground or in the lunchroom – was crucial to this study as this was the first step in gaining access to the school site. But more importantly, this presence helped me to better understand the situ-ated context of the different spaces within the research site, gain valuable insights and build important and meaningful relationships with the par-ticipants of the study. The staff, administration and fifth and sixth grade students knew me because of my sustained presence at the school and engagement in the different classrooms. Much like a classroom teacher, this physical presence at the school and in the classroom – as a classroom researcher – created routine and consistency which in turn sometimes helped to develop a level of trust with the teachers and youth (Hones, 2002). This was especially important for relationship building with the youth of this study, as some students were labeled as 'refugee' and had relocated from refugee camps in Africa where they experienced unstable and dehumanizing living conditions, while others were homeless, sometimes living in the family car or the local homeless shelter. Some youth attended the school without legal documents and lived in constant fear of deportation, while other youth were US citizens who frequently transferred from school-to-school throughout the year. Indeed, all the youth that participated in this study had experienced some form of linguistic, cultural and economic conflict in (and out of) school – and at times, this positioned some youth as vulnerable – though I frequently documented that the youth demonstrate agency throughout their learning experiences and the research process (see also Bernstein, this volume). My regular presence then, contributed to a sense of consistency, stability and routine, which I now believe helped to demonstrate my commitment to the school but also helped to establish the strong foundation needed to support and sustain positive relationships with the youth and teachers.

Data Collection and Analysis

In January 2012, I received permission from the school district (i.e. principal, teachers and youth of New Frontiers Elementary School) to collect data for a study that focused on teacher and EL youth perspectives on the reclassification processes and the monitoring period associated with the four-hour ELD block. Specifically, the research questions were:

(1) What do teachers say about reclassification policies and practices (AZELLA testing, mainstream placement, and monitoring)?
(2) What do teachers do in their classrooms once students have been reclassified and placed in a mainstream classroom?
(3) What do students say about reclassification policies and practices? What do they say and do in response to their teachers' pedagogical choices?

To understand the teachers' perspectives and experiences regarding the restrictive educational language policy in Arizona, I worked with four mainstream classroom teachers; Ms Rocio (fourth/fifth grade), Mrs Williams (fifth grade), Mr Kasey (sixth grade) and Mr Peterson (sixth grade). For three to five days per week, I worked with 12 fifth and sixth grade youth with recent reclassification from the four-hour ELD block to the mainstream classroom to examine how the youth responded to such policies and practices in the mainstream classrooms. The youth included

fifth graders Abilyn, Ishamel, Joseph, Malik, Raija and Terrell, in addition to sixth graders Brisa, Felipe, Joaquin, Anayeli, Catherine and Juan.
All youth participants of this study were between the ages of 10 and
13 years old, and collectively, they represented the linguistic and cultural diversity of the school and mainstream classrooms. I conducted
classroom observations, participant observation, interviews and a focus
group (with only the four mainstream teachers). I also collected relevant
artifacts from both teacher and youth participants (e.g. photographs of
student work, standardized test scores, and school documents). In all,
I observed and documented (via fieldnotes and audio-recordings) more
than 60 content-based lessons and over 150 hours of audio-recordings of
classroom observations, interviews, and interactions (on the playground
and in the lunchroom).

Nearly all 150+ hours of audio-recordings were transcribed, indexed
and thematically coded based on the research questions that guided this
study. Additional codes were created to represent emerging themes found
across the data set. The following school year (2012–2013), I continued to
volunteer in the classroom of Mrs Williams, visit the teachers and youth and
share my findings and emerging analysis with the teachers I had observed
and interviewed in order to confirm my understanding, check for accuracy,
and/or add details.

Researcher Positionality

I came to this study with experience teaching bilingual and
EL-designated youth in elementary and middle school classrooms in
Michigan, Texas and Arizona. Most of my teaching experience had been
with US-born and immigrant Spanish-speaking youth, though I have
worked with students from a variety of cultural, ethnic and linguistic backgrounds. My six years of bilingual, English-as-a-Second Language (ESL),
and SEI classroom teaching, coupled with my graduate-level coursework
in curriculum and instruction, language teaching and language learning,
influenced the different roles that I took up during this study. I understood
how policies (such as Arizona's restrictive language policy) impacted
teaching and learning in the classroom. Schools and classrooms were a
very familiar and comforting place for me, and this school was no exception. For these reasons, I was able to develop and maintain relationships
of understanding, solidarity and trust with both the teachers and youth
throughout the study. However, in spite of my experiences as a classroom
teacher and my growing understanding of restrictive language policies
(e.g. the prescribed curriculum), I discovered that I still had much to learn
about the local context. For instance, I had never taught students enrolled
in the four-hour ELD block, nor had I worked with students who had
been recently reclassified as English-proficient through such instructional
approaches. Though I had much experience working with ELs from a

variety of contexts, I had never taught in a community with such a large number of refugee families, or with refugee youth from so many different linguistic, cultural, and religious backgrounds. For these reasons, I quickly came to realize that even though schools and classrooms were generally familiar to me, I also had much to learn about this new teaching landscape and how the teachers and youth navigate their relationships, roles and understandings within it – all the while learning how to become a classroom researcher, too.

Rethinking Aspects of Data Collection

Researchers must deliberately select research methods that will facilitate the process of collecting trustworthy data sources that help to answer the proposed research questions. But what happens when a research method does not work in the immediate research context? What happens when a research method does not promote humanizing efforts that contribute to building and *sustaining* 'relationships of dignity and care' (Paris, 2011: 137)? To answer these complicated questions the researcher must assess the situation and revise the research method, while still maintaining rigor with trustworthy data generation practices.

Modifying the Interview Process

Interviewing the youth turned out to be complicated, as it was challenging, clumsy and awkward for all of us. At the onset of the study, I attempted to employ Seidman's (2006) framework for in-depth interviewing, an interview series approach that consists of three 90-minute interviews that focus on the participant's life history, the details of a particular experience or phenomena, and finally, a reflection on the meaning of the interview. Though Seidman (2006: 19) cautions researchers to 'respect the structure' of the interview, during initial planning for the youth interviews, I made modifications to this structure so that it would be more appropriate for the youth. For example, I selected a limited number of interview questions (five), reduced the amount of time designated for the interview (from 90 minutes to 20 minutes), drafted questions based on previous conversations (so that students would be familiar with the topics), interviewed the youth in (what I perceived to be) comfortable locations (e.g. a couch in the library and at a table in the school's courtyard) and attempted to interview youth in pairs. I also planned to conduct all interviews in English due to the formal and informal restrictive language policies in place at the school and because all of the youth who participated in the study were considered 'proficient' in English per the AZELLA test.

On two separate occasions, I tried to employ Seidman's (2006) modified in-depth interview approach with the youth. Initially, I arranged to interview Catherine, a sixth grader with 'refugee' status from Mr Kasey's classroom. I met Catherine during the 2010–2011 school year when she was classified as an EL student in Mrs Williams' ELD classroom. She was a participant in a previous study that I conducted in the ELD classroom that centered on youth talk, so we had known each other for over a year and she was familiar with the interesting roles I took up in her classroom (i.e. 'Miss Daisy' – a classroom volunteer and classroom researcher). She was also accustomed to my iTouch (used for taking photos of student work and recording conversations), classroom audio-recorders and notebook for fieldnotes, so I assumed that because of prior experiences together, she would be a great participant to begin the interview process. I spent much time planning our first formal interview together, and determined it would take place in the school's library, as this was a comfortable space where we could talk openly about her learning experiences. Unfortunately, this turned out to be a colossal failure. Even with the most careful planning, each question that I posed to Catherine (e.g. *Can you tell me more about what you didn't like in the ELD class with Mrs Williams last year?* [awkward silence] *So what didn't you like?*) was answered with more silence or a seemingly forced response (e.g. *I don't know … I just didn't like it.*) – although the questions had stemmed from rich conversations between us just days prior to the interview. From there, I took time to reflect on what I believed went wrong and to regroup on future interviewing approaches. I determined that Catherine might have felt isolated or powerless and so I thought it was better to move forward by interviewing the youth with a partner participant to help alleviate potential power/status hierarchies between the youth (as student participants) and I (as an adult researcher participant).

Utilizing this newly modified approach, I asked Raija and Malik, fifth grade learners with 'refugee' status from Mrs Williams' class, if I could interview them – and both boys readily agreed. Though this was the first year I had worked with Raija and Malik, they too, had grown used to my presence in their classroom – as well as the methods and tools that I used for classroom research (e.g. observation, participation observation, fieldnotes, audio-recorders, etc.). Both boys were outgoing and talkative – and I naively assumed these characteristics would shine during the interview. However, once we arranged ourselves outside in the courtyard and I began to ask the boys questions, the mood shifted from lively and curious to apprehensive and tense. There was no deep exchange of information between us or nuanced discussion, only mumbled phrases (at best), awkward silence and averted eyes. Reading the nonverbal cues and hearing the paralinguistic codes of silence, to me, both boys appeared nervous (as though they were in trouble) and they made very little eye contact with me, which was also quite unusual for the boys. I understood that formal interviews were a new and unfamiliar instructional routine for the youth in this study, particularly when such interviews were conducted (and audio-recorded) in the school context, but the process of conducting formal interviews seemed insincere, uncomfortable and potentially dehumanizing for some youth. After careful reflection, I was unsure about the types of previous experiences that some youth might have had with interviewing. Catherine, Raija and Malik came to their US schooling experiences under 'refugee' status, so it is plausible that the interview process itself created the awkward and tense exchanges, as refugees (and asylum seekers) must be interviewed by various government officials in order to be considered for relocation. Such interviews can create stress and tension due to the high stakes consequences for resettlement processes – if the interview is not compelling, relocation might not occur. Perhaps Catherine, Raija and Malik felt coerced to engage with me because of their prior experiences with the interview process during relocation. I wondered whether it made sense to ask the youth to share their feelings and thoughts with me if they didn't feel comfortable with me or with the questions I was asking or by engaging in the interview process. In my fieldnotes, I reflected on my growing concerns regarding this approach, and worried that continuing to utilize formal interviews might destabilize the relationships that we (the youth and I) had worked to develop and maintain. (For more on other blunders I made while interviewing youth, see Fredricks, 2017).

This methodological setback provided an opportunity for me to critically reflect on and assess the process of collecting data with the youth, and it inspired and challenged me to reconsider how I utilized formal interviewing throughout this study, particularly with the youth. In hindsight, I realized that even after the unsuccessful and awkward interview experiences with Catherine, Raija and Malik, the youth often initiated everyday conversations with me. These conversations occurred in and out of the classroom, and though they were common but sometimes calculated (on my end), the overall content felt insightful, rich, consistent and sincere. Moving forward, I thought it would be best to focus on the youths' everyday storytelling and conversations (Ochs & Capps, 2001), as these conversations regularly took place between the youth and I during every visit to the school – typically during participant observation in the classroom or when helping the youth on class assignments, walking students to intervention sessions, eating lunch in the cafeteria, hanging out at recess, attending school functions, or sometimes simply coming by the school to say hello. After I learned that the playground was an excellent space to talk and interact with the youth, I made sure to schedule my visits so that I could observe youth in the classroom and spend time hanging out during lunch and recess (Ibrahim, 2014). Initially, I received countless stares from both the adult playground monitors, as well as the students – especially when I played 4-square or sat at the metal table in the shade overlooking the soccer field, or when I chatted with the youth and their friends (who were often curious about my presence on the playground). This somewhat unconventional approach to data collection seemed to yield increased understanding and trust between the youth and me – and also served to humanize the research approach, as the youth signaled the types of inter-action routines they felt comfortable with (e.g. casual conversations) and I responded to their requests.

Hanging Out with Youth

Similar to the work of Ibrahim (2014), who engaged in a *hanging out methodology* (2014: 17) with continental African communities in Canada, the goal of this work was to engage the youth in genuine conversations with the purpose of constructing a 'complex space of research, power, and dia-logue' (2014: 18). For example, each recess, different students approached the table to say hello or to sit and talk and then move on when they wanted to. Some youth, like sixth grader, Anayeli, consistently sat with me at our table in the shade. We spent this time together talking about everyday topics – school, the weather, our families and friends and upcoming plans for the weekend. Other youth, like sixth graders Catherine and Juan, and fifth graders Malik and Abilyn would ask me questions about my children, my house and going to college, just as I had asked them questions about school, language, and learning.

It was during these informal conversations or 'dialogic spirals' (Kinloch & San Pedro, 2014: 30) that I learned about the youth and they learned about me. For example, I learned that Anayeli had a family friend who often helped her on her homework and upcoming projects, as her father worked long hours, her mother had passed away and her older siblings were consumed with high school, community college and sup-porting the family (Fieldnotes from lunch, 12 April 2012). Abilyn lived with nine of her family members in a nearby apartment and had recently been moved up in her math class, which she was not happy about because her new teacher taught her 'stuff that [she] don't know' (Fieldnotes from recess, 12 April 2012). Juan and his mother were both elated when Juan passed his English language proficiency test – his mom even posted his test scores on the family's refrigerator (Fieldnotes, 1 June 2012). Sometimes the youth would look at photos of my family on my iTouch (which I also used to record our conversations) and ask me personal questions – *Who is this? How many kids do you have? How old is your son? Where is your house?* – which I responded to.

Though our time together on the playground and in the lunchroom was brief, typically 10–15 minutes at most, our conversations were rich, honest, and real. It was in and through such conversations that I would ask the youth about their (language) learning experiences in school – *How are things going in Mr Peterson's class? Did you get your AZELLA scores back? What book are you reading now?* – as well as genuine questions about life – *What did you do this weekend? How did your basketball game go? How was your brother's birthday party?* No prepared questions or interview protocols were needed as we engaged in genuine dialogue about things that mattered to us. We took turns asking and answering questions, sharing stories and personal experiences all the while building relationships with each other. According to Ibrahim (2014: 18), it is within these complex spaces where genuine dialogues can take shape and transform the construct of research to an 'act of love' by which research can be carried out *with* the communities that we serve.

Discussion

While engaged in everyday conversations about topics of mutual interest and genuine concerns, the youth and I spent time together talking, listening, and sometimes, simply being silent, or what Kinloch and San Pedro (2014: 30) might refer to as the 'dialogic spiral'. These engagements served to humanize the research process, as these informal exchanges, fleeting conversations, and moments of hanging out required that the youth and I work together to learn more about each other through listening to and taking part in conversations – and such acts help to establish and sustain relationships, reciprocities, and for some youth, trust (Hones, 2002; Ibrahim, 2014).

This modified approach to data collection also contributed to the growth of 'relationships of dignity and care for both researchers and participants' (Paris, 2011: 137). For example, I recognized that the interview process made the youth (in this local context) feel uncomfortable (which made me feel uncomfortable, too). In response to both explicit messages and indirect signals from the youth, I deliberately moved away from scheduled and scripted interviews toward a dialogic approach because I was invested in building positive relationships with the youth and I was concerned that the formal interview method did not contribute to such efforts.

I believe that my conscious effort to modify this research approach also helped to disrupt the power imbalances that can exist between the researcher participant and the participant(s). Because my presence at lunch or on the playground invited – but did not require – the youth to approach me (or not), the interaction itself was their choice. The youth could talk with me when they felt comfortable, not only when I requested to speak with them. Often, the youth initiated conversations and asked me questions (e.g. *Miss Daisy, have you ever cheated in school?*), which offered a more genuine dialogue between us and also served to humanize the researcher (me) to the youth participants. These endeavors often challenged and contradicted the inherent power structures associated with youth learning experiences in schools (e.g. adults typically determine what youth will do, when they will do it, and how they will do it) – including the daily discourse and interactional practices – where teachers determine topics for discussion and tend to dominate the talk time. The shift from interviews toward dialogue challenged these institutional norms because we took turns asking and answering questions and sharing stories, which invited a certain level of reciprocity and also alleviated some of the power differentials between the youth and I.

I came to recognize that the information the youth shared with me during these encounters was just as meaningful and valid as the information that I tried to elicit from the youth while interviewing them. Often, they shared stories and insights that I would not have thought to ask during an interview. Paris (2011: 137) says that humanizing the research approach – particularly through dialogic engagements – can 'increase the validity of the truths we gain through research'. The relationships that we developed coupled with the everyday conversations that we had and the common stories that we shared over time, all contributed to understanding how restrictive language policies and classroom practices impacted the youths' learning experiences in mainstream classrooms. For example, I learned that the youth of this study believed the four-hour ELD block helped prepare students to learn English, but the youth loathed being placed in the ELD classroom as it was 'boring' and often considered a stigmatized learning space associated with academic failure. Moreover, the youth still struggled with the language associated with content area instruction after reclassification to the mainstream classroom. I also learned that some youth were actively seeking ways to learn and share languages other than English – despite the restrictive language policies in place. The important findings of this study would not have been possible without a modified approach to the original research process, as students often shared similar versions of a story or experience (over time) – sometimes sharing counter narratives as well – all of which added to the complexity of the restrictive educational language policies as practiced in this local context.

Conclusion

This chapter highlights important practices that contributed to humanizing the research process (e.g. being present at the school, building meaningful relationships, engaging in genuine dialogue, attempting to equalize the power balance) and analyzes the ways that I modified the interview process with youth in order to support such approaches. The reflections that I share in this chapter represent my understanding of what it means to humanize research in order to rethink and reconstitute the types of processes and interactions that took place between the youth and I – while also establishing rigor and trustworthy data practices. The reflections illustrate the need for all researchers to be mindful of their local research contexts, considerate of the needs of the individual participants, and prepared to adapt and modify particular research practices if needed. Each researcher must make sense of their local contexts, participants and relationships in order to come up with their own way of carrying out projects that promote humanizing research efforts. Being engaged, over time, in the local context with the participants in meaningful and authentic ways can create opportunities to develop, maintain (and hopefully sustain) 'relationships of dignity and care' (Paris, 2011: 137). Engaging in genuine dialogues with the participants can help to contribute to such relationships over time, but such conversations can also have other types of positive implications, like planting seeds of affirmation and hope between (researcher) participants, or disrupting larger ideological forces that might play out in a learning context. Humanizing the research process can be quite complicated in practice, but it is worthwhile and essential, particularly for working in schools and communities with marginalized and vulnerable populations.

References

Arias, M.B. and Faltis, C. (eds) (2012) Introduction. *Implementing Educational Language Policy in Arizona: Legal Historical and Current Practices in SEI* (pp. xxiii–xxviii). Bristol: Multilingual Matters.

Fredricks, D.E. (2017) Reflections on qualitative research with English language learner youth in restrictive language contexts. In S.A. Mirhosseini (ed.) *Reflections on Qualitative Research in Language and Literacy Education* (pp. 157–170). Dordrecht: Springer.

Fredricks, D.E. and Warriner, D.S. (2016) '*We speak English in here and English, only!*': Teacher and ELL youth perspectives on restrictive language education. *The Bilingual Research Journal* 39 (3–4), 309–323.

Fredricks, D.E. and Warriner, D.S. (2015) 'Talk English!': Refugee youth and policy shaping in restrictive language contexts. In E. Feuerherm and V. Ramanathan (eds) *Refugee Resettlement in the United States: Language, Policy, Pedagogy* (pp. 134–150). Bristol: Multilingual Matters.

Gándara, P. and Orfield, G. (2010) A return to the 'Mexican room': The segregation of Arizona's English learners. *The Civil Rights Project at UCLA*. Retrieved from http://civilrightsproject.ucla.edu/research/k-12-education/language-minority-students/a-return-to-the-mexican-room-the-segregation-of-arizonas-english-learners-1/gandara-return-mexican-room-2010.pdf. (accessed 7 May 2017).

Grijalva, G. and Jimenez-Silva, M. (2014) Exploring principals' concerns regarding the implementation of Arizona's mandated SEI model. In S.C.K. Moore (ed.) *Language Policy Processes and Consequences: Arizona Case Studies* (pp. 108–132). Bristol: Multilingual Matters.

Hones, D. (2002) (ed.) *American Dreams, Global Visions: Dialogic Teacher Research with Refugee and Immigrant Families*. Mahwah: Lawrence Erlbaum Associates.

Ibrahim, A. (2014) Research as an act of love: Ethics, émigrés, and the praxis of becoming human. *Diaspora, Indigenous, and Minority Education* 8 (1), 7–20. DOI: 10.1080/15595692.2013.803464.

Kinloch, V. and San Pedro, T. (2014) The space between listening and storying: Foundations for projects in humanization. In D. Paris and M. Winn (eds) *Humanizing Research: Decolonizing Qualitative Inquiry with Youth and Communities* (pp. 21–42). Los Angeles: Sage.

Krashen, S., MacSwan, J. and Rolstad, K. (2012) Review of 'Research summary and bibliography for structured English immersion programs' for the Arizona English language learners task force. In M.B. Arias and C. Faltis (eds) *Implementing Educational Language Policy in Arizona: Legal Historical and Current Practices in SEI* (pp. 107–118). Bristol: Multilingual Matters.

Lillie, K.E. and Markos, A. (2014) The four-hour block: SEI in classrooms. In S.C.K. Moore (ed.) *Language Policy Processes and Consequences: Arizona Case Studies* (pp. 133–155). Bristol: Multilingual Matters.

Lillie, K.E. and Moore, S.C. (2014) SEI in Arizona: Bastion for states' rights. In S.C.K. Moore (ed.) *Language Policy Processes and Consequences: Arizona Case Studies* (pp. 1–27). Bristol: Multilingual Matters.

Long, M.H. and Adamson, H.D. (2012) SLA research and Arizona's structured English immersion policies. In M.B. Arias and C. Faltis (eds) *Implementing Educational Language Policy in Arizona: Legal Historical and Current Practices in SEI* (pp. 39–58). Bristol: Multilingual Matters.

Ochs, E. and Capps, L. (2001) *Living Narrative: Creating Lives in Everyday Storytelling.* Cambridge: Harvard University Press.

Paris, D. (2011) 'A friend who understand fully': Notes on humanizing research in a multiethnic youth community. *International Journal of Qualitative Studies in Education* 24 (2), 137–149.

Paris, D. and Winn, M. (2014) To humanize research. In D. Paris and M. Winn (eds) *Humanizing Research: Decolonizing Qualitative Inquiry with Youth and Communities.* Los Angeles: Sage.

Ruíz, R. (1984) Orientations in language planning. *NABE Journal* 8 (2), 15–34.

Rumberger, R.W. and Tran, L. (2010) State language policies, school language practices, and the English learner achievement gap. In P. Gándara and M. Hopkins (eds) *Forbidden Language: English Learners and Restrictive Language Policies* (pp. 86–101). New York: Teachers College Press.

Seidman, I. (2006) *Why interview? Interviewing as Qualitative Research* (3rd edn). New York: Teachers College Press.

Wiley, T. (2012) Foreword: From restrictive SEI to imagining better. In M.B. Arias and C. Faltis (eds) *Implementing Educational Language Policy in Arizona: Legal Historical and Current Practices in SEI* (pp. xiii–xxii). Bristol: Multilingual Matters.

Part 3: Relationships, Ethics, Power and Equity

9 Ethics in Practice and Answerability in Complex, Multi-participant Studies

Katie A. Bernstein

Introduction

This chapter reports on a year-long ethnography in a preschool classroom where the majority of the students were learners of English as a new language as well as members of families who had moved to the US as refugees. Unlike a typical research paper, this chapter does not present findings from the original study (those can be found elsewhere; see Bernstein, 2014, 2016); rather it is a reflection about the on-the-ground ethical challenges of carrying out research with this population of children, their families, and their teachers. It explores issues of reflexivity and reciprocity in complex, multi-party, multi-layered research in which all of the participants – children, parents, teachers – are in some way 'vulnerable'. It also introduces Bakhtin's notion of answerability, posing the question, 'To whom am I answerable right now?' as a question of ethics in practice. Finally, it presents guiding questions to assist researchers in making decisions about answerability on the ground.

Using the original study as a tool, this chapter asks the following questions:

(1) How might reciprocity-in-practice and reflexivity-in-practice support ethical research with vulnerable populations?
(2) In what kinds of ethically important moments might reciprocity-in-practice and reflexivity-in-practice fail to account for the complexities that arise in multi-party research?
(3) How can the notion of answerability help with on-the-ground decision making in those instances?

In the next sections, I introduce key ideas – vulnerability, reciprocity, reflexivity, and answerability – that will guide the rest of the chapter.

Vulnerability

Historically, vulnerability in research has been understood in terms of: (1) capacity to give consent and (2) susceptibility to coercion (Block, Riggs *et al.*, 2013: 6). These are the main ways that the United States Code of Federal Regulations section on the Protection of Human Subjects (2009; 45 CFR § 46) understands vulnerability, as well. The groups of federally recognized vulnerable populations – children, prisoners, pregnant women and fetuses and persons with questionable cognitive capacity to consent – are all recognized as being vulnerable in one or both of those ways.

I knew, even before I met them, that many of the participants in my study would indeed be at risk in both senses. Young children – in this case, three- to five-year-olds – are vulnerable in that they may not have much say in where researchers find them – in their classrooms, perhaps, or through their parents – and it may be difficult for them to understand why they are participating in research, what the research will entail, and what the risks, benefits and outcomes will be. Additionally, the children in my study would be just beginning to learn English. Many of their parents, too, might be new to the United States and to the English language. They may not be literate in their first language, and they would likely be new to the research and consent process. Finally, while researchers do not often think of teachers as a vulnerable population, federal code also understands that all workers taking part in workplace studies are vulnerable, in that they are dependent upon their work for income. If their employer encourages participation in research, workers may feel obligated to participate or risk job loss or other sanctions if they do not. Additionally, in a workplace study, findings can have negative implications for a worker, particularly if they are about his or her job performance. This is no less true for teachers, and in fact might be more so in the current climate in the US, where, as Hatch (2015) put it bluntly, 'Teacher bashing has become a national pastime' (2015: 10). Additionally, preschool teachers tend to be the least well-paid educators, making less than $20,000 year in some places, and therefore may be economically insecure.

Ethics in Research with Vulnerable Populations

Accounting for these kinds of vulnerability by obtaining permission in comprehensible and non-coercive ways and by taking extra precautions with confidentiality and data security is the minimum that a researcher must do to satisfy the requirements of federal regulations. In my study, permission forms were translated and parents had the option to have them read aloud. Parents were given the chance to hear me explain the research in everyday language and to hear that the research was not tied to school enrollment (consent forms were not required 'school forms'), so that they could say 'no' without consequence or offense. Teachers were assured that the study was about children's learning and not their teaching skill, and that my writing would reflect that. Children were told that they could tell me 'I don't want you to watch me' or 'I don't want you to film me' whenever they wanted and that they could turn the camera away. Parents, children, and teachers all learned about pseudonyms and secure video storage. These safeguards amount to what Guillemin and Gillam (2004) called 'procedural ethics' or the ethical decisions required of researchers by various research ethics committees such as the university IRB. The procedures that make up procedural ethics take place primarily at the start of a research project, before data collection begins (e.g. informed consent) or after, in terms of the handling of data (e.g. encryption and storage) and reporting of findings (e.g. using pseudonyms).

Procedural ethics do not, however, account for the day-to-day decision-making in which researchers engage, over the course of a given project. Guillemin and Gillam (2004) give the example of an interviewer who, in the course of an interview about heart disease, learns of the sexual abuse of a child and must decide, first how to respond in the moment – stop the interview or keep recording? Engage or try to steer the conversation back to the topic of the interview? – and then, afterwards, whether to breach participant confidentiality to report the abuse. Guillemin and Gillam use the term 'ethics in practice' to describe these 'everyday ethical issues that arise in the doing of research' (2004: 263). They propose that while the IRB is the answer to procedural ethics, ethics in practice require different tools. Two tools that they suggest are reflexivity and reciprocity. In the next section, I address each in turn.

Ethics in Practice: Reflexivity and Reciprocity

Reflexivity is the acknowledgement and examination of the researcher's role, power, and position in the research process and relative to participants. While, in qualitative research, reflexivity is often considered a tool for rigor, Guillemin and Gillam propose that it can also be key to resolving dilemmas that arise in what they call 'ethically important moments'. They explain: 'Being reflexive in an ethical sense means acknowledging and being sensitized to the microethical dimensions of research practice and in doing so, being alert to and prepared for ways of dealing with the ethical tensions that arise' (2004: 265). This is particularly important in cross-cultural and cross-linguistic research, where reflexivity can both remind the researcher of the contextual, relational, and hierarchical processes of knowledge construction as well as potentiate awareness and subversion of power relationships between researcher and researched (Caretta, 2015).

In order to truly affect power relationships, however, reflexivity cannot be limited to a post hoc analysis during writing as a kind of correction to power imbalances (Nencel, 2014). Instead, a researcher must account for relational positionality as part of the whole research process, from conception to fieldwork to data construction to writing. In this sense, to extend Guillemin and Gillam's terminology, the traditional 'role of the researcher' section of a research paper might be viewed as *procedural reflexivity* – the minimum necessary – while reflexivity carried out throughout the research process can be seen as *reflexivity in practice*.

A second tool for ethics in practice, related to reflexivity, is reciprocity. Trainor and Bouchard (2013) divide definitions, or discourses, of reciprocity into two families. The first includes one-time, 'pay-to-play' definitions of reciprocity: Research subjects give us data; we compensate them fairly for their time and risk. This *quid pro quo* stance draws on discourses of transactions and market exchange. It is this view that is encouraged, if unintentionally, by many ethics boards, such as IRBs, who frame the question of reciprocity in terms of compensation rather than reciprocation, aligning with Guillemin and Gillam's 'ethics as procedure' view. Trainor and Bouchard (2013) instead argue for reciprocity as 'value, method, and lens', connected together in an overall reciprocal stance. From this view, reciprocity is not a one-time exchange, nor can it be defined ahead of time. Although reciprocity might still be 'a relationship in which each contributes something the other needs or desires' (2013: 986), both the relationship and the need/desires are continually redefined throughout the research process and thus reciprocation is ongoing. This is the view that I take up in this chapter. To extend Guillemin and Gillam's terminology one last time, one might call this definition of *reciprocity in practice*.

At its most potent, reciprocity-in-practice might entail doing research with and for participants, with the aim of social transformation (Hugman *et al.*, 2011; Pittaway *et al.*, 2010) This approach has been particularly powerful with populations such as refugees who, in addition to all of the other ways they are vulnerable, have been vulnerable to 'grab and go' researchers, who drop in for data collection without understanding the needs and desires of these groups, may traumatize with their questions, and may not realize the negative consequences that their work can have for their participants (Block, Warr *et al.*, 2013). Yet, even in cases where engagement in full collaborative research with participants is not possible or not desired, reciprocity-in-practice can still occur, if researchers are attentive to how their research and presence contribute to or benefit participants, and if researchers are open to evolving possibilities for contribution.

Yet, when researchers move beyond procedural ethics to ethics-in-practice, roles and relationships – simple when participants are just subjects and reciprocation is just payment – can multiply and become more complex. It may not always be clear who exactly the researcher is *answerable* to and in which way.

Ethics in Practice: Answerability

Answerability is an idea that comes from Bahktin's early work (1990, 1993) and is often considered a precursor to his notion of dialogism, the notion that utterances, and also selves, are always already responding to others. In his early work, Bakhtin introduced the idea that when two people look at each other, each can see something that the other cannot, what he called one's 'excess of seeing'. Because my excess of seeing is the other's lack, it is only in the eyes of 'the other' that we can ever come to know ourselves fully, to be whole. Thus, even before we act or speak, we are always already in dialogue with the other. When we act in the world, then our actions are always in anticipation of or in response to the other. In that sense, our actions are always *answering* to the other.

However, perhaps more importantly for Bakhtin, we must also answer to ourselves. Each time we act, we have to account to ourselves for our actions, based on our unique, individual, moral perspective at a given time and place. As Juzwik (2004) put it, 'Answerability highlights how utterances (and texts) are acts that do ethical work through the active intonations of once-occurrent selves in the event of being' (2004: 551). This means that the concept of answerability moves us away from seeing ethical action as action that follows a pre-determined moral code and instead sees ethical action as action that one can answer for – to oneself and to others – in an actual given time and place, or the 'unitary and unique world that is experienced concretely [...] a world that is seen, heard, touched, and thought' (Bakhtin, 1993: 56). Thus, the answerable (ethical) act is always a response to the concrete and current world, to actual others, by the present self. Answerability is therefore always answerability-in-practice.

Bakhtin took care to say that even when one is acting in as an official representative, backed by the authority of an institution, one does not abdicate one's responsibly to answer for one's actions. 'Being a representative does not abolish but merely specializes my personal answerability' (1993: 52). Thus, even when researchers and their work have been vetted by the IRB, a granting organization, or a school district, it does not relieve them of their obligation to act in a way that is answerable to themselves and to the others in their studies. Yet, when a researcher aims to act answerably in a study involving multiple participants in multiple interacting roles, tensions can arise. The question 'To whom am I answerable right now?' may not always have a definitive response.

In the next sections, I describe my entry into the research setting and some of the ways I engaged in reciprocity-in-practice with participants. I then present four vignettes in which, at the time, it was not clear to whom I was answerable. I use these vignettes to propose steps that researchers might take to prepare for on-the ground decision-making around answerability in these ethically important moments.

Entering the Field: Unanticipated Vulnerability

My original project sought to understand how young English language learners navigate the social world of their preschool classrooms and how their positions within the social fabric of the class connect to their English learning. I was in graduate school in California at the time that I conceived of my project, and I had planned to conduct the research locally. However, before I settled on a research site, an opportunity arose to instead carry out my research across the country, in Pittsburgh, Pennsylvania. I jumped at the chance to go 'out in the field', and to explore a new educational context. I left for Pittsburgh in spring of 2012, not sure who exactly I would find there as my young English learners. One of the first people I spoke to in the city was the director of English as a second language (ESL) services for a local school district. When he told me that the top three languages spoken by students receiving ESL services in the district were Nepali, Spanish and Swahili, I was surprised. I imagined that Spanish would be in the top three, but Nepali and Swahili? He explained in passing that in the last decade, many refugees have been resettled in Pittsburgh, and that the largest group were ethnic Nepali people from Bhutan. *Refugees? Resettled? Bhutan?* As I hung up the phone, I realized that my project was about to get bigger. During the summer before the start of the school year, I dove headfirst into a seemingly bottomless pool of questions: *What happened in Bhutan? What is a refugee, technically? How does resettlement work? Who, exactly, does the resettling? Why Pittsburgh?*

The more I learned about the conflicts that brought refugees to Pittsburgh and about their forced migration, relocation, and resettlement, the more I realized that several other kinds of vulnerability, falling outside of my IRB's concerns with consent and confidentiality, might be relevant, particularly for the parents in my study. Refugees, for instance, have no choice as to the country and city of their relocation. Many may have been holding out in hopes that the conflict would end and they could return home. Thus, many resettled refugees may not have wanted to come to the US at all, may have feared moving here, and may be suffering from acculturation stress (Benson *et al.*, 2012), but may be afraid to say so to a researcher, fearing a loss of benefits or rights. Additionally, refugees may have experienced extreme violence and trauma. Many experience symptoms of post-traumatic stress disorder (PTSD), depression and anxiety (Ao *et al.*, 2016; CDC, 2013). Their stories would have also been told again and again and again, to official after official as part of the asylum-seeking and relocation process (Bureau of Population, Refugees, and Migration, 2013; Refugees, n.d.), and it might be unethical to obligate families to tell me once more what had brought them here. Yet, I also learned that not all refugee experiences are the same and that even for people who had experienced the same conflict, potential vulnerabilities – and the potential for resilience and agency in the face of these – could vary greatly (Block, Riggs *et al.*, 2013; Mackenzie *et al.*, 2007; Perry, 2011).

One important source of information was the local resettlement agencies in Pittsburgh. These agencies partner with the US government to provide on-the-ground services, such as housing, job training, and assistance registering for schools, for refugees arriving in the US. A director at one of these agencies, who himself had come to the US as refugee years before, helped me to understand the process through a long conversation in his office. At the end, he smiled and not yet standing up from his desk, told me, 'We always need volunteers.' That is how my first connection with the refugee community of Pittsburgh began: as a volunteer home educator. In that capacity, I visited newly-arrived residents, with an interpreter by my side, to talk about how to work the stove, where to do laundry, how to interact with a landlord, how to pay rent, why one does not mail cash to a utility company, and how to stay warm in this new, very cold season of winter without creating an excessive heating bill. I got to know all of the apartment complexes and neighborhoods where newly-arrived families lived, and I became intimately familiar with the material conditions of arrival in the US as a refugee. I learned that most calls to landlords could be avoided if I brought along a set of tools, a plunger, a drain snake, and some 9 volt batteries (not a single smoke detector in any apartment I visited ever had a working battery). I became an advocate for the families I visited, calling doctors' offices and negotiating with property owners. I also became friends with the interpreters with whom I most often worked. These interpreters had also come to Pittsburgh as refugees, and they became key to my understanding of what it means to arrive in the US that way.

Reciprocity-in-Practice

Although I did not see it then, this volunteer job, which began around the time I entered the classroom as a researcher and continued for more than a year afterwards, was the first and longest kind of reciprocity I engaged in during dissertation research. Although I never directly worked as a home educator for the families who participated in my study, as they had all been in the US for several years, I often worked in their apartment complexes with people that they had known in their camps, or who were friends of friends or cousins of cousins. This work does not easily fit within the discourse of procedural, or *quid pro quo*, reciprocity, as it did not directly compensate my research participants, but it amounted to what one might call indirect reciprocity, or reciprocity with a community in which my participants lived.

But what about reciprocity with the participants who were directly involved in my project? The classroom where I spent a year as a researcher was a mixed-age preschool classroom with two teachers and 17 three-to five-year old children, 12 of whose families had come to the US as refugees. This meant that my participants were two teachers, 16 children (one child declined to participate) and nine parents who agreed to do an interview with me.

With parents, my chance for reciprocity came when I brought an interpreter and sat down with parents for one-on-one interviews. In these interviews, parents shared their views about their children's language learning and schooling and about living and working in Pittsburgh. As a gesture of procedural reciprocity – albeit one I put a great deal of thought into – I gave each parent a Nepali-English bilingual children's book, a Bhutanese folktale written down and illustrated by a group of refugees who had resettled in New England (Tiwari & Rai, 2013). During the interviews, however, parents also expressed worries about balancing the demands of acculturation to the US and acquisition of English with the maintenance of their ways of speaking and living. I reassured them that their inclination to preserve Nepali at home was backed by much research and that being bilingual and bicultural had many social, emotional, cognitive, and familial benefits. Many of the mothers also wanted to know how their children were doing at school, whether they were good and what they did all day, but because of the mothers' nervousness with English, they were afraid or unable to ask the teachers. I told them what I had seen in the months I spent with their children, particularly times when their children had been kind to friends, clever problem-solvers and good listeners. I had not planned on sharing information about language learning or about classroom life as a way of giving back, but both became a very important moment of reciprocity-in-practice, and from January, when the interviews took place, until the end of the school year, my relationship with those parents was closer and warmer than it had been before.

I did not have to wait as long to engage in reciprocity with teachers and children. Immediately upon entering the classroom as a researcher, myriad tiny ways of contributing emerged. As a participating observer involved in day-to-day activity in the classroom, I tied shoes, wiped down tables, wiped noses, opened milk cartons, wrote names on artwork, held hands and cut up hundreds of apples and oranges for snacks. As anyone who has been in a classroom knows, there is always something that an extra pair of hands can be doing, and in between taking notes and setting up the video camera, I looked for as many ways to contribute as possible.

Balancing Reciprocity with Power and Positioning: Reflexivity-in-Practice

My reciprocal actions in the classroom benefitted students and teachers in small, but frequent ways – saving the teachers a few seconds of work; getting the students their milk a few minutes earlier – yet I was also always aware that each action positioned me, the teachers, and the students in relation to one another in particular ways. I had discussed with the teachers early on that I would not act as a third teacher in the classroom in any managerial or disciplinary capacity. It was important that I be able to observe students teasing, fighting, and rule breaking, and therefore that they did not see me as an authority figure. I also made clear to teachers that I was not there to evaluate their teaching or to tell them what to do, but that I was there to learn from them. Negotiating and maintaining these relational positionings meant that not all forms of reciprocity were possible. For instance, the teachers would have appreciated it if I had prevented one student from knocking over another's block tower or if I had kept another from slowly pouring sand onto the floor. And the students probably would have appreciated it if I had questioned the classroom rules of limiting the number of people at the sand table or of not letting the children run in the grassy area of the playground. But since these actions on behalf of one group (teachers vs. students) would have interfered with my positionality (as a non-teacher and non-evaluator) with the other, I avoided them.[1]

Sometimes though, when only teachers or only students were present in an interaction, I could engage in reciprocal activity that would have unbalanced my positionality with the other group. For instance, before the children arrived in the morning, or when they were sleeping in the afternoon, I engaged with teachers in the teacher-like reciprocal activity of bringing coffee, empathizing about paperwork and district policies and wages, or discussing a challenging student. And when, during meals or free playtime, the teachers were off in another part of the room, I engaged with students in ways that would have positioned me as questioning the rules and decisions of the teachers, had the teachers seen them. For example, I let students write and draw in my field notebooks, even when they were not in the writing corner, and I let them do it with pen, a tool meant for adults only.[2] Once, I joined them in playing 'Wedding' even as they drew pretend *mehndi* all over their hands and arms with marker, clearly breaking the 'we only write on paper' rule. Perhaps most importantly, in an otherwise English-only classroom, I reciprocated students' interest in my language: I smiled when they spoke Nepali around me, I went home and looked up words that they used, I tried out Nepali words and I played language games with the words we both knew in both languages ('Sister, *didi*! Water, *paani*!'). When I was only with students or only with teachers, it was easy to engage in on-the-ground reciprocal action without upsetting the balance of relationships that I had worked so hard to establish.

For this reason, negotiating reciprocity and positionality with the parents was easy: our interactions were bounded, taking place mostly during one-on-one interviews through an interpreter, without students or teachers present. Those interviews, of course, also required

reflexivity-in-practice and some negotiations of our respective positioning. There was the time, for instance, when a grandmother expressed
shame that she could not yet speak English, and I responded, trying
to show empathy, by telling her that it was okay, and that if she was
ashamed, then I, too, should be, since I had spent a lot of time listening
to the children speak Nepali and had hardly learned any. She replied,
'It's ok for you not to know Nepali, but I have to speak English because
everybody here speaks English', swiftly contesting my admittedly somewhat disingenuous negation of power relations. For the most part,
however, as I interacted one-on-one with parents (sometimes with my
interpreter, a Nepali woman around my and the mothers' ages), there
was no tension between reciprocal action with parents and positionality
with students or teachers.

When I was in the classroom, however, particularly when multiple
kinds of participants (parents, teachers, children) were present in the
same interaction, it was sometimes less clear how to balance reciprocity
with relationships. On several occasions, when reciprocity with one kind
of participant would have meant contradicting the relational positioning
with another, I struggled with what to do. In these situations, it was not
always clear whether I was acting answerably or to whom.

The Limits of Reciprocity and Reflexivity: Multiple Answerabilities in Conflict

In this section, I turn to four brief vignettes that illustrate this tension
between answerability to myself and to different kinds of participants.
Each begs the questions: To whom, if anyone, were my actions answerable? Looking back, to whom *should* I have been answerable?

Vignette 1: 'When in Rome'

*As a teacher was serving lunch one day, she sighed about needing separate
tables for the meat eaters and the non-meat-eating Nepali students. She
expressed that it would be nice if when they were at school, the students
ate meat like everyone else. 'When in Rome', she said. 'Right?'*

*I hesitated. Then asked if anyone told her that the students were vege-
tarian for religious reasons. She said no. I said, laughing, 'Imagine if some
made you eat meat on a Friday during Lent!' She laughed and said she
could never do it.*

Vignette 2: Helping and not helping

*Parents often stayed in the classroom during breakfast. The teachers
encouraged them to sit with their children, but not to feed them or help
them too much, as school was a place for learning to be independent.*

One day, a parent could not open the cereal container for her son, as she was also holding her baby. She passed it to me. As I began to open it, the teacher said, 'Let's let [the child] try it himself first.'

I looked at the teacher, the parent, the child. 'Let's do it together,' I suggested. He and I both peeled the paper back and when it seemed inevitable that it would open, I let him finish. Everyone seemed satisfied, and parents began using 'doing it together' as way to help that was also acceptable to teachers.

Vignette 3: Hand holding

One day, I was sitting in the morning circle time (the time of day when the whole class meets to talk about the schedule, the calendar, attendance, etc.) when Kritika, one of my Nepali-speaking focal students, took my hand. The teacher glanced over and told her to keep her hands to herself, because she might need them to participate during circle time. After the teacher looked away, Kritika tried to take my hand again.

Without thinking, I pulled back and whispered to her that I would hold it later. She crossed her arms in front of her body and said, 'I sad. I SAD.' I felt awful.

Vignette 4: Paint mixing

A teacher was working one-on-one with children as they created self-portraits on paper plates with paints, markers, and yarn. The first step was to use a variety of skin-toned paints to paint the plates. The teacher helped the children mix paints until it matched their hands.

Joy, the only African American child in the class, was the sixth student to have a turn. While she and her family identified as Black, her skin was lighter than two or three of the Nepali students. The teacher asked Joy which color she should start with, and Joy pointed to the bright white paint. The teacher laughed and looked at me across the table, 'White, she says!' The teacher (laughing) and Joy (serious and confused) both looked at me.

In that second, I thought of what both of them might be thinking and about language and race in America. I couldn't laugh back. The teacher seemed annoyed.

Multiple Answerabilities in Conflict: Discussion

In Vignette 1, 'When in Rome,' tension arose as the expertise and experience of the teacher came into contact with the culture and beliefs of the students and their families. The parents were not there at lunch to represent their perspective on meat-eating, and the children were not likely to protest. I realized I could not let the teacher continue thinking that the students and families were simply being difficult. Yet, I could also not directly contradict her. My time in the classroom and in conversation with the teacher about her own background gave me an idea: posing a parallel situation, in which asking the Hindu families to eat meat in school might feel as impossible to them as it would be for her to breach the Catholic no-meat-Fridays rule. I was therefore able to act answerably toward the teachers, the families, and to myself, by finding a third way out.

In Vignette 2, Helping and not helping, the discourse of school – students must learn to be independent – came into conflict with the beliefs of the families – that three-year-olds must still be taken care of. Rather than choosing between just helping (valued by the parent) or just letting the child try alone (valued by the teachers), I again found a third way out, a way that still allowed the child to start eating. In this case, I managed to answer to everyone in my response, and my 'third way'[3]became a lasting compromise.

In the Hand holding and Paint mixing scenarios (Vignettes 3 and 4), I did not manage to find such a way out. In Vignette 3, had I answered to Kritika (and myself) and taken Kritika's hand, I would have represented Kritika's act as a welcome gesture of friendship, but I would have also risked positioning myself as judging, or even outright defying, the teacher. I instead answered to the teacher, choosing not to take Kritika's hand. In doing so, I positioned myself as a rule-enforcer, but also Kritika as a rule-breaker and Kritika's action as a deviant one. In Vignette 4, if I had defended Joy's choice, it would have meant positioning myself as evaluating and as questioning the teacher's judgment, in addition to making her comment a racial (perhaps racist) one. Yet, had I laughed with the teacher, I would have positioned Joy's choice as ridiculous, as well as ignored what 'white' and 'black' have meant and mean in the US. So I froze and did not answer to anyone, least of all to myself.

As much as I insisted (privately and publicly) during my time in the preschool classroom that we were all there to learn from each other, these examples make plain my power as a researcher to shape context. I had the power to create a way of helping/not helping at breakfast. I also led the teacher to see the children's food choices in a new light. But I also had the power to make Kritika's hand-holding a deviant act and the teacher's comment a racist one. One of the invisible findings of this project, then, is that in a complex research ecology, where multiple groups of people from multiple backgrounds are present in multiple, interconnected social roles, it is impossible to be equally answerable to everyone all the time.

What *Should* I Have Done?: Answerability as a Guide in Ethically Important Moments

Just as social positioning is always negotiated across time, requiring reflexivity-in-practice, and reciprocal ways of helping emerge and fade, requiring reciprocity-in-practice, answerability, too, shifts with context and interlocutors. This idea is built into the very notion of answerability: 'The world in which an act or deed actually proceeds, in which it is actually accomplished, is a unitary and unique world that is experienced concretely: it is a world that is seen, heard, touched, and thought, a world permeated in its entirety with emotional-volitional tones of the affirmed validity of values' (Bakhtin, 1993: 56). For Bakhtin, answerable action was always answerable in the lived moment.

This does not mean, however, that it is impossible to prepare for instances in which multiple 'others' call for contradictory answerable acts. There are commonalities across instances in which I was able to negotiate ethical action that was answerable to all, including myself. In these instances, such as the first and second vignettes, I acted on behalf of those least able to speak up for themselves and with the least relational power in the research ecology – the children and then their families – yet in a way that allowed me to maintain my delicate relational balance with the teachers, as well. I accomplished this by avoiding an either-or solution but instead finding a third way out.

I propose, therefore, that answerable action in complex, multi-party, multi-layered research might include two components. First, even when accountabilities are shifting and multiple, it is necessary to have a hierarchy of to whom it matters most to be answerable. Of course, as Bakhtin wrote, answerability is first and foremost answerability to oneself: Do I *stand by this action? Will I answer for it?* After that, I suggest that even when everyone in a study is in some way vulnerable, researchers must next be answerable to their most vulnerable participants (here, the children, then parents, then teachers, then school/district). However, even if this goal to support the most vulnerable first remains stable, the approach to reaching that goal must be navigated in *situ*. This is the second component of answerable action in research: negotiating tensions in answerability by looking for the 'third way', or the path that allows the researcher to support the most vulnerable, while respecting relationships with all parties. In the Helping and not helping example, this meant accomplishing the outcome of getting the student his breakfast without disrupting my positionality as a non-teacher to the students and non-evaluator of the teachers. This was accomplished by avoiding the binary of 'open the cereal' (and contradict teachers) or 'don't the open cereal' (and contradict parents), but finding a third way: doing it together. In the 'When in Rome' example, answerable action meant working on behalf of families toward the outcome of teacher understanding of students' dietary needs, but avoiding directly questioning the teacher's judgement or expertise. Here, too, I skirted the binary of 'agree with teacher' or 'disagree with teacher' and instead simply provided a missing piece of information and a helpful analogy. The two questions, therefore, that

I suggest could be asked to support on-the-ground decision making as part of answerable action are:

(1) What is the <u>outcome</u> here that answers first to the most vulnerable participant(s)?
(2) What is the <u>approach</u> to that outcome that allows me to maintain my relationship with all of the participants, i.e. the third way?

Together, these questions might have helped me react differently in the last two vignettes. In the Hand holding scenario I might have determined that the desired outcome (answer to Question 1) was reciprocation of Kritika's gesture of friendship. I might have realized, too that the approach (answer to Question 2), did not have to mean deciding between either holding her hand or letting go of it. What if I had let go, but let go in order to give her a tight hug? Or let go, but to draw a heart for her in my field notebook? Or what if I had held on for three more seconds and let go with a wink and a squeeze? Unlike the action I chose in real life, any of those responses are actions that I would stand by.

In the Paint Mixing vignette, I might have concluded that the desired outcome (answer to Question 1) was to make Joy's choice of paint seem like a fine choice. In terms of approach (answer to Question 2), rather than thinking of my two choices of action as either laughing or explicitly contradicting the teacher, I might have said 'What a good place to start!', acknowledging to Joy that white was a fine choice and to the teacher that it was still far from Joy's skin tone. Or maybe I should have asked if I could start with white, too, and began mixing my own paint. Both acts would exhibit answerability to myself, as well as to my most vulnerable participant, while still finding a way not to alienate the other participant, the teacher.

Conclusion

Ethics in practice is made up of the multiple, day-to-day, on-the-ground decisions that researches must make. This on-the-ground ethics involves learning to recognize and engage in diverse ways of reciprocal action. It also involves engaging in reflexivity-in-practice throughout the research process to account for power and positioning in researcher-participant relationships. Additionally, in ethically important moments where tensions arise between reciprocity and reflexivity, the notion of answerability might help researchers negotiate satisfactory – if never perfect – solutions. When applied through each of the two questions posed above, the idea of answerable action might help researchers prioritize the most vulnerable while maintaining relational positionalities with all participants. Most importantly, it might help researchers choose ethical action: action by which they can stand and for which they are proud to answer.

Notes

(1) Of course, if someone was going to get hurt or hurt someone else, I stepped in. And when the fire alarm went off one day and only one teacher was in the room, I abandoned my rule of non-teacher-like behavior and helped her get the students in a line and out the door.
(2) However, see Bernstein, 2016 for an account of the very positive outcomes of this rule-breaking.
(3) Although this is not exactly what Bhabha (1994) or Gutiérrez *et al.* (1999) meant by Third Space, their work certainly deserves credit for its role in my thinking here.

References

Ao, T., Shetty, S., Sivilli, T., Blanton, C., Ellis, H., Geltman, P.L., Cochran, J., Taylor, E., Lankau, E.W. and Cardozo, B.L. (2016) Suicidal ideation and mental health of Bhutanese refugees in the United States. *Journal of Immigrant and Minority Health* 18 (4), 828–835. https://doi.org/10.1007/s10903-015-0325-7 (accessed 17 September 2018).

Bakhtin, M.M. (1990) *Art and Answerability: Early Philosophical Essays*. Austin: University of Texas Press.

Bakhtin, M.M. (1993) *Toward a Philosophy of the Act*. Austin: University of Texas Press.

Benson, G.O., Sun, F., Hodge, D.R. and Androff, D.K. (2012) Religious coping and acculturation stress among Hindu Bhutanese: A study of newly-resettled refugees in the United States. *International Social Work* 55 (4), 538–553. https://doi.org/10.1177/0020872811417474 (accessed 17 September 2018).

Bernstein, K.A. (2014) Learning English as an L2 in PreK: A Practice Perspective on Identity and Acquisition. PhD Thesis, University of California at Berkeley.

Bernstein, K.A. (2016) Writing their way into talk: Emergent bilinguals' emergent literacy practices as pathways to peer interaction and oral language growth. *Journal of Early Childhood Literacy*. http://dx.doi.org/10.1177/1468798416638138 (accessed 17 September 2018).

Bhabha, H.K. (1994) *The Location of Culture*. London: Routledge.

Block, K., Riggs, E. and Haslam, N. (2013) *Values and Vulnerabilities: The Ethics of Research with Refugees and Asylum Seekers* (p. xvii). Samford Valley: Australian Academic Press.

Block, K., Warr, D., Gibbs, L., and Riggs, E. (2013) Addressing ethical and methodological challenges in research with refugee-background young people: Reflections from the field. *Journal of Refugee Studies* 26 (1), 69–87. http://doi.org/10.1093/jrs/fes002 (accessed 17 September 2018).

Bureau of Population, Refugees, and Migration. Department of State. The Office of Website Management. (31 January 2013) Refugee Resettlement in the United States (Press Release|Fact Sheet). http://www.state.gov/j/prm/releases/factsheets/2013/203578.htm (accessed 13 September 2016).

Caretta, M.A. (2015) Situated knowledge in cross-cultural, cross-language research: a collaborative reflexive analysis of researcher, assistant and participant subjectivities. *Qualitative Research* 15 (4), 489–505. http://doi.org/10.1177/1468794114543404 (accessed 17 September 2018).

Centers for Disease Control and Prevention (CDC) (2013) Suicide and suicidal ideation among Bhutanese refugees – United States, 2009–2012. *MMWR. Morbidity and Mortality Weekly Report* 62 (26), 533–536.

Guillemin, M. and Gillam, L. (2004) Ethics, reflexivity, and 'ethically important moments' in research. *Qualitative Inquiry* 10 (2), 261–280. http://doi.org/10.1177/1077800403262360 (accessed 17 September 2018).

Gutiérrez, K.D., Baquedano-López, P. and Tejeda, C. (1999) Rethinking diversity: Hybridity and hybrid language practices in the third space. *Mind, Culture, and Activity* 6 (4), 286–303. https://doi.org/10.1080/10749039909524733 (accessed 17 September 2018).

Hatch, J.A. (2015) *Reclaiming the Teaching Profession: Transforming the Dialogue on Public Education*. Lanham, MD: Rowman & Littlefield.

Hugman, R., Pittaway, E. and Bartolomei, L. (2011) When 'do no harm' is not enough: The ethics of research with refugees and other vulnerable groups. *British Journal of Social Work* 41 (7), 1271–1287. https://doi.org/10.1093/bjsw/bcr013 (accessed 17 September 2018).

Juzwik, M. (2004) Towards an ethics of answerability: Reconsidering dialogism in sociocultural literacy research. *College Composition and Communication* 55 (3), 536–567. http://doi.org/10.2307/4140698 (accessed 17 September 2018).

Mackenzie, C., McDowell, C. and Pittaway, E. (2007) Beyond 'do no harm': The challenge of constructing ethical relationships in refugee research. *Journal of Refugee Studies* 20 (2), 299–319. https://doi.org/10.1093/jrs/fem008 (accessed 17 September 2018).

Nencel, L. (2014) Situating reflexivity: Voices, positionalities and representations in feminist ethnographic texts. *Women's Studies International Forum* 43, 75–83. http://doi.org/10.1016/j.wsif.2013.07.018 (accessed 17 September 2018).

Perry, K.H. (2011) Ethics, vulnerability, and speakers of other languages how university irbs (do not) speak to research involving refugee participants. *Qualitative Inquiry* 17 (10), 899–912. https://doi.org/10.1177/1077800411425006 (accessed 17 September 2018).

Pittaway, E., Bartolomei, L. and Hugman, R. (2010) 'Stop stealing our stories': The ethics of research with vulnerable groups. *Journal of Human Rights Practice* 2 (2), 229–251. https://doi.org/10.1093/jhuman/huq004 (accessed 17 September 2018).

Refugees, UNHRC for. Resettlement Procedures: The Case Identification and Determination Process. http://www.unhcr.org/en-us/protection/resettlement/3bd58ce9a/resettlement-procedures-case-identification-determination-process.html (accessed 14 September 2016).

Tiwari, H. and Rai, D. (2013) *The Story of a Pumpkin: A Traditional Tale from Bhutan.* (N. Adhikari & T. Farish, Trans.) (Bilingual Nepali-English ed. edition). Concord, N.H.: New Hampshire Humanities Council.

Trainor, A. and Bouchard, K.A. (2013) Exploring and developing reciprocity in research design. *International Journal of Qualitative Studies in Education* 26 (8), 986–1003. http://doi.org/10.1080/09518398.2012.724467 (accessed 17 September 2018).

US Department of Health and Human Services. *Code of Federal Regulations – Title 45 Public Welfare CFR 46.* http://www.hhs.gov/ohrp/regulations-and-policy/regulations/45-cfr-46/ (accessed 14 May 2016).

10 Weaving Reciprocity in Research with(in) Immigrant and Refugee Communities

Nicole Pettitt

'Teacher, teacher!' Sahra waved a piece of paper in the air, attempting to get the attention of Joy, her English teacher. Joy walked slowly toward Sahra without missing a beat. 'Who is this again?' Joy asked the entire class of refugee women, pointing at a picture of Martin Luther King, Jr. that appeared in the women's citizenship preparation book. Joy paused long enough to skim one side of the piece of paper and ask if I could take Sahra to the hall to help – an unremarkable request. After several months conducting participant-observation in Joy's classroom, she regularly took me up on my offer to provide the kinds of reciprocity she found most meaningful, e.g. making tea for break time, providing one-on-one support to her students, making copies, helping to host a class Christmas party in her home, and more.

As I made my way toward Joy, I saw the paper had lines and small boxes. *A form. Of course.* In many community-based adult English programs in the United States, it is not uncommon for teachers' work to spill over into tasks akin to social work or advocacy. In these cases, learners' requests frequently center on the language and literacy demands of every-day life (e.g. Perry, 2009), such as making sense of mysterious items that arrive in the mail; accessing public transportation; or communicating with healthcare providers, children's schools, cell phone providers, and so on. Or, in Sahra's case, filling out a form.

As Joy handed me the paper, I saw the title, 'Medical Information'. I paused. I had assisted many former students, family members, and friends who had migrated to the US in filling out forms. But I had never done so as an educational researcher. I began to feel uneasy. *As a university researcher, am I allowed to do this? What if I say no? What about my commitment to offering the kinds of reciprocity that Joy and her students feel are most meaningful to them?* Sahra was already walking toward the hallway. In a split second, I decided to continue. *Okay, let's see where this goes.*

During these few moments of class, as my positionality shifted from classroom observer to participant, I faced unexpected ethical questions surrounding reciprocity. Conducting research with Joy and her former students has played an important role in shaping my evolving understandings of reciprocity, specifically its multi-layered, complex, and sometimes-contradictory nature. In this chapter, I explore methodological tensions that can arise when shifts in positionality bring reciprocity and ethics into contradiction.

Reciprocity and Positionality

Multiple qualitative research traditions seem to agree on one point surrounding reciprocity, namely that it, 'refers to a cooperative exchange of help in which two parties strive for an arrangement where everyone benefits' (Curry, 2012: 92). Beyond this, many questions remain, such as, what constitutes 'cooperative exchange'? What criteria can we use to determine that 'everyone benefits'? Who is 'everyone'? And perhaps most importantly, who gets to answer these questions? My own attempts at enacting reciprocity with Joy, her students, and others at their school underscored for me that the answers are not necessarily readily apparent and may shift during the research process. In this chapter, I focus my attention primarily on the first of these questions.

In his book-length philosophical treatment of reciprocity, Becker (2014) argues for reciprocity as a moral virtue (2014: 4), common across social groups and types of interactions despite potential ambiguity: '… what is universal is merely exchange under some sort of requirement that good be given for good received. Other considerations are needed to give definition to the requirement' (2014: 81). Understanding reciprocity in this way leads Becker to ground his views of reciprocity in justice and fairness, contending that humans should be disposed to reciprocate, the point of which is 'to create and sustain balanced social relationships' (2014: 107). Such a disposition includes two elements that are particularly salient for elucidating the tensions discussed in this paper: fittingness and proportionality.

While fittingness pertains to if and how one's attempts at reciprocity are truly good for a recipient ['good for good' (Becker, 2014: 107)], and to the ways a recipient perceives those attempts, proportionality centers on balanced exchange, highlighting the notion of fairness or 'equal benefits and sacrifices' (2014: 111) for all parties. The latter also entails two questions and a caveat: what does it cost each party to make a gift?, what benefit does each party derive from receiving a gift?, and the caveat that when costs and benefits in exchanges cannot balance, we should prioritize balanced benefits (2014: 112). For example, the benefits I reap from my dissertation should match the benefits Joy and her students received from my presence in their classroom. However, I maintain this is not the case and never will be; like other researchers who have carried out similar work, I feel I benefit most.

Many critical and feminist researchers have engaged with the above or similar questions, highlighting a diverse array of ontological, epistemological, and axiological positions that may underpin conceptualization(s) of reciprocity (see Trainor & Bouchard, 2013). Like many qualitative researchers, I attempted to reflect upon my own positions prior to and during the classroom-based phase of dissertation data collection, but had not considered these questions for *other* stakeholders in my research. In retrospect, I see that stakeholders in community-based research may include participants, gatekeeping entities (e.g. school boards and administrators), thesis examiners and committees, research funders and Institutional Review or Ethics Boards, as well as participants' family members (even when research participants are 'of age' according to dominant US norms), community leaders or elders, community organizations, and more. Further, each of these stakeholders lives and works within a web of commitments and constraints that shape their/ our desires and concerns in myriad ways, as previous scholars have described. For example, the distinct needs and desires for reciprocity of gatekeeping groups in Junqueira's (2009) school-based research in Brazil necessitated carrying out different kinds of reciprocity for each group (e.g. parent leaders, district officials, school administrators). Similarly, in their participatory work within Indigenous communities, Thorne *et al.* (2015) discuss balancing the sometimes-competing priorities of tenure-track faculty (or their institutions) and the Indigenous teachers and leaders with whom they work. And Hermès (in Dance *et al.*, 2010) recounts that, as she moves her research into new communities, each with its local concerns and strengths, she 'expects (her) research questions will be reframed as they are co-constructed anew by each community' (2010: 337); she goes on to demonstrate how differing goals for reciprocity can be complementary at times, even when these originate from different ontological and epistemological positions.

Thus, as researchers attempt to enact reciprocity in community-based research, many times we are tasked not solely with negotiating a two-way relationship as Curry (2012) and Becker (2014) describe, but with navigating several varied and sometimes-divergent stakeholder priorities. It seems that to do so in ways that are in alignment with local social practices and perspectives (e.g. community leaders, tribal entities), while balancing top-down (e.g. university, funder, IRB) constraints, would demand a great deal of sensitivity, flexibility, cultural knowledge, and ethical grounding.

Cultural Intuition and Subjectivity

Dance *et al.* (2010) refer to the above constellation of qualities (i.e. sensitivity, flexibility, cultural knowledge, ethical grounding), as well as to the sometimes-competing priorities of research stakeholders, when they describe and call for 'improvisation' (Dance *et al.*, 2010: 332) in research with/in historically marginalized individuals and communities. Improvisation requires, they argue, both 'cultural intuition' (2010: 332) and knowledge of academic discourses. The latter are generally learned during graduate programs, but the former must be learned on the ground, experientially (2010: 332). Drawing on Delgado-Bernal (1998), the authors explain that cultural intuition involves:

> hav(ing) some degree of experience and understanding with/in the discourse community being researched ... This intuition means you have enough life experience, affinity, and relationships to understand the community that you study in a lived way – enough experience to create something that is both understood by and new to that discourse (Dance *et al.*, 2010: 332).

When I began the research described in this chapter, I thought my previous professional and personal experiences had provided some amount of cultural intuition surrounding adult English education in US. I had worked for over a decade in community-based adult English as an Additional Language (EAL) settings, performing various roles including volunteer, teacher, curriculum writer, administrator, assessment coordinator and grant writer. My work frequently entailed collaborating with local college and university researchers, faculty, and service-learning staff; the most productive partnerships – the ones I was most inclined to continue year after year – were those in which university partners did not attempt to impose their projects upon our school(s), but rather made efforts to understand the immediate needs of our stakeholders from insider perspectives. Although I did not realize it, those partners were teaching me lessons about (not) sharing power and voice in community-university partnerships, which I would later attempt to draw on in my research, with uneven outcomes (Dillard & Pettitt, 2017).

   During the same time period, I also supported my immigrant family members and friends in navigating the language and literacy demands of life in the United States. As those experiences unfolded, they simultaneously deepened my cultural knowledge. For example, as I assisted immigrant family members, friends, and students through processes that required them/us to 'negotiate many cultures' (Dance *et al.*, 2010: 332) such as immigration proceedings, advocating for oneself after a car accident, escaping an abusive spouse, finding culturally-appropriate mental health care and more, I found myself alternating between comfort with the familiar practices surrounding such tasks and stepping back to reflect when asked the uncomfortable question, 'Why do Americans do it that way?' As I spent more time living and working predominantly outside of the white, middle-class, English-dominant, protestant, US-citizen-born communities in which I had grown up, the practices and perspectives of newcomers in my community began to make more sense to me, little by little – especially as I was given more access to witnessing (but admittedly not 'wholly understanding or identifying with', (Visweswaran, 1994: 100)) the contexts in which they unfolded.

Yet, my thinking remained ambiguous. I remained convinced that learning English and taking up dominant practices were key for newcomers to accomplish their goals. I had only brief flashes of witnessing how broader power structures operate to obstruct and marginalize, regardless of linguistic ability or adopted cultural practices. For instance, when a family member from Mexico was pulled over because his tabs were supposedly expired, yet I had placed updated tabs on the car three days prior, my positions of privilege allowed me to view this as an isolated incident. Only after this same family member was pulled over more times in one year than I had been in my lifetime did I begin to see systemic injustice.

Later, my graduate work helped me begin to make sense of these experiences. I was especially challenged to think about my own positionality within power and privilege and the ways I contribute to and benefit from injustice and inequality. As I began to take up and craft my researcher identities, I was also learning that my knowledge is partial, contingent, and informed by my locations (Alcoff, 1991). These ideas resonated with my prior experiences working on the community side of community-university partnerships. I began thinking about ways former university partners had worked to de-center their perspectives, experiences, and epistemological stances (Tuhiwai-Smith, 2012) and I resolved to do the same, although I wasn't sure how. I assumed that I would need to listen and attempt to hear what de-centering looked like across myriad social contexts so that my research had a chance of coming closer to being congruent with local practices – just as my most-appreciated university partners had done. In terms of reciprocity, I assumed this meant asking the community-based research partners what kinds of reciprocity were most meaningful to them and offering to provide those.

As I envisioned my dissertation research, I desired to bring the above perspectives, for example, attempting to share power by blurring the lines between researcher and participant, listening, questioning that which is taken for granted, and uncovering and de-centering my assumptions in ways that appear to be congruent with local contexts. In principle, these are the stances I continue to value, although I stumble through dilemmas and tensions as I attempt to enact them in my research, including that shared in this chapter: a community-based EAL family literacy class for women who migrated to the US as refugees. And, unsurprisingly, I sometimes find myself acting in ways that are contrary to what I've described, as the vignette below shows. I hope that readers will find that my stumblings and contradictory actions reflect the ambiguity and uncertainty I continue to feel about my positionality in the research I share here.

Reciprocity and Weaving

I include the above reflections in order to demonstrate how positionality was implicated as I began to develop cultural intuition in a specific cultural context and, in conjunction with the vignette about Sahra and her paper (which I continue below), to show some of the ways this construct is interwoven with reciprocity. I purposefully take up the metaphor of weaving, reflecting on the different tools and steps involved in creating a physical weaving, as well as the diverse materials that might be incorporated into a woven item and the fundamental need for knots and working at cross-directions (i.e. warp and weft). Weaving helps me to understand reciprocity as a process and part of a whole, rather than a utilitarian exchange of goods, services, or money.[1]

This is not to say that weaving, either real or metaphorical, unfolds unproblematically or always produces beautiful items. While working at complementary cross directions produces the strength of a weaving, it is also intricate work and requires careful attention – whether weaving threads into fabric or reciprocity into research. And flipping over a partially-completed weaving reveals the mess at the back: myriad hanging strings that need to be woven back through the piece and trimmed.

The vignette in this chapter is a figurative flipping over of the partially-completed 'weaving' of my dissertation research. In my telling, I don't seek a coherent tale or to hide errant strings (dilemmas) by weaving them back through and trimming, as real-life weavers would do. My goal is not to force the details of untidy stories into orderly storylines, but rather to show the messy underside of my work, to reveal some of the hanging strings (unresolved dilemmas) surrounding reciprocity in my research, and to explore some questions these dilemmas present.

Initial Negotiations of Reciprocity

From October 2014 to May 2015, I collected ethnographic and discourse data in Joy's classroom – an English class for 20 women who had migrated to the Southeastern United States as refugees within the previous two years. The class was embedded in a small community-based family literacy program, 'Refugee Education Center' (REC), a program I had become familiar with the previous year through conducting some teacher professional development on a volunteer basis. When I approached the administrator 'Julia' regarding my proposed dissertation research in early fall 2014, I felt comfortable sharing my approach to reciprocity: I desired to 'give back'[2] to her and REC, as well as to the refugee women and teacher in whose classroom I would collect data. Simple, I thought. This approach was in line with my professional and personal values, as well as what I had learned in research methods courses. My previous experience in a role like Julia's told me that small community-based organizations' staffing and funding can be stretched thin, so welcoming in researchers may be a burden. I did not want to presume to know what Julia, Joy, or others at REC might consider meaningful reciprocity, so I purposely asked for their input; I wanted to present myself as flexible, sensitive to their concerns to fittingness in reciprocity (Becker, 2014). Overall, I felt I was attempting to enact a 'principle of respect for persons' which 'entails a responsibility on the part of researchers to try to understand and engage with the different perspectives and life experiences of research participants and to construct research relationships that are responsive to their needs and values' (Mackenzie *et al.*, 2007: 301). In order to do this, I was prepared to modify informed consent documents via IRB amendment if needed.

When Julia later asked for feedback on plans for teacher professional development, as well as on a grant, I took it as an indication she believed my offer to support her in the ways she desired. She began including me on emails to teaching staff, invited me to a staff and volunteer potluck in her home, and said I was welcome to attend teacher meetings, although meetings were not part of data collection nor my research questions. Similarly, Joy invited me to be her classroom assistant/researcher for the remainder of the school year. She expressed feeling this could be helpful both for her and the refugee-background women in the class, and initially introduced me to class as another English teacher 'here to help us'.

These invitations – and discursive positioning of me both inside and outside the research space – permitted me to gradually shift my role from sometime-volunteer to participant-observer, a change I welcomed. I felt it would enable REC participants and me to develop more complex relationships than we might otherwise have. It did, in ways I hoped for and also in ways I did not expect. As we began to blur researcher-researched and insider-outsider dichotomies, I was admittedly thinking not of the ethical dilemmas we might eventually face, such as those I describe below. Rather, I was thinking primarily of the (supposed) promises of close reciprocal relationships in ethnographic research, for instance, working against traditional research hierarchies; increased trust and equality; and the potential to gather more complex ethnographic data (Hayman *et al.*, 2012). (For a more extensive list of researchers' claims of the benefits of reciprocity, see Hayman *et al.*, 2012.) I knew the insider-outsider boundaries had become blurry for me and others at REC when one of the non-focal teachers sent me a text message to ask if I knew whether school would be cancelled due to inclement weather that day.

One of the dilemmas that Joy and I encountered centered on the ethical tensions that arose surrounding my participant-observation in the classroom and, more specifically, as my positionality shifted between these two roles. Of course, the kinds of reciprocity a researcher can ethically engage in both overlap and differ from the contributions a full participant may make in a classroom. While there are instances in which these roles converge, academic researchers – unlike other classroom participants – are rightly constrained by disciplinary codes of conduct and university institutional/ethics review boards (Kubanyiova, 2008). The shades of difference that may produce dilemmas might not become noticeable until a critical incident occurs as shifts in positionality occur in response to bids for reciprocity. The incident with Sahra's paper continues below, and is drawn from my field notes, classroom audio recordings, and researcher journal. As above, italics represent my internal voice.

Sahra's paper

Sahra and I walked out of the classroom and sat side-by-side on folding chairs in a hallway nook. I agreed to help partially because I was familiar with the demands of schools like REC: waiting until classes finished to offer learners one-on-one assistance was frequently incongruent with the workday reality of REC's teachers and administrators, whose contracts were all part-time. Teachers usually left the school building immediately after REC's classes in order to attend to other commitments. Joy in particular held two other part-time teaching jobs to make ends meet, one of which began on the heels of finishing at REC. Learner requests, then, were frequently handled quickly during class time, as in the case of Sahra's form.

I looked over the form. It was from her children's elementary school and appeared to request information I already knew, such as the family's address, phone numbers, and names and ages of children. I guided Sahra through those seemingly-simple, but painstakingly difficult for her, questions. When I flipped over the form, the questions became more complicated. First, the form asked whether Sahra's children had received flu shots earlier in the school year; if not, did community nurses have her permission to administer these when they visited the school? Sahra seemed to understand the school was asking permission to give her kids shots, but wasn't sure which ones or why.

As I stumbled through attempting to explain, I started to question whether I should continue helping Sahra. *What would my professors say? What about the online 'responsible conduct of research' course I took? What about my commitment to fittingness, my promise to the women in Joy's class to assist in the ways they found most helpful?* In retrospect, I see that, although my research training had taught me to 'do no harm' to research participants (Mackenzie *et al.*, 2007), it had not critically engaged with the questions surrounding benign neglect. I wanted to walk carefully, but could not immediately discern what course of action was most ethical. *What if helping Sahra is the most meaningful way I can enact reciprocity with her right now? What are the potential consequences for her if the form isn't completed or completed incorrectly? Overall, what is harmful: helping or not helping?* I couldn't tell and, in short, these questions surrounding reciprocity were tightly woven with both ethics of care and macro-ethics (Kubanyiova, 2008).

I sensed Sahra's exasperation. The school had already sent home forms asking for immunization information, she lamented. Why did she have to do this again? I sighed sympathetically, 'I don't know why they ask for the same information over and over.' *How many times have I heard this complaint? Don't schools and doctors' offices and government agencies and employers understand how stressful this can be?* Sahra pulled the piece of paper close and pointed at each box requesting her response to the flu shot question, 'Yes? No?' then shoved the paper back toward me, 'I don't know! What do, teacher?'

I stopped. Literacy brokering for Sahra had become a request for providing medical advice. *Now I can't do this. I'd better not do this.* My thoughts shifted to worst-case scenarios involving Sahra's children getting hurt, me losing permission to conduct research with human subjects, being thrown out of my PhD program, or worse. *Staff. Someone on staff needs to handle this.* I told Sahra I wasn't sure what she should do and that we should look for Julia. We walked downstairs to REC's tiny administrative office and Julia's assistant took over helping Sahra with the form.

As I climbed the stairs back toward the classroom, I mentally rehearsed talking with Joy about this incident. Helping learners fill out forms did not present ethical tensions, as long as I wasn't asked to provide guidance on sensitive issues that could make me liable in some way. *Okay, what are 'sensitive issues'? What might make me liable?* I didn't really know, but I knew I should say something to Joy.

As Joy was packing her bag and gathering her coat to leave, as she did most days immediately after class, I briefly mentioned that I wasn't sure if I should help students fill out forms that may contain sensitive issues. Joy had taken a research methods course during her graduate-level coursework, and wondered out loud about what the boundaries might be, 'How does helping with forms make a researcher liable? Does IRB say researchers can't do that?' I had a difficult time putting into words the reasons I had experienced discomfort earlier. Our conversation lasted less than two minutes because Joy needed to leave for her second job, so we agreed to talk about the incident again later. We wouldn't have the opportunity to do so again for several weeks.

After this event, Joy's and my differing roles in the classroom, as well as our distinct experiences with research ethics and training, created some challenges as we attempted to work out reciprocity in our context. Specifically, my enactment of meaningful reciprocity in Joy's classroom was partially dependent upon her telling me the ways I could be most useful, that is, expressing what she felt was most fitting (Becker, 2014). For her, this entailed discerning on a case-by-case basis which activities might pose an ethical quandary for me, and avoiding asking me to do those – a significant amount of responsibility for a teacher whose primary work centers on her students' learning and development. Understandably, she appeared to prefer an up-front delineation of what I could and couldn't do, while I wanted to work with general ethical principles, rather than a list of do's and don'ts.

It took a few weeks of reflection, but I ultimately proposed what I felt was middle ground: a blanket reprieve from providing assistance surrounding students' medical concerns. I could help with other student questions and requests and, if additional ethical tensions arose, I could address those in situ. Even though a blanket do/don't statement felt a bit excessive, it seemed to be a clear and manageable boundary, and I hoped it would reduce any stress Joy was experiencing. In reality, that boundary didn't entirely resolve the blurriness of reciprocity-in-action for us. Throughout the remainder of the school year, before asking me to assist students with any non-instructional request, Joy would first ask if I felt comfortable carrying out the task. For instance, I agreed to help several students to comprehend items they had received in the mail, and to fill out end-of-year forms that were internal to the school; I declined to help a student navigate complications surrounding her and her husband's taxes. Each time Joy asked if I was comfortable assisting with such tasks, I was given another opportunity to examine my ethical positions. Likely without intending to, she was weaving additional threads onto the loom, revealing to me that reciprocity, ethics, and positionality are tightly interwoven (Trainor & Bouchard, 2013) – and highly situational/context-specific.

This incident, as well as my and Joy's ongoing negotiations of reciprocity, demonstrated to me some of the ways that reciprocity-in-action can be slippery, unpredictable, and complicated. As a community-based ethnographic researcher, I cannot always know ahead of time what I might be asked to do at a particular moment. Requests for assistance may emerge unexpectedly and involve unforeseen tasks or topics, especially when stakeholders, participants, and I are attempting to work flexibility and nimbleness into our reciprocity or, as Dance *et al.* (2010) would say, when attempting to improvise (2010: 328). Further, as I discussed above and attempted to show in this vignette, reciprocity in ethnographic and community-based research is not necessarily a simple give and take between two parties as Curry (2012) writes. Rather, reciprocity entails giving within sometimes-competing constraints (T. Holbrook, personal communication, March 5, 2016) and, at times, negotiating amongst three or more stakeholders. In this incident for example, I brought the constraints of a university-based graduate student researcher; Joy, those of a part-time teacher in a small, underfunded and understaffed community-based adult English program; Sahra, those of a woman recently-arrived to a new country, attempting to navigate a medical literacy task in a new language for the benefit of her children. Our positions and roles were certainly not at counter purposes by definition, but the concerns and desires they entailed came into conflict as we went about enacting reciprocity together at a specific moment, for the purposes of a specific task.

Connections to Research With/in Immigrant and Refugee Communities

I find that reciprocity can be especially unpredictable, multi-layered, and challenging in research with/in organizations like REC, that is, small, community-based English programs for adults who have migrated to the US. Frequently, these programs operate with very small budgets (McKenna & Fitzpatrick, 2004) and thus small and underpaid staffs with few or no benefits (e.g. health insurance, retirement accounts), which can contribute to high staff turnover. For instance, Julia, the head administrator at REC, did not take a salary for a period of time in order to pay the part-time teachers and keep the school open. As Perry and Hart (2012) discuss, delivering educational services with few resources also frequently entails relying on large numbers of volunteers – with varied levels of training as educators – to carry out instruction, as well as on relationships with faith communities, libraries or community centers for classroom space, which is commonly shared with other organizations or religious groups, as was the case at REC. Logically, these challenges translate into having different kinds of capacity than what many educators and researchers may be accustomed to in other educational settings, such as K-12 or higher education in the US. For example, at REC, funding was not available to have paid social workers, counselors, nurses, interpreters/bilingual staff, or classroom aides on staff. That work fell to volunteers and part-time staff members who stepped in out of goodwill, and frequently without as much training or experience as their counterparts in K-12 or higher ed. (Exceptions were the cases when professionals or service-learning programs gave their time to carry out these tasks.) In my previous work in a small, community-based adult English program, staff and volunteers frequently commented that we never knew what might come our direction; the same seemed to be true at REC. For example, one day, Julia noticed one of the babies in the nursery had a croupy cough. She called his mother out of class and recommended the mother take her baby to the doctor. The next day, I found out Julia had driven the mother and baby to the ER, and then stayed with them for seven hours because the mother did not feel comfortable there alone and did not have a language broker to assist her that day.

In short, the needs in small adult English programs can be quite different from other educational contexts, and the kinds of work that some staff and volunteers feel called to engage in may involve close relationships and intense levels of giving. Perhaps this is one reason the women with whom I interacted at REC said their school felt like a family. But these intense levels of giving may also produce dilemmas for some university researchers, who, like me, intentionally seek to blur the lines between researcher-researched and insider-outsider. For instance, our blurring may give the impression that we can sink into no-holds-barred, family-type reciprocal relationships (such as those that volunteers and staff like Julia and Joy have with their adult students) without pausing to consider the potential ethical questions of doing so. At the same time, holding back from such close relationships may present other ethical dilemmas, since doing so may also entail holding back from responding to immediate and urgent social needs. Such tensions may lead some researchers to feel they are in a no-win situation, or to altogether shirk research methods that blur traditional research roles (e.g. researcher/researched).

I also wondered about the public ways that I managed the contradictions between what I wanted to do from an ethics of care perspective (i.e. when requested, jump into students' personal situations without pause) and what I felt I should do from a macro-ethical perspective (i.e. walk circumspectly). My concern was rooted in the consciousness that, when I engaged in professional work outside of the university, including at REC, I was known as 'Nicole from Georgia State University'. In other words, I didn't just represent myself or even my academic department. I represented my university. Thus, my ability to enact reciprocity that was sensitive and meaningful to the people at REC (participants *and* non-participants) could have myriad repercussions for other Georgia State University researchers and other academic departments or offices (e.g. community engagement office, student clubs' service projects), both at the present time and in the future. Julia had grown weary of 'tourist researchers' (Kiluva-Ndunda, 2005: 28) and even declined requests from some other university researchers to carry out their work at REC based on her previous negative experiences with individuals from those institutions. Thus, I knew my actions left a footprint; I had a role to play in keeping open the research doors at REC (and other organizations in REC's tightly-knit community) for others who may be identified as 'X person from Georgia State University'. I perceived that my responsibility to institutional colleagues (even those I may never know) included publicly navigating ethical dilemmas surrounding reciprocity in ways that, ideally, resonated with all stakeholders. This was a significant challenge that I know I have not accomplished, as my vignette shows, and likely may not.

Lingering Questions

I continue to have many questions related to reciprocity in my research, like threads that hang off the back of a weaving-in-progress. First, as I discussed above, Mackenzie *et al.* (2007) write that the 'principle of respect for persons' involves 'construct(ing) research relationships that are responsive to (participants') needs and values' (2007: 301). I wonder, then, when I (co)create blurry insider-outsider relationships in ethnographic research, only to re-draw some boundaries when requests for reciprocity pose potential ethical quandaries, what is the effect on participants' perceptions of my respect for them as persons? On the possibility of others from my institution to enter the same community spaces, whether for research or service, in both the short and long term?

Second, if we agree with Dance *et al.* (2010) that enacting reciprocity in research with/in historically marginalized communities demands improvisation, and this, in turn, requires significant previous experiences in those communities, what should the expectations be of (novice) researchers vis-à-vis their/our cultural intuition of the community research settings they/we have in mind? Is it unethical or simply irresponsible for (novice) researchers to enter historically marginalized communities, such as immigrant and refugee communities, to carry out research without significant previous experiences in those spaces or, at minimum, similar ones? If so, what is the role of mentoring in this? That is, how would we know when we are 'ready' and able to improvise reciprocity in culturally-responsive ways?

Finally, I continually revisit the critical and challenging questions I posed at the beginning of this chapter: What counts as 'cooperative exchange'? What criteria can we use to determine that 'everyone benefits' from research? Who is 'everyone'? And most importantly, who gets to answer these questions?

Notes

(1) A reviewer asks how reciprocity and compensation are similar and different. The multiple answers to this question hinge on the philosophical stances adopted by researchers in their work. I take the position that reciprocity is woven throughout research processes and cannot be reduced to compensation.

(2) Here, 'give back' appears in scare quotes to signal that I question its appropriateness in discussions of reciprocity. An anonymous reviewer reminds that 'give back' implies returning something that belonged to another, which is not an accurate description of researchers' intent.

References

Alcoff, L. (1991) The problem of speaking for others. *Cultural Critique* 20, 5–32. doi:10.2307/1354221.

Becker, L.C. (2014/1986) *Reciprocity*. New York: Routledge.

Curry, M.W. (2012) In pursuit of reciprocity: Researchers, teachers, and school reformers engaged in collaborative analysis of video records. *Theory into Practice* 51 (2), 91–98. doi:10.1080/00405841.2012.662858.

Dance, L.J., Gutierrez, R. and Hermès, M. (2010) More like jazz than classical: Reciprocal interactions among educational researchers and respondents. *Harvard Educational Review* 8 (3), 327–352.

Delgado-Bernal, D. (1998) Using a Chicana feminist epistemology in educational research. *Harvard Educational Review* 68 (4), 555–582.

Dillard, B. and Pettitt, N. (March 2017) (De)legitimating teacher voices in community-engaged scholarship. Paper presented as part of colloquium at annual conference of American Association for Applied Linguistics, Portland, Oregon.

Hayman, B., Wilkes, L., Jackson, D. and Halcomb, E. (2012) Exchange and equality during data collection: Relationships through story sharing with lesbian mothers. *Nurse Researcher* 19 (4), 6–10. doi:10.7748/nr2012.07.19.4.6.c9217.

Junqueira, E.S. (2009) Feminist ethnography in education and the challenges of conducting fieldwork: Critically examining reciprocity and relationships between academic and public interests. *Perspectives on Urban Education* (Spring), 73–81.

Kiluva-Ndunda, M.M. (2005) Reciprocity in research: A retrospective look at my work with Kilome women. *Counterpoints* 275, 221–233.

Kubanyiova, M. (2008) Rethinking research ethics in contemporary applied linguistics: The tension between macroethical and microethical perspectives in situated research. *Modern Language Journal* 92 (4), 503–518. doi:10.1111/j.1540-4781.2008.00784.x.

Mackenzie, C., McDowell, C. and Pittaway, E. (2007) Beyond 'do no harm': The challenge of constructing ethical relationships in refugee research. *Journal of Refugee Studies* 20 (2), 299–319. doi:10.1093/jrs/femOO8.

McKenna, R. and Fitzpatrick, L. (2004) *Building Sustainable Adult Literacy Provision: A Review of International Trends in Adult Literacy Policy and Programs*. Australia: The National Centre for Vocational Education Research.

Perry, K.H. (2009) Genres, contexts, and literacy practices: Literacy brokering among Sudanese refugee families. *Reading Research Quarterly* 44 (3), 256–276.

Perry, K.H. and Hart, S.J. (2012) 'I'm just kind of winging it': Preparing and supporting educators of adult refugee learners. *Journal of Adolescent & Adult Literacy* 56 (2), 110–122.

Thorne, S.L., Siekmann, S. and Charles, W. (2016) Ethical issues in indigenous language research and interventions. In P. De Costa (ed.) *Ethics in Applied Linguistics Research: Language Researcher Narratives* (pp. 142–160). New York: Routledge.

Trainor, A. and Bouchard, K.A. (2013) Exploring and developing reciprocity in research design. *International Journal of Qualitative Studies in Education* 26 (8), 986–1003. doi:10.1080/09518398.2012.724467.

Tuhiwai Smith, L. (2012) *Decolonizing Methodologies: Research and Indigenous Peoples* (2nd edn). New York: Zed Books.

Visweswaran, K. (1994) *Fictions of Feminist Ethnography*. Minneapolis, MN: University of Minnesota Press.

11 Anonymity, Vulnerability and Informed Consent: An Ethical-Methodological Tale

Kristen H. Perry

The experiences, and the thinking around them, that I present in this chapter do not represent an 'untold story', as such. Rather, they represent a sequel to an already-told story, as I consider one question posed by the editors of this volume: 'What ethical dimensions are involved with collecting information, stories, and views of those often marginalized or excluded from the pursuits of social science?'

Prologue

My work with refugee communities, and my scholarly interest in the ethical issues inherent in refugee research, have both been somewhat serendipitous. My work with refugees began as I sought to fill the empty-seeming months between the end of my Peace Corps service in southern Africa and the start of my doctoral program. When my mother mentioned that a local resettlement agency was looking for volunteer tutors for some orphaned refugee youth (the so-called 'Lost Boys of Sudan'), I jumped at the chance. I assumed that this community service would be something I did simply for personal fulfillment while I pursued the 'real' work of my doctoral studies and prepared to return to Lesotho for my dissertation research.

Life, like qualitative research, is messy and unpredictable: the more deeply involved I became with the Sudanese community in Michigan, the more deeply I became convinced that addressing the educational needs of the ongoing influx of refugees, many of whom had limited or interrupted formal schooling, *was* my real work. My doctoral program required students to complete a practicum research project prior to qualifying exams and the dissertation; as I prepared to do my practicum, I also was enrolled in a seminar that required us to conduct an ethnographic case study of literacy practices in a community. My study of the Sudanese youths' literacy practices (Perry, 2009a, 2009b, 2014) not only fulfilled both requirements, but it also cemented my commitment to the local Sudanese community. By the time my dissertation proposal rolled around, I had completely abandoned my plans to return to southern Africa, instead remaining in Michigan to study literacy brokering among Sudanese families with young children (Perry, 2009a, 2009b, 2014).

When I embarked on these projects, I did not expect that research ethics, particularly questions related to vulnerability and naming/anonymity, would also become a storyline in the narrative arc of my scholarly work. Yet, surprising ethical questions inserted themselves in my research from the very beginning. I had expected to explore questions related to literacy; I did not expect to confront the ethical issues that:

> ... arise from a range of intersecting issues including those of power, consent and community representation; confidentiality; trust and mistrust; harms, risks and benefits; autonomy and agency; cultural difference; gender; human rights and social justice; and in the worst cases, oppression and exploitation. (Mackenzie *et al.*, 2007: 300)

Questions related to these ethical issues wormed themselves so deeply into my brain that simply addressing them as part of the research process was not enough – I also needed to explore them from a scholarly perspective.

Chapter 1: Rethinking Anonymity

As a graduate student and novice researcher, I dutifully completed the research ethics training required by our university's Institutional Review Board (IRB). Like most orientations to research ethics, this training focused on what Guillemin and Gillam (2004), and later Kubanyiova (2008), refer to as 'macro ethics', or the specific procedures required to satisfy both government regulations and IRBs. This training reviewed the history of unethical research, such as medical experimentation by the Nazis or the Tuskegee syphilis study, as well as psychological studies such as those by Stanley Milgram and Zimbardo's prison experiment at Stanford (Bailey, 2014). The training also introduced the three guiding principles of ethical research involving humans, codified by the Belmont Report (DHHS, 2016): (a) respect for persons, which requires that 'individuals should be treated as autonomous agents, and second, that persons with diminished autonomy are entitled to protection' (n.p.), (b) beneficence, or the obligation to 'do no harm, and maximize possible benefits and minimize possible harms' (n.p.), and (c) justice, in which the advantages and burdens of research should be equitably distributed. Finally, the training covered the ways in which these principles corresponded with regulations and were applied in research practices, such as selecting research participants and obtaining informed consent.

Armed with both the ethics training certification and the IRB's stamp of approval for my research project (along with the certainty that I generally acted in an ethical manner), I naïvely assumed that I had covered all of the necessary ethical bases related to my work. When I began recruiting Sudanese youth to participate in the study, I was astonished when one young man refused to participate in my project, precisely *because* I was going to change his name. How could this possibly be? I was following the ethical rules, after all, which said that I was supposed to protect participants' identities! And, as a refugee, didn't this young man need *more* protection than other types of participants? As I described in my first publication on the issue (Perry, 2007b), the young man stood fast in the face of my clumsy explanations for the IRB's requirements, insistent that 'I have something important to say, and I want the world to know that I am the one who said it' (2007: 138). Unfortunately, his insistence on using his real name was out of line with the university's stipulations for my work, and we had to part ways.

Not only was this man's refusal to participate in my research because of the anonymity issue disappointing – as a leader among the Sudanese youth community, his perspective would have provided valuable insights – but it also fractured the seemingly-secure foundations of my ethical knowledge. I began to wonder:

> Why is anonymity the 'default' assumption in research? What is privacy, and who really is being protected by current guidelines for anonymity? What does it mean to 'protect' participants? When is anonymity truly necessary, and when does it actually silence participants' voices? When, and why, should participants' real names be used? Who should have control over issues of naming and anonymity in research – researchers, IRBs, or the participants themselves? Do participants fully understand the implications of this decision? For that matter, do researchers or IRBs? (Perry, 2007b: 138)

Neither the IRB-required ethics training I had received, nor my research methods coursework, had prepared me to think about these questions. This was the first 'ethically important moment' (Guillemin & Gillam, 2004) in my work, as I began to wrestle with what I would later learn was the distinction between *macroethics* and *microethics*, also referred to as *procedural ethics* and *ethics-in-practice* (Guillemin & Gillam, 2004). Guillemin and Gillam (2004) describe procedural ethics as the regulations that must be met and the procedures that must be approved by a research ethics board, while ethics-in-practice are the 'everyday ethical issues that arise in the doing of research' (2004: 263), which typically cannot be anticipated and also are not covered by standard ethics-board procedures.

As a result of this experience, I began to question my naïve acceptance of the IRB's macroethical principles and to acknowledge that, despite the required training, I had a pretty limited understanding of the real-world ethical issues that might emerge in the necessarily-messy process of researching human activity in general, and refugee communities in particular. At about the same time, I attended a workshop at the University of Lancaster on ethnographic literacy research. When Anita Wilson, one of the facilitators, happened to bring up the issue of naming and anonymity in qualitative research, the questions that had been quietly nagging at me suddenly became more insistent. Wilson shared other sources that had challenged the taken-for-granted practice of using pseudonyms in qualitative research (e.g. Grinyer, 2002), and I felt called to add my own voice to this movement (Perry, 2007b).

Exploring the methodological and ethical literature helped me to understand that research ethics, while presumed to be universal, are in fact a cultural product of Western, Enlightenment-era thinking (Christians, 2000). Enlightenment epistemologies not only emphasized the fact-based, value-free nature of knowledge, but they also reflected beliefs in privacy's 'nonnegotiable status' and a focus on the 'sacred innermost self' (Christians, 2000: 139). As these Enlightenment values became formally coded as ethical principles, emphases on privacy and individual rights were translated into unquestioned assumptions about anonymity for research subjects. Lahman and her colleagues (2013) observed that the practice of assigning pseudonyms is 'seen as integral (and by some required) to the social science research process' (2013: 1), and the ubiquity of pseudonyms results in little reflection by scholars. In fact, I would argue that masking participants' identities has become such a standardized expectation that researchers who do identify participants are seen, or at least questioned, as somehow deviant or abnormal.

My early reading helped me understand that not only are specific ethical guidelines related to respect for persons, beneficence, and justice a product of one culturally- and historically-situated context – the Enlightenment in Western/Northern countries – but the interpretation of those principles is also shaped by culture. For example, Honan and her colleagues (2012) noted that notions related to *privacy* vary greatly by cultural community. Many cultural communities emphasize collective, rather than individual, values; in a collectively-oriented culture, a sense of privacy is not absent, it is just perceived and enacted differently (Honan *et al.*, 2012). Despite different cultural orientations, 'ethics rules and expectations are generally informed by hegemonic sociocultural norms' (Honan *et al.*, 2012: 3). From one perspective, the principle of 'respect for persons' could be interpreted as an absolute requirement to protect individual privacy, but from another, it could be understood as allowing those individuals to self-determine the ways in which they are represented. As a result, I began to see automatic assumptions about anonymity in research as rather paternalistic, as supposedly more-knowledgeable researchers (and IRBs) made decisions on behalf of others. Indeed, Lahman and her colleagues similarly speculated that expectations for pseudonym use are 'more likely a preference by researchers who are from a white, Western, male orientation' (Lahman et al., 2013: 2).

My encounter with a black African potential research participant, thus invited me into an emerging understanding of the roles of perspective, privilege, and power in research ethics. I committed, then, to giving participants ownership over how they were represented, to honoring their voices, and to giving them clear credit for having 'something important to say'.

Chapter 2: Rethinking Vulnerability

Feeling that the scales had fallen from my eyes with respect to automatically assigning pseudonyms to research participants, I embarked upon my dissertation research with a steely resolve to honor my participants' choices in how they were represented – to take seriously what Mackenzie et al. (2007) argued is the researcher's responsibility 'to try to understand and engage with the different perspectives and life experiences of research participants and to construct research relationships that are responsive to their needs and values' (2007: 301).

In filling out the required IRB paperwork, I carefully delineated the scholarly argument for allowing participant choice in naming decisions, included as many citations for this rationale as I could possibly find, and thoroughly outlined the procedures I would follow in obtaining my participants' informed consent, such as having them indicate directly on the consent form whether they wished to use their real names or a pseudonym. I had heard many horror stories of the IRB's nit-pickiness when it came to reviewing research protocols and, under the assumption that I would be facing an uphill battle, I was fully prepared to be filled with righteous scholarly indignation and to fight to hold my ground on principle. However, I was once again thoroughly taken aback when the IRB rubber-stamped my protocol without question.

Feeling as though I was finally on solid ground with respect to my understanding of research ethics, particularly involving refugees, I merrily went about my research way. Despite my prior experiences, I was truly surprised that all adult participants in the project wished to use their real names:

> I was surprised largely because I knew the histories of these families – their lives had not been easy, and they had sought refuge in the United States as a result of great oppression and violence… I expected that most would choose to protect their identities, given what they had endured. (Perry, 2007b: 147)

I was particularly surprised when Viola, one of the mothers in the study, claimed that she didn't have any 'political problems or anything to hide our names'. *Really*? Viola, the daughter of a former government minister, feared that she would be assassinated if she ever returned to Sudan, and her own sister (still in Sudan) was engaged in underground work for Christian organizations. Yet, Viola's explanation is the perfect example for why researchers (let alone IRBs) cannot automatically categorize participants as vulnerable, nor presume to make decisions about anonymity on their behalf. Not only did Viola apparently not perceive herself as particularly vulnerable, she also saw participation in my research project as an important form of empowered advocacy: 'We need people to know what is going on in our country and how we are suffering here ... We need them to know our culture, our tradition, because of our kids' (Perry, 2007c: 50).

Throughout the project, I continued to encounter the ethically-important moments (Guillemin & Gillam, 2004) that are inherent in any research design that involves developing close relationships with participants. I did not see any of these micro-ethical decisions – Should I lend this mother money? Should I bail that father out of jail? Should I intervene with that child's school? – as being substantially different from the kinds of issues I might face with any participants. In other words, I did not perceive the microethical issues I was facing as being somehow inherent in work with refugees, immigrants, or other linguistic minorities.

About the same time, I happened to meet a man who had been recently hired in an upper administrative position with the university's IRB. A professor in my program eagerly introduced me to the official and suggested I tell him about the interesting research I was doing with refugees. The man immediately shut me down by saying, 'You can't do research with refugees; it's not ethical.' Wait – *what*? How could my research not be ethical? After all, didn't I already have the IRB's stamp of approval? Because refugees are in a vulnerable position in refugee camps, the official asserted, research with them is inherently unethical. I did not know it at the time, but my experience with an IRB official who had little understanding of the complexities of refugee contexts was not unique (Mackenzie *et al.*, 2007). The official's position echoed that of some (e.g. Jacobsen & Landau, 2003; Mackenzie *et al.*, 2007) who view refugee contexts as highly problematic and warranting careful ethical considerations of vulnerability:

> Although Jacobsen and Landau (2003) write from the perspective of large-scale quantitative studies undertaken in refugee camps, they rightly argue that 'the political and legal marginality of refugees and IDPs [internally displaced people] means that they have few rights and are vulnerable to arbitrary action on the part of state authorities, and sometimes even the international relief community' (187). (Perry, 2011: 900)

Yet, refugees resettled in a third country experience a very different context than those who are living in camps. When I explained that I was working with resettled refugees, and not in camps, he backed off and grudgingly acknowledged that my research *could* be ethical.

This encounter once again knocked me off of what I had assumed to be a solid ethical foundation. This administrator, an older man, had years of experience in thinking about research ethics and passing judgment on the ethicality of innumerable research projects. I, on the other hand, was a young, female graduate student embarking upon the research study that would determine whether I completed my doctoral degree. This difference in power and position caused me to question my study, and to worry that I might be engaging in unethical work. Indeed, writing about this encounter after a decade still has the power to make my pulse race and my palms sweat! Even at that time, though, I could not shake the feeling that he was wrong about all refugee research being inherently unethical. In fact, I discovered that our disagreement reflected a lively debate regarding the ethicality of research with refugees.

After I successfully completed my dissertation, earned my degree, and was comfortably employed in a tenure-track faculty line, I returned to the scholarly literature to better understand the ethical dimensions of *vulnerability* in research participants, particularly those who are refugees. Specifically, I wondered:

> Are refugees somehow inherently more vulnerable than other types of participants? What does *vulnerable* truly mean? Are negative perceptions about the inclusion of refugees in research widely held, or are they localized? If existing ethical guidelines are doing a disservice to refugee research populations, how can qualitative researchers address this problem? (Perry, 2011: 899–900)

To explore these questions, I analyzed the websites of 32 university IRBs to understand how the IRBs conceptualized and defined *vulnerable populations,* and the guidelines they offered with respect to research with participants whose English proficiency may be limited (Perry, 2011). I found that IRBs vary widely in how they conceptualize vulnerability, and that many lumped refugees and other linguistic minorities together with children, adults with intellectual disabilities and others with 'impaired' capacity to consent. IRBs offered little guidance on conducting research with participants whose first language was not English, and even less on conducting research with refugees.

This project was not only my first study that had ethics at the heart of its inquiry, but it was also the first that introduced me to the body (or bodies) of literature that explored ethical-methodological questions related to including refugees, immigrants, and linguistic minorities in research, especially qualitative designs. I found comfort among a community of scholars who not only wrestled with the same questions, but who also believed that research involving refugees was both important and at least had the potential to be conducted ethically, despite real ethical pitfalls. Not only did scholars assert that refugee research in the social sciences was an essential tool for solving the real-world problems that refugees faced (Hynes, 2003; Rodgers, 2004), but many also believed that participating in research could potentially empower those refugees:

> Refugees are quite often glad to tell their histories to researchers, particularly if they have politicised the experience and recognise it in a political context. In fact, it has been argued that the telling of their stories, or 'bearing witness' actually assists in the process [of empowerment]. (Hynes, 2003: 4)

Yet, sprinkled among these voices that clearly shared my perspective also were those who raised new issues that prickled at my comfortable conclusion that I was, after all, an ethical researcher.

Chapter 3: Rethinking Informed Consent

After having delved into the ethical-methodological literature regarding refugee research, I felt I had a much better grasp of ethical issues related to naming/representation and vulnerability. However, several years removed from the deep ethnographic involvement with the Sudanese communities I had studied, I was surprised to find myself *less* comfortable with some of the decisions I had made in those studies. Had my participants really understood the research process and what they were consenting to?

Even asking this question made me uncomfortable, and not simply because I was worried about what the answer might be. Because of the common conflation of English learners with impairment (Perry, 2011), would publicly wondering about the participants' understandings of the research process inadvertently imply that I, too, was questioning their intellectual capabilities? Although the adult participants in the family study represented various educational levels, my experiences with them had proved time and again that they were both smart and savvy about the world. It was obvious to me that these adults, despite their different levels of English ability, had the capacity to make competent, well-informed decisions when information was presented to them in comprehensible ways.

But, I began to wonder, does that necessarily mean that potential research participants (regardless of whether or not they are refugees) understand what *research* is, or what will actually happen to the information they share by opening up their lives to ethnographic research? And, even if they do understand the nature of research, do they understand all of the possible ramifications of their decisions? (And, equally importantly, can researchers themselves, even, truly understand these ramifications?)

While my dissertation research was under way, a number of interactions across the families led me to conclude that while they may not have understood the nuances of American academia, the parents did, in fact, have a solid understanding of my research purpose. All of the parents were active in different aspects of Sudanese community life in Michigan, and parents in two of the three families had even been elected to leadership positions in Sudanese community groups. Viola's quote, above, represented the parents' perspectives. The parents appeared to view their participation in my research as another agentive form of community activism – participating because 'we need people to know' and 'because of our kids'. They also appeared to understand that I would be publicly writing about them, as they kept referring to the 'book' I was writing. At the time, this felt sufficient to ensure that I was engaging in ethical research, and that participants had an understanding of the research process and what they were agreeing to when they stated that they wanted to use their real names.

Yet, the world does not stay the same. In the decade since the end of data collection for that study, the landscape of digital information and access has changed exponentially. For example, in 2006, the same year that my data collection ended, Facebook opened to public use and the verb 'google' was entered in both the *Oxford English Dictionary* and the *Merriam-Webster Collegiate Dictionary*. The subsequent introduction of smartphones and tablet computers has put access to all of this information at the quick swipe of a fingertip. Not only could just about anyone access the articles I had published, but they potentially could also easily connect to a whole host of other personal information about the participants.

As a result, the implications of using these participants' real names now feels radically different. I began to wonder, given all of the changes in media and access, would those participants still have made the same decisions regarding using their real identities in my work? Even if they still felt that using their real names was important, were there bits of information or particular events that they might rather I hadn't included? Given the greater connectivity of the world, might using participants' real names have an impact on any of their family and friends who weren't directly participating in the study? These questions are similar to those raised by Lahman and her colleagues (2013), who suggested that researchers need to consider the potential implications of identifying participants from relational (e.g. 'when real names are used, the persons directly connected to the participants are also known'), developmental (e.g. 'as time passes, will the participants still wish they had used their name?') and economic (e.g. 'could there be unanticipated impact on current or future work?') perspectives (2013: 9).

These questions clearly connect to the nature of informed consent. At the time of the research project, I understood informed consent as an ethical *procedure* – that is, a box to be checked off at the beginning of the study. In line with ethics training, my understanding of informed consent was macroethical, in that I assumed that informed consent simply meant (a) ensuring that individuals were not coerced into their research participation, and (b) documenting that the required research-related information had been presented. However, as Guillemin and Gillam (2004) argued, 'signed consent forms do not constitute informed consent, they merely provide evidence (perhaps of questionable value) that consent has been given' (2004: 272). Similarly, as Hugman and his colleagues (2011) pointed out, providing consent 'depends on the capacity of people to exercise their rights. It assumes knowledge, confidence, and other personal and social resources to understand and be able to claim redress should the need arise' (2011: 659). Did the participants in my research have these resources? I knew (perhaps, believed?) that they trusted me, but this is not the same thing as having the resources, or being empowered to, exercise rights. Moreover, neither the participants nor I had the capacity to know what could be on the horizon, in terms of possible ways privacy could be breached.

Based upon my own experiences, coupled with my ethical-methodological reading (e.g. Guillemin & Gillam, 2004; Lahman *et al.*, 2013; Mackenzie *et al.*, 2007), I now understand consent as an ongoing, iterative process. Lahman and her colleagues (2013) referred to this concept as *process consent*, which 'means the researcher is committed to ongoing consent, not simply a one-time signature at the outset of a research relationship' (2013: 9). 'From an ethical point of view', Mackenzie *et al.* (2007) argued, 'such a process gives real content to the principle of *respect for persons*' (2007: 307). Process consent, as I see it, appears to be an important method for addressing the very real vulnerabilities of research participants. Lahman and her colleagues (2011) took the notion of process consent and extended it to *process responsiveness*, which they defined as 'an all-encompassing stance whereby one is committed to a reflexive methodology that calls for the researcher to check in with the participants and fellow researchers regarding everyone's comfort with all aspects of the study' (2011: 9). Iterative models of consent and process responsiveness sound logical, and perhaps even easy to implement, yet they likely represent a substantial shift in business-as-usual for many (if not most) researchers. These approaches 'involve a series of fundamental conceptual shifts in research ethics: from subjects *of* research to participants *in* research; from harm minimization to reciprocal benefit; from informed consent to the promotion of autonomy; from researcher-directed to participant and community-negotiated' (Mackenzie *et al.*, 2007: 311).

When I reflect upon my work from the perspective of process consent, I must admit to myself that my research with these three families was not as ethical as it could have been. Sure, I built mutually respectful and trusting relationships with the families, and I spent a great deal of time acting as an academic tutor and cultural mentor to the families, so that they would also be receiving clear benefits from the enormous amount of time (and data) that they were gifting to me. Sure, I worked hard to honor the participants' choices and voices, even threatening to pull a manuscript from a Tier-1 research journal when the editor kept insisting that I needed to mask the participants' identities. Sure, I was careful about the ways I portrayed the participants in presentations and publications, using language that (I hope) showed the rich and warm textures of their lives, and excluding specific incidents that might be misinterpreted or unintentionally cast them in a poor light. But all of these good intentions and ethical behaviors were not enough: I did not continually seek their consent, at least not explicitly. Although I engaged in some member-checking with participants, these consultations were about the content of the data and my analytic interpretations, not about whether they still wanted to use their real names or whether there were any bits of data that I should exclude.

Chapter 4: Still Rethinking...

Although I have conducted other research studies since these early projects, none has matched the same level of deep, lengthy involvement with participants as the two studies with Sudanese orphaned youth and families. Not coincidentally, none of my subsequent studies has raised challenging ethical-methodological issues, either. Yet, the ethical issues that arose in my early work have continued to percolate in my brain and, more importantly, have pushed me as a researcher and as a scholar. As a tenured associate professor, I believe I'm now officially classified as a 'mid-career' scholar. When I think back to myself as a novice researcher, I see someone who had great confidence in her ethical knowledge and who believed that most ethical-methodological dilemmas had fairly obvious solutions. The older, (hopefully) wiser, me would like to kindly pat that younger version of myself on the head and say, 'Oh, you sweet, naïve young thing – how much you still have to learn!'

Where I once saw ethical decisions as clear-cut, I now see a complex, nuanced ethical-methodological landscape. Where I once believed most issues to be either clearly ethical or obviously unethical, I now understand that there are always ethical and unethical aspects to any decision in research. Is it even possible, I now wonder, that no decision or action is ever wholly ethical? Where I once thought that my required ethics training and the stamp of approval from the ethics board were enough for my research, I now understand the importance of Guillemin and Gillam's (2004) notion of *ethical competence*, or 'the researcher's willingness to acknowledge the ethical dimension of research practice, his or her ability to actually recognize this ethical dimension when it comes into play, and his or her ability to think through ethical issues and respond appropriately' (Guillemin & Gillam, 2004: 269). My experiences have led me to believe that it is critically important to go beyond the IRB-based ethics training for novice researchers. As a result, I now extend beyond the required procedural ethics when teaching courses in qualitative research methods and, when asked to write methodologically-oriented questions for doctoral students' qualifying exams, I expect those students to push their ethical thinking with respect to their work. My intent is for students to have the opportunity for 'substantive discussions about the nature of ethical research and how those ethical principles can be translated or interpreted in cross-cultural contexts' (Honan *et al.*, 2012: 12). My hope is that the students I teach will be less naïve and at least somewhat better prepared to face the inevitable micro-ethical dilemmas in their own work.

I think I now am better able to accept that, no matter how many scholarly articles I read or how many research experiences I have, my understanding of research ethics will always only be partial. Or, to put it perhaps another way, I may have developed a strong(er) ethical foundation, but that foundation is only a basis from which to approach the real, messy and unpredictable ethical issues that will inevitably arise in my work with real, messy and unpredictable human beings. And, of course, now that I once again feel reasonably confident in my ethical foundations, I will probably be faced with a new ethical dilemma that will force me, once again, to question my knowledge, perspective, and practice.

Epilogue

People who have read my studies of Sudanese refugees often approach me to ask how those participants are doing now. One of my biggest research regrets, both ethically and personally, has been losing touch with the Sudanese participants with whom I had been so deeply involved. Although I had intended to stay in contact, I lost touch with all of the participants after I left Michigan in 2007. The invitation to write this book chapter added fuel to the flames of my regrets. I belatedly realized that, not only did the social media revolution mean that *others* could potentially locate the identified families, it also meant that I could do so, too. Thanks to Facebook, I established contact with one of the mothers from the family study. Early in our initial, extended instant messaging conversation, she asked, 'Did you made your book yet?' I explained that I hadn't quite managed a book (other than the bound text of my unpublished dissertation), but I had published several articles and book chapters from the project. The conversation moved on, as we caught each other up on our lives. Although I felt somewhat reassured that this mother, at least, had some understanding of what I had done with her data, I am once again left to ponder ethical-methodological questions: A decade down the line, how does this mother view her family's participation in my research? Would she still make the same decisions if the study were conducted today? Would the explosion of social media affect her decision-making? Have I portrayed her, and her family, accurately and fairly? Does she feel that I was ethical? I don't yet know the answers to these questions, but I hope to have this conversation with her in time.

References

Bailey, L.R. (2014) History and Ethical Principles (Collaborative Institutional Training Initiative Program). https://www.citiprogram.org/members/index.cfm?pageID=805& intModuleID=490 (accessed 17 September 2018).

Christians, C.G. (2000) Ethics and politics in qualitative research. In N.K. Denzin and Y.S. Lincoln (eds) *Handbook of Qualitative Research* (2nd edn). Thousand Oaks, CA: Sage Publications.

Grinyer, A. (2002) The anonymity of research participants: Assumptions, ethics, and practicalities. *University of Surrey Social Research Update*, 36. See http://sru.soc.surrey.ac.uk/SRU36.html (accessed 17 September 2018).

Guillemin, M. and Gillam, L. (2004) Ethics, reflexivity, and 'ethically important moments' in research. *Qualitative Inquiry* 10, 261–280.

Honan, E., Hamid, M.O., Alhamdan, B., Phommalangsy, P. and Lingard, B. (2012) Ethical issues in cross-cultural research. *International Journal of Research & Method in Education* 35, 1–14.

Hugman, R., Bartolomei, L. and Pittaway, E. (2011) Human agency and the meaning of informed consent: Reflections on research with refugees. *Journal of Refugee Studies* 24 (4), 655–671.

Hynes, T. (2003) *The Issue of 'Trust' or 'Mistrust' in Research with Refugees: Choices, Caveats, and Considerations for Researchers*. UNHCR.

Jacobsen, K. and Landau, L.B. (2003) The dual imperative in refugee research: Some methodological and ethical considerations in social science research on forced migration. *Disasters* 27 (3), 185–206.

Kubanyiova, M. (2008) Rethinking research ethics in contemporary applied linguistics: The tension between macroethical and microethical perspectives in situated research. *The Modern Language Journal* 92 (4), 503–518.

Lahman, M.E., Rodriguez, K., Moses, L., Fiedler, K., Brady, B.M. and Yacoub, W. (2013, April) A rose by any other name is still a rose?: Problematizing pseudonyms in research. Paper presented at the annual meeting of the American Educational Research Association, San Francisco, CA.

Mackenzie, C., McDowell, C. and Pittaway, E. (2007) Beyond 'Do no harm': The challenge of constructing ethical relationships in refugee research. *Journal of Refugee Studies* 20 (2), 299–319.

Perry, K.H. (2007a) Sharing stories, linking lives: Literacy practices among Sudanese refugees. In V. Purcell-Gates (ed.) *Cultural Practices of Literacy: Case Studies of Language, Literacy, Social Practice, and Power* (pp. 57–84). Mahwah, NJ: Lawrence Erlbaum.

Perry, K.H. (2007b) 'I want the world to know': The ethics of anonymity in ethnographic literacy research. In G. Walford (ed.) *Developments in Educational Ethnography* (pp. 137–154). London: Elsevier.

Perry, K.H. (2007c) 'Look, You Have to Sign': Literacy Practices among Sudanese Refugee Families. Unpublished doctoral dissertation,Michigan State University, Lansing, Michigan, USA.

Perry, K.H. (2008) From storytelling to writing: Transforming literacy practices among Sudanese refugees. *Journal of Literacy Research* 40 (4), 317–358.

Perry, K.H. (2009a) Genres, contexts, and literacy practices: Literacy brokering among Sudanese refugee families. *Reading Research Quarterly* 44 (3), 256–276.

Perry, K.H. (2009b) 'Lost Boys', cousins & aunties: Using Sudanese refugee relationships to complicate definitions of 'family'. In M. Dantas and P. Manyak (eds) *Home-School Connections in a Multicultural Society: Learning from and with Culturally and Linguistically Diverse Families* (pp. 19–40). Mahwah, NJ: Lawrence Erlbaum.

Perry, K.H. (2011) Ethics, vulnerability and speakers of other lnguages: How university IRBs (do not) speak to research involving refugee participants. *Qualitative Inquiry* 17 (10), 1–14.

Perry, K.H. (2014). 'Mama, sign this note': Young refugee children's brokering of literacy practices. *Language Arts,* 91 (5), 313–325.

Rodgers, G. (2004) 'Hanging out' with forced migrants: Methodological and ethical challenges. *Forced Migration Review* 21, 48–49.

12 The Emotional Dimensions of Qualitative Community-Driven Research: How Interactions and Relationships Shape Processes of Knowledge Production

Katherine E. Morelli and Doris S. Warriner

Although qualitative researchers now routinely reflect on the ethical dimensions of their processes of discovery, very little has been written about how personal or emotional dimensions of a researcher's experience influence their decisions about *whether* to pursue a research agenda in the first place, *how* to engage with community partners, and *what* kinds of research practices might be used in response. As Denzin (1984) and others have argued, 'emotionality lies at the intersection of the person and society, for all persons are joined to their societies through the self-feeling and emotions they feel and experience on daily basis,' and for this reason, 'the study of emotionality must occupy a central place in all the human disciplines' (1984: x; see also Lupton, 1998). If emotionality does lie at this intersection between person and world, then it would make sense that emotions are and should be a central aspect of social research, and that it is important for qualitative researchers to see their emotional and cognitive functions as inseparable from each other (Dickson-Swift *et al.*, 2009).

In this chapter, Morelli (a doctoral student at the time) and Warriner (her faculty advisor) examine how and under what circumstances emotions contributed to our understandings, practices, relationships and ways of knowing while exploring a series of cross-institutional exploratory partnerships and taking into consideration the collaborative projects each partnership might allow or facilitate. We examine when and how 'emotionally-sensed knowledge' (Hubbard *et al.*, 2001) shaped our relationships, understandings, goals and priorities; how relationships, goals and priorities shifted over time; and some of the ways that our decisions were inevitably shaped by our attachments to and interactions with contacts located in different community-based and institutional settings.

In order to better understand the role of emotions in the research process, we reflect on a handful of illuminating experiences that are often excluded from more sanitized accounts of the research process, and how an enhanced understanding of the role of emotion continues to influence our practices, relationships and emerging agendas. We consider how we might develop emotionally-sensed knowledge as a way of *being* and *knowing*, as researchers, how we might recognize or identify when emotion has *epistemological significance,* and how it may function as a heuristic for responsible practice.

In her introduction to *Improvising Theory: Process and Temporality in Ethnographic Fieldwork,* Cerwonka (2007) observes that what we know is not only dynamic and emergent but also the product of uneven processes of knowledge production:

> ... the tempo of ethnographic research (like most knowledge production) is not the steady, linear accumulation of more and more insight. Rather, it is characterized by rushes of and lulls in activity and understanding, and it requires constant revisions of insights gained earlier. (2007: 5)

In this chapter, we reflect on how certain 'rushes of and lulls in activity and understanding' permeated some of our early interactions and influenced our decisions on what steps to take next, including who to talk with and how to present ourselves. We describe how our particular process of discovery yielded both 'anxiety and euphoria' and how 'the uneven tempo of analytical understanding and systematic research' (Cerwonka, 2007: 5) characterized our collaborative, community-based research endeavor.

Theorizing Emotion Work and Emotionally-Sensed Knowledge

The concept of 'emotion work' was initially developed by Arlie Hochschild in her classic study, *The Managed Heart* (1983), where she made a distinction between two different components of emotion relative to research: emotional labor (i.e. used to refer to emotional management during work done for a wage) and emotion work (i.e. referred to work involved with dealing with other people's emotions). Hochschild (1983) argued that we 'infer other people's viewpoints from how they display feeling' and that emotion has a 'signal function' just as hearing and seeing, which acts as clues 'in figuring out what is real' (1983: 22). Others (e.g. Game,

1997; Hubbard *et al.*, 2001; Miller, 2004) have also argued that emotions are the means by which we make sense of, and relate to our physical, natural and social world. Put another way, emotion has *epistemological significance* (Game, 1997) because we can only 'know' through our emotions and not simply our cognition or intellect.

Hubbard *et al.* (2001) referencing Game (1997) observe that knowledge is not something 'objective and removed from our own bodies, experiences and emotions, but is created through our experiences of the world as a sensuous and affective activity' (2001: 126). This is to say our emotions are embodied in our experiences and the many decisions, paths, relationships and questions we pursue (or don't). By understanding the ways in which emotion contributes towards knowledge, researchers (particularly qualitative researchers) are able to listen and interpret and make sense of what we are hearing and seeing, and also how we might be using cognitive and emotional functioning simultaneously to potentially produce what Hubbard *et al.* (2001) call 'emotionally-sensed knowledge'. Affectivity is only *one way* in which we 'get in touch with the world' and make sense of our relation to others and things – thereby making connections essential to cultivating trusting relationships. Once we 'take up' and 'live' in a situation, rather than trying to distance ourselves or disconnect, we begin to close the gap between the world and our own consciousness. This view places emphasis on experience as the *relation between* things (Game, 1997: 393) rather than the unstable boundaries that create distance.

Other qualitative researchers argue that knowledge production involves choices that are 'entwined' with their own daily existence where a range of emotions are involved in the 'practice of understanding' (Cerwonka, 2007), where emotions enable the researcher to gain intuitive insight, and where 'inchoate knowledge arises' (Hubbard *et al.*, 2001: 127). According to Cerwonka (2007), it is important to examine the interpretative dimensions of this process – or the 'hermeneutic process as it relates to affective experiences such as doubt, hope, fear, confidence, exhaustion, energy, and projection, further complicating the common idea of a neat boundary between objective and subjective, abstract and concrete knowledge' (2007: 5). When researchers take time to examine the affective aspects of knowledge-building, they are better able to 'assess research practices in relation to shifting circumstances' (Cerwonka, 2007: 5) and also better equipped to arrive at a more nuanced understanding of the complex relational dynamics in research. This includes the 'many tensions and conflict' that arise between researchers, stakeholders, gatekeepers, service providers and how these can be understood as 'clashes between taken for granted values', or values that shape group identities (Gifford, 2013: 47). Although these 'muddy' (Lippke & Tanggaard, 2014) situations can cause uncomfortable feelings, they do not have to be dismissed or discounted; instead, they can become opportunities for researchers to evaluate their feelings (e.g. of doubt, fear, hope, confidence) in relation to their goals and to reconsider potential next steps. Without paying attention to the affective domain, the researcher may miss out on valuable ways of interpreting and learning from emotionally-generative situations (Dickson-Swift *et al.*, 2009), or restrict their capacity to act (or react) and perform ethically – particularly when the 'ethical choice' is not entirely obvious.

By routinely looking at our emotional responses to interactions, relationships, and information, we can better understand the *affective accumulation* of each emotionally infused interaction, insight or experience. In this way, emotion itself serves as an analytical tool that helps explain, for instance, how and in what ways we are able to gain 'interpersonal access' (Miller, 2004) or how emotion impacts interviews. Miller describes access as 'the extent to which researchers are able to actively engage community members as participants in their research' (Miller, 2004: 221). The degree and type of interpersonal access can qualitatively impact the kind of data collected and knowledge produced. Paying attention to emotional clues may help the researcher make an important distinction about the kind of access they are experiencing. This highlights the importance of acknowledging a wide range of emotions and recognizing 'the possibilities of an experiential knowledge in which affect has a central place' (Game, 1997: 398). It is often through the visceral display of emotion(s) that we are able to infer particular perspectives that might otherwise have gone unspoken or unnoticed.

In short, tuning into the affective experience provides another way of knowing about and acting in the social world that opens the self to others, and to the clues, cues and other emotionally-sensed or felt signals that enable us to infer others' viewpoints. These clues, cues and inferences may then be subject to deliberation, analysis and action (and reaction) that emerge transformed as embodied knowledge and inquiry. In order to do this kind of work effectively and with purpose, researchers need to become more practiced in recognizing and interpreting emotions, particularly those with epistemological significance in the research process. At this time, however, there is very little guidance for researchers to make emotion a more central aspect of our understanding of our social world (Hubbard *et al.*, 2001).

Getting Started: Early Interactions and Interpersonal Access

In the fall of 2014, Warriner was approached by the state's Office of Refugee Resettlement (ORR) and invited to explore questions and concerns about refugee families' access to healthcare services in order to devise ways to improve that access. With support from a university seed grant, Morelli (a first-year graduate student at the time) was hired to assist with the early stages of the project. For about 18 months, the team pursued three goals: reviewing the available literature on the topic of refugees and health care, conducting interviews with members of the local community who were involved in providing services to refugees living in the area, and making connections with other university-based researchers with shared interests and concerns. All of our efforts were guided by a desire to find out what was being said and done (by researchers, by health care providers, by representatives of the community) to facilitate refugee families' access to health care and health literacy.

While meeting with community-based experts (e.g. physicians, cultural health navigators, representatives of refugee resettlement organizations, caseworkers, leaders of ethnic community-based organizations, ESL teachers working with adult refugee learners of English, interpreters, the State Refugee Health Coordinator and staff from the ORR), we stated our reason for initiating the conversation, asked basic questions about refugees and healthcare, listened and took notes. To be transparent, we made explicit our outsider status. The responses to this approach were generally positive, warm, and welcoming. As we kept track of emerging themes and patterns (from our conversations and from the literature review), we also kept track of what we did and said that seemed to facilitate information-sharing, trust-building, and a willingness to collaborate. After our interactions with these local experts, we often reflected on what approaches and strategies elicited useful information about refugee families' access to health care and health literacy, and we kept track of the questions we asked, responses, our reactions to the information we gathered, the decisions we made, and what seemed to influence those decisions. Over time, we began to notice that our decisions were often partly influenced by our emotions, and we wondered whether those emotions might be shaping and informing what we knew and how we knew it – i.e. the kind of knowledge-work that we were pursuing. For instance, we reflected on how 'well' certain meetings went – e.g. whether a relationship was being established, what we thought/felt about the potential for that relationship to grow, and why we thought or felt that way. We evaluated the agendas and goals we had communicated, how different contacts had responded, and whether the idea of a future collaboration seemed to be valued. We noticed that we often made decisions about who to talk with again (or next) in part in response to such feelings.

Our process of discovery and the knowledge we gained helped us understand that questions about access to health care were complex, daunting and important. Because we were not already involved in providing healthcare to refugees, our understanding of the challenges and constraints was limited. To figure out what was going on, we asked many questions that were open-ended, and it seemed our outsider status opened doors to certain people and information. We felt encouraged and hopeful every time someone shared with us new information, agreed to meet again at a later date, or made recommendations to us (e.g. who else to contact and talk to). We began to equate warmth with support and evasion with skepticism, and we decided to keep track of which stakeholders seemed interested in our questions, even as we worked to build relationships with them. In these ways, our values, priorities and feelings seemed to influence not only who we spoke with but, also, what they shared with us and the kinds of relationships we were establishing through these interactions. While some people that we interviewed seemed to have similar assumptions and expectations (e.g. in situations that were more 'comfortable' for us), others seemed to question our goals, agendas, priorities (during interactions that felt more 'tense' to us). In such ways, our knowledge was both 'emotionally-sensed' and arising out of what we later came to understand as ethically uncomfortable situations that prompted us to pause and evaluate the affective dimensions of our experiences and the ethical implications of our decisions about process and procedure. While reflecting on what had transpired, we paid attention to 'clashes' that emerged (e.g. between our questions, assumptions or concerns and theirs) and wondered whether the points of tension we were noticing reflected a difference in our 'taken for granted values' (Gifford, 2013) and theirs.

Even though a lot of what we did was very careful – based on extreme sensitivity to the quandaries and paradoxes that were emerging within particular situations – we do not believe that our heightened awareness in and of itself could fully account for or mitigate the tensions we experienced – some of which we never did overcome. As university-based researchers with academic training in the humanities and social sciences (rather than in health sciences or public health), we came to learn that our ways of seeing, asking questions and generating knowledge were distinct and unfamiliar to many of those we spoke with. We noticed that the ways we responded were influenced by our institutional identities, professional pursuits and lived experiences.

Understanding the Role of Emotionally-Sensed Knowledge in our Practices and Priorities

After about six months of listening, learning and taking stock of what we had discovered so far, we initiated contact with some of those who had been most receptive to and supportive of our interests and commitments to see if they might be willing to facilitate introductions to refugee families in the community. Because we had been wanting to learn from refugee parents about their children's access to healthcare, we placed great importance on talking with them directly and were actively looking for ways to make this happen. Although we initially used some of our community-based contacts to expedite this process, we later realized that relying on others to facilitate introductions and access to an already-vulnerable and underserved community would be quite complicated and fraught. We share some of the details of this experience here to illustrate the challenges of the situation we found ourselves in, our emotional responses to it, and decisions we then made about how to proceed.

Recall that, as part of our process of discovery, we routinely talked with health care providers serving refugee families in the metropolitan area. Early in our process, we had been invited to attend a meeting attended by health care providers and local stakeholders. During this meeting, we were positioned by the convener as potential partners, and this helped us to establish rapport with those at the meeting. We eventually met a number of people who were invested in providing support to refugee families, facilitating their access to local services, and improving their experiences as new immigrants – including the manager of an apartment complex that housed many refugee residents. By the end of the meeting, the manager had invited us to meet her at the complex so we might learn more about the work she was doing to serve the refugee families living there.

During the meeting at the complex the manager took time to describe the many connections and collaborations that had been established with different local and community based organizations and how such partnerships enabled her to provide a variety of important services to the residents (e.g. ESL instruction, classes on domestic violence and reproductive health, and assistance enrolling in health insurance plans through the state's Medicaid agency). We also learned that she had immigrated to the US in the 1970s and, prior to taking on the managerial position at the complex in 2008, had worked for two local refugee resettlement organizations. After meeting with her twice, and in response to her warmth and enthusiasm, we felt optimistic and excited about having made a connection with an advocate who was providing resources to refugee families. Her enthusiastic responses to our goals and priorities filled us with excitement and optimism. We decided to ask whether we might meet some of their residents in order to learn more about their experiences with health and the health care system. In these ways, our meetings with the manager provided opportunities to establish some affinity, trust, and a willingness to take risks with each other. Grateful for the manager's encouragement and assistance, we proceeded to schedule a handful of listening sessions and hire interpreters to facilitate communication. We believed that the listening sessions would both complement and extend what we had already learned through earlier conversations with providers and other stakeholders about refugee families' experiences accessing healthcare, what accommodations had been helpful to them and their children, and what challenges they had encountered finding out about accessing health-related services. As we worked closely with the welcoming and responsive manager to plan these sessions and to identify interpreters for the languages that would be spoken, we felt both anxious and excited.

While drafting questions to ask refugee families, our goal was to be accessible and transparent. We solicited feedback from a handful of providers and community-based stakeholders we had already spoken with to find out how our questions would translate and whether such questions would elicit informative responses. We also wondered whether our concerns would be shared by the residents and what kinds of conceptions of 'health'and 'healthcare' might emerge during the conversation. After obtaining feedback from established and trusted contacts in the community on the questions we planned to ask, we proceeded with scheduling three listening sessions with residents (who were grouped by language) and hiring an interpreter for each.

On the day of the scheduled sessions, we came prepared with our questions and notebooks. As the residents slowly entered the 'classroom' where we waited, we noticed that the apartment manager referred to many of them by their apartment numbers rather than their names. We both independently felt uncomfortable about this but also realized that we couldn't do much about it given the situation. We bracketed our discomfort and proceeded with our plans. We welcomed residents, introduced ourselves and explained why we were there. Our desire to be transparent influenced our decision to say we were there to listen and to learn but not to present solutions. At the same time, we didn't really like saying that out loud. While our goal was to ask relevant and important questions, it wasn't entirely clear (to us or to them) why we were asking those questions. Afterwards (that day and on another day), in response to our feelings of anxiety and unexpected frustration, we began to ask ourselves more reflective questions about the long silences and looks of confusion that had emerged during each of the meetings. We wondered out loud whether our questions were too personal and if we had a right to ask such questions of people we had just met. On the other hand, we also felt encouraged by the eager and enthusiastic responses of some residents who seemed to welcome our presence and the discussion of the challenges they faced trying to access healthcare.

After reflecting on and discussing what we had learned and felt – and our discomforts with how we had come to learn what we now knew – we decided to revise our plans for next steps and not move forward with additional sessions. We came to realize that we both felt uncomfortable with asking refugee families questions about health and health care under these circumstances. We considered the contradictions and tensions that seemed to exist between our goals and those of the apartment manager, as well as the challenges presented by our role as 'outsiders', and we worried about how our values and assumptions about people and their circumstances seemed to clash with those of the manager. We talked with each other about the problems that emerge when putting our agenda and trust in others' hands; about the fact that the residents did not seem to know why we were there, or why they were there either; and how surprising and disappointing this was. When we discovered that the residents who participated in our sessions had been instructed to go to 'class' with no other information provided, we felt even more misrepresented and misunderstood, and we decided to try to attend to our emotional reactions to what went well and what didn't go so well. This attention prompted us to reconsider the ethical dimensions of the situation and the practices we were engaging in and how we might move forward differently.

The Emotional and Logistical Complexities of Cross-Institutional Collaborations

Having confirmed (through reviewing literature; interviewing providers, agency staff and other local stakeholders, and also through talking with refugee residents of the apartment complex) that language, literacy and culture were major contributors to the challenges that refugee families routinely faced when accessing health care or information about health care, we increasingly focused our efforts on exploring these issues. Although we had also learned about other contributing factors (e.g. transportation, childcare), we decided to focus on how language, literacy, communication and miscommunication might influence providers' and refugee families' experiences with health and healthcare – in and outside of the clinical setting. With this emerging focus in mind and building on the knowledge, understandings and relationships that gave us hope and confidence, we returned to a handful of contacts to share insights, solicit feedback and gather additional information. This circular process of gathering information from a variety of sources then returning to those sources to share in our understandings demonstrated our willingness to continue listening, learning and reciprocating (e.g. by sharing new information or understandings). This regular and sustained contact with a smaller group of providers yielded more trusting and reciprocal relationships, some of which have led to partnerships and agendas we are continuing to pursue today.

One such partnership went through a series of changes and renegotiations. This partnership began with a meeting suggested by a trusted contact at a healthcare facility serving a large number of refugee patients, and included a physician and cultural health navigator working in the pediatric clinic within the facility. We had learned that the clinic was continuing to see an increase in refugee families seeking care, and we felt through this suggestion to meet that we might be of value to this clinic. It was during this first meeting that we asked what we hoped were well-informed and relevant questions about the work they were doing and how they were doing it. Over the course of three meetings, we came to feel great alignment with their priorities, and we were embraced warmly and enthusiastically. The idea of partnering emerged, and we began to articulate a potential research agenda whereby we might play a role in documenting and analyzing some of the work that this pediatrician and cultural health navigator were doing (with their colleagues) to address the kinds of challenges facing refugee families and providers at the clinic. Over time, as we shared perspectives, resources and understandings, our emotional attachments, trust and knowledge expanded; our interactions became more regular; and our optimism grew. Eventually, we drafted a proposal to conduct research together with our community partners working in this clinic. Unfortunately, the physician we had been collaborating with ended up leaving this facility to work in a different setting focused on a different population. Even more disappointing, her transfer occurred just as we were getting ready to submit a proposal. While this temporarily took the wind out of our sails and demanded a reset (emotionally and logistically), we eventually re-evaluated, re-grouped, and moved forward by working closely with a different physician in the clinic to identify and pursue shared interests and questions. Through meetings (in person and by phone) and regular correspondence, we again worked deliberately to establish relationships, trust and a sense of shared priorities; and these discussions facilitated interactions that ultimately influenced a couple of research projects that we decided to pursue in collaboration with the physician and the Cultural Health Navigators working with her to serve refugee families.

These projects would focus on the practices of Cultural Health Navigators serving refugee families in the pediatric clinic and their understanding of those practices. By exploring the language, literacy and communication dimensions of healthcare encounters and interactions, we hoped to identify, describe and analyze what was going on and how we might build on existing practices to improve refugee families' access to health, health care and information about health and health care. Having received approvals from physicians, cultural health navigators and other staff from the clinic, we worked closely with the academic affairs unit of the hospital to obtain IRB approval to conduct our research projects in the clinical setting. We were supported in our efforts to make a contribution by advocates and allies on the ground who were immersed in providing health care or information about health care to refugee families and were open to our input and insights.

Although we remain outsiders in many ways, we have gained more legitimacy and respect over time – as we continue to show up, listen, and show an ability and desire to contribute in relevant and meaningful ways. We have moved from listening and learning to offering ideas and suggestions (even as we continue to listen and learn). With each step of the process (discovery, design, implementation), we endeavor to contribute (based on what we know) and to collaborate (because of what we don't know). This has all been received warmly and enthusiastically so far, and the excitement and enthusiasm we feel as a result helped us manage the challenges and tensions that continue to emerge at almost every step of the process required to develop and sustain a cross-institutional collaborative research agenda. Patience has indeed been our asset, as we struggle to make sense of institutional and bureaucratic barriers on both fronts. As complications and tensions continue to emerge, we are challenged to find appropriate ways to respond to those complications and challenges while also attending to the affective insights we gain throughout each step of the process.

Conclusion

According to Hubbard *et al.* (2001), emotions are not a purely individual phenomenon, they are 'created and managed through inter-actions with others' – and this includes participants and those within the research team (Hubbard *et al.*, 2001: 134). In this chapter, we have explored the power and potential of more actively and deliberately engaging with the affective experience in research and the value of cre-ating spaces where researchers are able to explore the emotional nature of the work they do and its implications for knowledge production. We have found that emotional ways of knowing can shape what we want to know, how we pursue those questions, what we learn, who we learn from, how we learn, and the value of that knowledge (to us and to our partners). As we reflect back on the many twists and turns we have taken, and the many stops and starts we have experienced, we realize that exploring the emotional dimensions of our experiences has helped us recognize and then pay closer attention to issues and concerns that are a priority to our community-based partners while also aligned with our own commitments.

By illuminating how the emotional and relational dimensions of the research process have shaped our understanding of the focus and the scope of the project, the plans we created, and the choices we made, this chapter contributes to ongoing conversations in the social sciences about the challenges that emerge as researchers attend to the concerns, responses, decisions, and practices of other researchers and stakeholders. For both of us, it has been both challenging and illuminating to con-sider the *value* of emotions and to allow ourselves to pause, take stock, and allow the feelings that surface to help guide conversations, reflec-tions and deliberations. Although certain emotional dimensions of our experiences have influenced what decisions we made about process, it is also true that we allowed ourselves to be influenced by the scholarship we were reviewing, how we proceeded with next steps, what we learned from those experiences, and what challenges remained (in spite of what we were learning). Understanding that the 'push-pull' of 'emotionally-sensed knowledge' (Hubbard *et al.*, 2001) is both normal and productive, we believe we have evolved into researchers who are now better able to recognize the hidden dimensions of discomfort, the ethical implica-tions of emotions, and the value of paying attention to them even it if means taking a detour or delay in relationship-building or knowledge production.

Looking back now, we realize that our emotion has become more than just another abstract concept from the literature; it has become a key way of being and knowing (Hubbard *et al.*, 2001: 135). We argue that theorized reflections on the emotional dimensions of the inquiry process are not only important but essential to the ethical pursuit of research agendas that are both university-based and community-driven. As Hubbard *et al.* (2001) note:

> ... unless emotion in research is acknowledged, not only will researchers be left vulnerable, but also our understandings of the social world will remain impoverished. The challenge therefore is how to construct meaning and develop understanding and knowledge in an academic environment that, on the whole, trains researchers to be rational and objective, and 'extract out' emotion. (2001: 119)

By writing this chapter, we have come to better understand what factors and forces seemed to influence the practices we engaged in and the priorities ultimately pursued, and we hope that sharing our self-conscious reflections here will be useful to others who are embarking on research endeavors in complex circumstances, about complicated topics, or with vulnerable populations. In such ways, we hope to have shown how 'emotionally-sensed knowledge' paves the way for new ways of looking, listening and making sense. Our careful and systematic process of gathering information and soliciting input from a variety of perspectives together with our willingness to attend to the affective dimensions of knowledge production has contributed to relationships, understandings and partnerships that are founded on trust and transparency. Our agendas are now more focused, and we have gained more solid footing in terms of understanding and articulating to our community-based partners what we might contribute, how we might proceed, and the expected benefits of doing so.

References

Cerwonka, A. (2007) Nervous conditions: The stakes in interdisciplinary research. In A. Cerwonka and L.H. Malkki (eds) *Improvising Theory: Process and Temporality in Ethnographic Fieldwork* (pp. 1–43). Chicago: The University of Chicago Press.

Denzin, N. (1984) *On Understanding Emotion*. Jossey Bass.

Dickson-Swift, V., James, E.L., Kippen, S., Liamputtong, P. (2009) Research sensitive topics: Qualitative research as emotion work. *Qualitative Research* 9 (1), 61–79.

Dona, G. (2007) The microphysics of participation in refugee research. *Journal of Refugee Studies* 20 (2), 210–229.

Dyregrov, K., Dyregrov, A. and Raundalen, M. (2000) Refugee families' experience of research participation. *Journal of Traumatic Stress* 13 (3), 413–426.

Game, A. (1997) Sociology's emotions. *Canadian Review of Sociology* 34 (4), 385–399.

Gifford, S.M., Bakopanos, C., Kaplan, I. and Correa-Velez, I. (2007) Meaning or measurement? Researching the social contexts of health and settlement among newly-arrived refugee youth in Melbourne, Australia. *Journal of Refugee Studies* 20, 414–440.

Gifford, S. (2013) To respect or protect? Whose values shape the ethics of refugee research? In K. Block, E. Riggs and N. Haslam (eds) *Values and Vulnerabilities: The Ethics of Research with Refugees and Asylum Seekers* (pp. 41–59). Toowong QLD: Australian Academic Press.

Hochschild, A. (1983) *The Managed Heart: Commercialization of Human Feeling.* Berkeley: University of California Press.

Hubbard, G., Backett-Milburn, K. and Kemmer, D. (2001) Working with emotion: Issues for the researcher in fieldwork and teamwork. *International Journal of Social Research Methodology* 4 (2), 119–137.

Lippke, L. and Tanggaard, L. (2014) Leaning in to 'Muddy' Interviews. *Qualitative Inquiry,* 20 (2), 136–143.

Lykes, R. (1997) Activist participatory action research among the Maya of Guatemala: Constructing meanings from situated knowledge. *Journal of Social Issues* 54 (4), 725–746.

Lupton, D. (1998) *The Emotional Self: A Sociocultural Exploration.* Thousand Oaks: SAGE.

Marmo, M. (2013) The ethical implications of the researcher's dominant position in cross-cultural refugee research. In K. Block, E. Riggs and N. Haslam (eds) *Values and Vulnerabilities: The Ethics of Research with Refugees and Asylum Seekers* (pp. 85–102). Toowong QLD: Australian Academic Press.

Mayfield-Johnson, S. (2011) Adult learning, community education, and public health: Making the connection through community health advisors. *New Directions for Adult & Continuing Education* 2011 (130), 65–77.

Miller, K.E. (2004) Beyond the frontstage: Trust, access, and the relational context in research with refugee Communities. *American Journal of Community Psychology* 33, (3–4), 217–227.

13 Perspectives on Power and Equity in Community-Based Participatory Action Research Projects

Martha Bigelow, Jenna Cushing-Leubner,
Khalid Adam, Mikow Hang, Luis Enrique Ortega,
Shannon Pergament, Amy Shanafelt
and Michele Allen

This chapter will explore some of the quandaries our team of university and community researchers grappled with as we worked across hierarchies, disciplines and roles on a community-based participatory action research (CBPAR) project focusing on helping teachers to recognize resilience among Somali, Hmong, and Latinx[1] adolescents and use those assets to support the students' academic progress. In the field of CBPAR, power dynamics are openly acknowledged and actively addressed, particularly with respect to dynamics between researchers and participants. However, less addressed in the field are power dynamics among researchers. Our power-related challenges, sometimes unresolved, are endemic to work involving many collaborators – the authors on the paper, as well as many other advisors, educators, parents and youth. We examine our experiences with such challenges here to inform other teams of researchers striving for ethical, equitable and productive collaborations in which collective assets and diversity can be leveraged for more productive processes and better project outcomes.

The goal of our multi-year, school-based, teacher professional development (PD) project is to promote teacher learning about their role in developing resilience among Somali, Hmong and Latinx secondary students. As we write about this project, Training for Resilience in Urban Students and Teachers (TRUST), the work is still evolving and unfolding. It started in 2010 and through re-funding is expected to continue at least until 2020, showing that our relationships with each other are long-term, evolving, and represent our individual and collective investment in the project and in working together. Institutionally, TRUST is a collaboration among the University of Minnesota's Medical School Program in Health Disparities Research, the College of Education and Human Development, the Somali, Latino and Hmong Partnership for Health and Wellness (SoLaHmo), a program of West Side Community Health Services, Inc., and various urban middle and secondary schools. This project began with a research period involving the Somali, Latinx and Hmong students[2] as well as teachers and parents. By design and in spirit, the project follows a CBPAR approach (Macauley et al., 1999) in which knowledge and research questions emerge from stakeholder community groups and evolve in conjunction with scholarly, interdisciplinary research. In the early stages of this CBPAR project, TRUST was an initiative launched by a small grant secured by faculty and community partners and then later systematically expanded through substantial funding from NIH.[3] These circumstances led to collaborations among people with different interests, priorities, home languages, cultures, educational backgrounds, and research experiences, among others. While it was not difficult for everyone to embrace our common goal of recognizing and using resilience among immigrant and refugee youth, the logistics of this ambitious and complex project presented us with a number of challenges, some of which we will explore in this chapter.

Overview of Project TRUST

Research shows that teachers, through positive relationships with youth, can help them develop assets that support their healthy development and academic success (Bernat & Resnick, 2006; Gavin et al., 2010; Resnick et al., 1997; Youngblade et al., 2007). These assets may include strong interpersonal skills, a positive view about the future, and the ability to recover from challenges. TRUST aims to equip educators with the tools they need to foster positive relationships with youth in order for them to engage in the educational process in individualized, and multiple positive and productive ways.

The phases of TRUST have involved a community and educator research phase, a curriculum development phase, and a piloting phase. Across these phases, there have been qualitative analyses of interview, focus group and survey data collected from high school teachers and Somali, Hmong and Latinx high school students. As we are writing this chapter, we have begun youth participatory action research (YPAR) and parent participatory action research (PPAR) in order to deepen the PD experience by legitimizing youth and family concerns through research. To capture some of the complexity of this work, we share the following diagram (Figure 13.1) to illustrate conceptual grounding of TRUST.

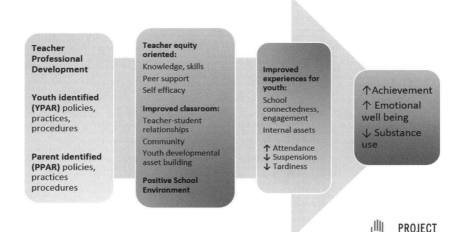

Figure 13.1 TRUST conceptual model

Overlapping Project Phases

In the first phase of the project, we conducted interviews and focus groups with Somali, Hmong and Latinx high school students, parents and educators. This three-year perspective-gathering phase involved a strong collaboration between university researchers and members of SoLaHmo (2010–2012). The full team co-developed the research protocol, methods and data collection tools and SoLaHmo was largely in charge of recruiting participants and gathering data about how educators can foster a sense of connectedness at school for immigrant background youth. Community- and university-based researchers co-conducted qualitative analyses of the transcripts of the interviews and focus groups with parents, students and teachers in order to inform the design and development of curriculum for educators. In addition, a second round of analysis was conducted by parents, students and teachers in an innovative concept mapping process in which ideas for action were ranked according to importance and feasibility (Allen, Shaleban-Boteng *et al.*, 2015). The results of this process guided the development of the themes for the PD experience for practicing teachers.

During the second phase of the project, we developed a curriculum for educators. Using the voices, experiences, and advice of youth, parents, and educators, the team established a nine-session PD experience for educators. The initial version of the curriculum (2014) focused on identifying tools teachers could use to connect with youth to build resilience through relationships, with a built-in process for reflexive discussions about implementation of the various tools. Other key components of the sessions include (a) teachers bringing in their everyday dilemmas on issues that they encounter; (b) showcasing Somali, Latinx and Hmong voices; and (c) the use of multiple supplementary resources (e.g. videos) and summaries of research studies on the session topics.

In a third phase, we piloted our nine-session PD curriculum with a group of six educators in the 2013–2014 academic year, and again with 47 educators in the following year. The PD effort focused on strategies for building trusting and respectful student-teacher relationships through resilience-oriented teaching through the following topics with more detail available elsewhere (Cushing-Leubner *et al.*, 2015):

(1) Factors for success – Resilience and positive youth development.
(2) Connecting with individual students in multiple ways.
(3) Building youth resilience through reinforcing family and community assets.
(4) Building and conveying trust – Maintaining mutual respect.
(5) Building trusting relationships through strong communication and listening.
(6) Growth mindsets.
(7) Resilience-oriented teaching overview.
(8) Resilience-oriented teaching – Commitment to care for students and their learning.
(9) Resilience-oriented teaching – Commitment to high expectations.

During the PD piloting phases, we gathered survey and focus group data from the teachers about the curriculum and from the youth about their feelings of connectedness at school. Currently, we are in a planning year for expanded implementation of another PD intervention phase, including increased levels of participatory action research with youth and parents. Now, we will explore and reflect on key pressure points that have emerged among us as we strive to carry out this CBPAR project.

Tensions, Dilemmas and Bumps in the Road

As we wrote this chapter together, our discussions of power and equity revolved around three main topics: (a) the often contested zone occupied by the TRUST coordinator; (b) our reoccurring debates emanating from the disciplinary or contextual spaces and positions we occupy; and (c) our ongoing challenge to disseminate our work in ways which are generative, hold true to the equity spirit of the project, and help those the project is designed to help.

Coordinating Project TRUST

Although the core community and university team members have remained stable over the course of the project, we have worked with at least five different TRUST coordinators and have noticed that this role is fraught with challenges, sometimes stemming from the positionality of the individual – whether they identify primarily with the university or the community. CBPAR partnerships must consider power dynamics between community and university. In this section, we examine some of the human elements of these tensions by reflecting on the example of the coordinator role. We chose to explore what was happening in terms of the coordinator role, because the people who stepped into this role needed to stand in both worlds – community and university – while being more at home in one or the other. We all could feel the tensions that emanated from this dynamic and slippery role, and we wanted to reflect on the ways that interpersonal and institutional factors were weaving together. We hope that our observations about the coordinator role in our particular project will help to illustrate one of the core challenges within CBPAR, particularly the ways relationships are put under pressure within the power dynamics of these institutional partnerships.

Study coordinators from the University of Minnesota, particularly in the Medical School, are often hired on a project-by-project basis, and their roles and responsibilities can change dramatically from one project to the next. The coordinator's role is to manage the project team timeline, track team communication and organize action items, manage university-related regulations and funder reporting processes, and manage the student recruitment and data collection processes. The less clear objectives for study coordination with TRUST relate to efficiency pressures and leading or performing other study activities such as operationalizing the intervention, carrying out process evaluations, and study communications with team members and others. The skill set involved with building relationships with the team is difficult to define, but the coordinator needs to understand and work with a decentralized, yet hierarchical team whose work is moving forward among the team at a fast clip. The coordinator, on the other hand, has the burden of figuring out the team dynamics, which have developed over many years. It is difficult to orient a new coordinator because so much of thelandscape of the teams' interpersonal dynamics are largely invisible to the team members. Furthermore, the coordinator reports to the PIs, yet is often given tasks by any member of the team. The complicated boundaries of the role, and the feeling of reporting to everyone, are challenging. To the coordinators, it sometimes feels overwhelming and disempowering.

In CBPAR, team members with direct community knowledge and expertise related to the study activities lead community work rather than a study coordinator or PI as in a traditional study team. For example, the intervention components of the TRUST study, teacher PD, YPAR and PPAR are led and carried out by team members who are teacher educators or school administrators, which adds depth and applicability to that work. Team members have different areas of expertise and thus different levels of input and responsibility across the phases of TRUST. This dynamic process is challenging for any coordinator to manage, both logistically in terms of who is responsible for what deliverables, as well as interpersonally in terms of knowing and respecting everyone's expertise.

The balance of university and community priorities can be a challenge for a study coordinator on a CBPAR study like TRUST in multiple ways. Sometimes, the coordinator is tasked with negotiating those priorities among the study leadership, which requires strong relationships with each member to understand what drives their decisions well enough to make 'on the fly' decisions. Often, quick decisions are not possible in the CBPAR structure and it is necessary to know when to move on something and when it is important to wait for corroboration. On a traditional study team, coordinators may need to receive approval for study decisions from the PI, or may even be able to act autonomously. For TRUST, getting to know those preferences takes care and attention and building relationships with everyone on the team, not just the PI. This is initially more work for the coordinator.

TRUST has had multiple coordinators – some who come from the immigrant and refugee communities we work with, and others who originate from connections through the university. Sometimes both. For instance, we had a coordinator from the Somali community in the Twin Cities, who began working in TRUST as a dynamic and key researcher with SoLaHmo. We were lucky to have him apply for and move into the coordinator role. However, in this transition, it seemed that this change of role resulted in his voice becoming less present and thus less powerful than when his voice came through SoLaHmo. (In fact, we are missing his voice on this paper.) As we reflect on this, we see how SoLaHmo has a very different dynamic than the CBPAR leadership team. While both groups are democratic, and the CBPAR team has a strong SoLaHmo representation, our leadership team does admittedly have hierarchies because of the roles of the co-principal investigators and co-investigators with respect to accountability. In other words, there is a small sub-set of the team responsible for moving the project forward and they are thus able to charge other members of the team with tasks. This is a power dynamic intrinsic to the working of the team. There is also the expectation that the supervision and mentoring of the person in the coordinator role is quite minimal, yet the coordinator needs to assertively move into highly collaborative and flexible ways of working with the team. We now see that having a SoLaHmo researcher in this role was a challenge for some members of the team. We see this as a failing of the team, but also recognition that the systems within which we are working are also very resistant to change. The team is well aware of how the university can be a self-perpetuating machine in which equity across hiring practices does not get institutionalized, even among us.

To compare, we have also had, and currently have, university-based coordinators – typically white and female. Among these white, female coordinators, some were very accustomed to working with NIH and university systems. However, most NIH funded studies in the Medical School are not participatory and tend to be directed by the professor who received the grant with a small research team including the study coordinator. In such arrangements, roles and hierarchies are typically well defined and the coordinator tends to manage all of the work. For TRUST, on the other hand, study coordinators have found it challenging to understand the shared leadership and decision-making process in TRUST as a CBPAR study. Thus, study coordinators have had to learn that it is necessary to adapt to this structure and let go of some of the management duties – relinquishing them to other team members to lead or, for the whole team to lead as a group. This balance can be very difficult for the coordinator because there is constant pressure to meet certain study benchmarks and stay on the study timeline. Coordinators can feel that they are not performing their job up to standard, while adapting to the unfamiliar territory of collaborative, complex decision-making processes.

The balance between community and university priorities in hiring a study coordinator is challenging for those leading studies. CBPAR studies require coordinators with strong and, ideally, personal knowledge of the communities involved in the study, but also, particularly in larger studies, methodological training and experiential skills with university-based research. Individuals with that broad set of skills are often difficult to find. There is a tension when compromises need to be made in terms of which skills to prioritize. We have noticed that, over time, as TRUST has become larger, research training and experience are more valued than immigrant/minoritized community membership and cultural and linguistic expertise. Ideally, those compromises can be offset by the skills of others around the table. The difficulty of finding individuals who can easily straddle the multiple contexts of a project like TRUST speaks to the larger societal need for a more diverse and community-focused work force.

While working as a study coordinator for Project TRUST comes with challenges, those challenges are present because of traditional study structures embedded in one's training and understanding as a study coordinator. Likewise, there is an ongoing need to create opportunities to build capacity among coordinators from the community, if a community member is not easily identified. This requires additional funds for training experiences and time for mentoring. The need to develop new and multiple lenses for those in the coordinator role, and their mentors, seems to be related to and sometimes influenced by the next challenge we often faced: findings ways for researchers from different disciplines to communicate and collaborate effectively.

Working across disciplines and contexts

The fact that CBPAR projects are often interdisciplinary is seen as an undisputed strength. Our research team from the university is intentionally diverse. The academic disciplines we come from (i.e. medicine, public health, education and applied linguistics) serve the team well in terms of content expertise. We have strengths in academic background about health disparities, immigrant education and teacher education. Aside from crossing campus to do our work, we also cross epistemological boundaries and this has led to rich discussion and debate. These differences, while critical to the success of TRUST, have also illuminated a number of structural and interdisciplinary challenges which we will explore here.

The collaborators on the project with medical and public health backgrounds (Allen, Hang, Pergament) come from disciplines that emphasize quantitative intervention work that prioritizes knowledge gained through randomized controlled trials. Although they embrace qualitative research and have done quite a bit of it – some think of themselves fundamentally as interventionists. They advocate for studies that are inherently action focused which fit with CBPAR in that regard. In fact, we use CBPAR because this approach is largely focused on navigating those challenges. The investigators from education (Bigelow, Cushing-Leubner) are deeply invested in epistemologies which are more qualitative. These members of the team prefer to understand the complex issues of the study through interpretive lenses. The different disciplinary grounding we bring offers a sort of balanced mandala of skills, which on the surface seems optimal for a CBPAR project. Nevertheless, we have experienced our disciplinary divide when trying to talk and write about our work in different academic venues across our disciplines. One explanation is that we have been socialized into our fields in ways which shape the ways we understand and write about our work. While disciplinary differences in discourse have been documented in the scholarly literature (e.g. Airey & Linder, 2008; Myers, 1989), it is different to experience it first hand when trying to contribute to each other's fields.

There are power dynamics at play as we do writing projects and encounter discomfort with being unfamiliar with genre and audience of our papers as we recast them in different ways for different purposes. While we welcome epistemological diversity among us, this brings some level of unease. For example, the qualitative researchers question or don't understand fundamental design decisions about who is included in the experimental and comparison groups or how analyses are conducted. The interventionists from the side of public health struggle need those from education to translate the work into the discourse used by those in that field (e.g. translanguaging, white supremacy, restorative justice).

Working across disciplines means also working across actual spaces on campus and in communities. For example, in the early days of the grant, we struggled over where to meet – on campus or in communities. This may seem trivial, but where we meet carries enormous symbolic weight in terms of who is perceived to have the most flexibility (i.e. can meet anywhere, park anywhere), who has the most pressing schedules, the most resources and ultimately the most power. Over time, we worked through these challenges and currently find community-located meetings, and optional conference calling the most facilitative of getting our work done while being mindful of these power differentials.

In this work, however, the various competing priorities that we have discovered among us pale in comparison to the competing priorities between us and the school partners. Our most significant challenge has been figuring out with school partners how to deliver the PD to the teachers. Schools face their own pressures and these pressures often drive the work they do as a district or a school-level staff. For instance, the district we are working with is focusing its efforts on one (also minoritized) student demographic while our grant focuses on immigrant and refugee background youth. This has been cause for us to expand our project scope in order to stay relevant to the school district. Other district currents cause the sands to shift when we find out that administrators who we have had close working relationships with leave or change roles. We often develop relationships with school and district leadership and suddenly that leadership shifts. Furthermore, NIH's funding cycle is not designed to coincide with the academic calendar year. Therefore, we are under pressure to reach milestones in our project at times when the decision-makers at school are not available. As we negotiate a new phase of the TRUST with school principals, it feels that they have all the power. Our free PD, YPAR, PPAR and community engaged project often just doesn't seem that interesting to some school leadership teams – they say it overlaps, they say they want to wait for YPAR results to come in before signing on. While it is exciting to see youth having a powerful role in the PD decisions made by administrators, we are often baffled by how to move forward with our school partners.

Dissemination of knowledge from CBPAR

In the midst of satisfying research grant and project deadlines, writing academic journal articles for publication, presenting at conferences and writing next-phase grant proposals, it is easy to allow community dissemination to fall by the wayside. In CBPAR projects, however, it is imperative that community dissemination be a priority. From the perspective of our community researchers, the opportunities for the dissemination of our research tend to be 'ready made' and widely available in academic venues that promote a single goal – to participate in academic conferences and publications – in English. These opportunities to disseminate our work serve the academics on the team in terms of reaching promotion and tenure goals, and following the norms and culture of information sharing within their professions. But what about community dissemination?

This reality and challenge of CBPAR dissemination has been noted in the literature (e.g. Chen *et al.*, 2010) with the recognition that academic publication outlets are often not accessible to our community members due to mode of dissemination. The language used is English, the mode is often written, not spoken, the genre is often formal, not conversational, the venue is often academic and remote and not located in communities. All of these facts create a dynamic in which dissemination is falling on the side of the powerful – English speakers with high levels of education who are located in universities.[4] As such, we know that our work is not reaching the participating communities as often as it is reaching academic peers. One reason CBPAR projects have routinely struggled with the challenge of community dissemination is because the outcomes of the projects are often seen as products, not processes, and because the products may be things that depend heavily on community input and involvement. In one CBPAR project focusing on reducing youth violence in urban areas, Vaughn et al. (2013) used digital animation as a way to disseminate their research findings to their community, as per advice from their community partners. This dynamic and engaging community dissemination strategy was high impact, but also high effort. It involved multiple steps such as turning youth quotes from the research into vignettes, linking the vignettes to the literature, engaging local artists in producing the digital animation, creating a youth advisory board to guide and vet the materials, which ended up including action steps that community members could take to reduce violence in the community. In this example, it seems that deliberate power sharing was initiated by the CBPAR team and promoted through dedicated resources, including time.

Vaughn et al.'s (2013) approach to involving youth in dissemination addresses a key structural issue in community dissemination. One issue is the lack of tangible career motivations that accompany successful community dissemination. In other words, it is important to identify the value of learning new skills (e.g. videography). It is also important to identify or create the spaces in which the dissemination work will take place in order to experience and even measure impact. In academia, community dissemination may not be valued by promotion and tenure committees, or lead to skills that community members are seeking to reach their own personal or professional goals. Yet, for CBPAR projects to be successful, ultimately the communities most impacted by the research findings must be made aware of and engaged in the outcomes and plans for future efforts in order for the uptake of new programs and interventions to be sustainable at the community level. Again, dissemination falls on the side of power.

In Project TRUST, we have made a deliberate effort to create parallel processes and strategies for academic and community dissemination. We are continually working on papers and presentations for teachers and other researchers, while simultaneously working on community dissemination activities. For instance, in 2015–16, we conducted six community dissemination activities, eight academic dissemination activities, and created a TRUST website in multiple languages. Our community activities have included participating in conferences such as the Twin Cities

Social Justice Education Fair (October 2015). In this event, and others like it, we offered participants the opportunity to experience what our resilience-focused PD is like. When we have shared our work with educators, we have seen the most interest and the highest levels of attendance. This is encouraging because the PD curriculum is designed for educators. We also have had TRUST community events in which educators, parents and TRUST members attended. Currently, we are hearing about research questions and methods of YPAR and PPAR participants.

While we can report dissemination activities back to the funder and our university and are encouraged by the positive responses we've been getting, we see many limitations in our efforts. As we strive to fulfill the expectations of our fields (i.e. public health, education) we are pressed to conform to the parameters of a journal or a conference presentation. Likewise, our non-academic partners often feel confined by the genre or mode of dissemination. Expectations of brevity, fitting information into formats that conform with academic venues (e.g. posters at conferences), can lead to dissemination that captures only a small slice of our project. We wonder what parts of our work are taken up by others and generative of new ideas. Could dissemination events or artifacts simultaneously reach community-university audiences in one venue and create opportunities for further community-academic engagement and dialogue?

Challenges unique to community dissemination are numerous, including but not limited to the following: (a) that there is limited time in a project grant cycle and teams can run out of steam at the end of a project as they gear up for the next grant submission deadline and new projects begin; (b) successful marketing of community events and meetings can be difficult, especially the logistics of finding a time that works for diverse participants; (c) community events require a budget for food, translation of documents and interpreters; and (d) making results interesting to community members is much different than framing results for an academic audience. On our team, we struggle with who is responsible for this work and it seems that the most complex, uncharted work falls on the team members who are more on the community side of the project.

Until funders require that grantees include community dissemination strategies as part of their grant proposal and budget, community-academic research partnerships need to be proactive in prioritizing community dissemination in tandem with more traditional dissemination activities. While sometimes easier said than done, this commitment should be discussed and decided upon early in a partnership and can even strengthen the partnership when the dissemination activities offer participants purpose and learning opportunities, like the previous examples of the educational materials created by and for youth. We have learned that dissemination throughout the project should be part of the proposal writing process and include timelines and budget considerations that are unique to a community setting (i.e. space rental, food/refreshments, advertising, translation/interpretation and project staff salary support) and strategies should be revisited as part of the Memorandum of Understanding or other collaborative agreement process.

As we reflect on these issues, we'd like to also discuss the issues related to commitments and distribution of resources whereby funds are weighted toward communities, and away from the university. TRUST has been successful in doing this in many ways (e.g. catering, site rental, translators) but unsuccessful in other moments because of forgetfulness or tight timelines that don't allow for enough lead time for a community business to respond compared to the university (e.g. printing services). In addition, we'd like to illuminate the fact that there are hidden costs of community-based labor. It takes time and funds to create dissemination events and materials that involve community members.

Finally, we have been finding that when TRUST uses direct quotes and narratives from our qualitative data, there are cross-over opportunities for dissemination to researchers and educators. For example, qualitative data is often presented in research papers and academic presentations through direct quotes from participants, as narratives, and as conversations. This way of talking about research findings resonates with people not trained as researchers, particularly educators who can 'hear' the voices of their students in the data and identify with the issues brought forward through qualitative data. It seems to us that the links among the student quotes from the data, the PD themes and the interactive workshop formats engage and inspire the teachers who show up in large quantities to our presentations at practitioner conferences. TRUST is reaching educators, a sub-community and stakeholder group that does not necessarily read academic journals on a regular basis. We see the potential for similar approaches to work with immigrant and refugee-background youth and families who can also 'hear' the voices of themselves in the data. In sum, by having a epistemologically diverse team, we have the skills to represent data in different ways for different audiences.

We wish to challenge ourselves and other CBPAR researchers to consider the problem academia has with disseminating findings of all sorts, to any audience. We seem to lack a robust open-access knowledge exchange which offers us feedback on our work, and reaches a large number of researchers working on similar topics, with similar teachers and youth. One promising direction is Community-Engaged Scholarship for Health (CES4Health) which offers teams like ours a peer-reviewed and open access outlet for our work (see http://ces4health.info/). CES4Health doesn't only publish reports on CBPAR work, they publish other sorts of products – videos, radio series, websites, etc. This sort of outlet may be the in-between space that TRUST needs to disseminate more broadly while the project unfolds rather than only after all the data are analyzed.

We are not the first to do CBPAR and these dissemination challenges have been documented in the literature, but we wonder how our dilemmas are unique and how our activities can contribute to the practice and the science of CBPAR. Likewise, we have noted that sometimes we have given presentations at a researcher-oriented conference with a very small audience. This may be a high prestige venue, but very low impact. While we are generating lines on our CVs, we are not necessarily (even) disseminating findings to fellow researchers. Perhaps we need to broaden what we ourselves understand as dissemination. Can dissemination be sharing our work with our closest classmates, peers, colleagues, and stakeholder groups? Perhaps by refocusing our efforts locally, we can have a broader and more impactful reach into our respective disciplines. Can we challenge the powerful systems of what is seen as legitimate modes of dissemination in CBPAR for *all* members of our team? Can we purposefully and creatively disrupt the power structures for greater impact and sustainability? These are some of our ongoing dilemmas.

Conclusion

One of our main discoveries in writing this chapter is that our CBPAR project is still struggling to work within rigid, larger systems of power. School, community, and university systems are not necessarily ready to work the way we work (Allen, Svetaz *et al.*, 2013). Nevertheless, we hope that by revealing a behind-the-scenes look at doing CBPAR for, with and as members of multigenerational and new arrival immigrant and refugee communities, we will inspire others to dive into this work with their eyes wide open. By critically reflecting on issues of hierarchy and power and limits of university-based research, we demonstrate the value of reflecting on the possibilities and challenges of the research process, the ethical and emotional dimensions of participating in collaborative research, and the 'untold stories' of research design, data collection, data analysis, and representation of findings.

We also have discovered that we have work to do. Some of our lingering questions are these:

(1) In terms of accountability, how can we (re)imagine processes that are focused on the healthy workings of community organizations, school partners and university partners? What are the ways that accountability might focus inwardly, on and by each partnership group, as well as synergistically across the partnering groups? How are we encouraging the voicing of procedural or interpersonal dynamics that team members find uncomfortable? How do we elicit ideas for making meetings or other process-oriented daily activities work better?

(2) In terms of issues related to hierarchies and power, what are the ways our partnerships take stock of and listen responsively to the pains of power as these play out in dynamics informed by institutional

histories as well as changing roles over time? How can we challenge institutional norms, including those of our funders, when this often means extra or different work for some or all of us?

(3) In terms of living cultural responsiveness among ourselves, how do our partnerships explicitly examine power dynamics that center differences in ways of being that may be informed by intersecting oppressive and silencing factors that fall across cultural practices, language differences and ideologies around race, gender and class? How do these inquiries take into consideration different interactional and performance contexts? How can we learn about or at least recognize that people are socialized differently across disciplines as well as cultural and linguistic ways of being?

(4) When there are failings – when ecologies of partnering become unhealthy – how do our partnerships respond? Who or what is the partnership willing to lose? What does this loss mean for the work? What does this willingness mean for the work?

By articulating these questions, we can better explore the nature of our partnerships and how we leverage institutional resources in solidarity with immigrant and refugee-background youth and communities. Maybe we can more faithfully embody some of the tenets of our curriculum for teachers (e.g. be assets-focused, continually (re)create respect and trust) amongst ourselves and our partners. We may need to take risks and challenge ourselves to explore these issues with each other, but it is our hope that our collaborations will be more ethical and fruitful. In the end, and with this hard work, we hope that our outcomes will be more positive, sustainable and powerful.

Notes

(1) As a team, at the time we wrote this chapter, we differed on our comfort with using Latinx (rather than Latino, Latin@ or Latina/o). We chose Latinx here in an effort to become more comfortable with the term, following discussions about the terms from, for example, these websites: We are Mitú https://www.wearemitu.com/mitu-voice/how-do-you-feel-about-the-label-latinx/; Latino USA http://latinousa.org/2016/01/29/latinx-ungendering-spanish-language/; and Coming to Terms with 'Latinx'http://www.refinery29.com/2017/03/147477/what-is-latinx.

(2) Many of the youth participants were born in the US and were children of immigrants. Some were immigrants themselves and some had refugee backgrounds.

(3) Research reported in this publication was supported by National Institute of Minority Health and Health Disparities of the National Institutes of Health under award number 1U01MD010586. The content is solely the responsibility of the authors and does not necessarily represent the official views of the National Institutes of Health. Additional funding came from the Universityof Minnesota Clinical Translational Science Institute Planning Grant # CTSI 15673, and theUniversity of Minnesota Program in Health Disparities Research Planning Grant # 2010-004.

(4) Decisions about language have emerged throughout the project. For instance, the contexts in which languages other than English are used in this project were slightly

different between the youth researchers and the parent researchers. The recruitment of parent researchers and the participants in the parent focus groups and surveys was done through multiple languages (Spanish, Somali, Hmong) while youth researchers were recruited from several different language backgrounds mainly though English. Likewise, the focus groups and interviews were conducted in English. The assent and consent processes were also done through multiple languages and a survey we used was available to students in Somali, Hmong, Karen, Spanish and English. The issue of language was discussed often and in depth throughout this effort with the youth researchers. A couple of the obstacles were the number of different languages found in each of the schools and the limited number of youth researchers at each school site. We are working to include more student voice from students of languages other than English.

References

Airey, J. and Linder, C. (2008) A disciplinary discourse perspective on university science learning: Achieving fluency in a critical constellation of modes. *Journal of Research in Science Teaching* 46 (1), 27–49.

Allen, M.L., Svetaz, M.V., Hurtado, G.A, Linares, R., Garcia-Huidobro, D. and Hurtado, M. (2013) The developmental stages of a community-university partnership: The experience of Padres Informados/Jovenes Preparados. *Progress in Community Health Partnerships* 7 (3), 271–279.

Allen, M.L., Shaleben-Boateng, D., Davey, C., Hang, M. and Pergament, S. (2015) Concept mapping as an approach to facilitate participatory intervention building. *Progress in Community Health Partnership* 9 (4), 599–608.

Bernat, D.H. and Resnick, M.D. (2006) Healthy youth development: Science and strategies. *Journal of Public Health Management and Practice* 12, S10–S16.

Chen, P.G., Diaz, N., Lucas, G. and Rosenthal, M.S. (2010) Dissemination of results in community-based participatory research. *American Journal of Prevention Research* 39 (4), 372–378.

Cushing-Leubner, J., Bigelow, M., Ortega, L., Pergament, S., Adam, K., Hang, M., Susens, S., Prifrel, R. and Allen, M. (2015) Promoting resilience in diverse classrooms: The answers are not in the back of the book. *MinneTESOL Journal*. http://minnetesoljournal.org/spring-2015/promoting-resilience-in-diverse-classrooms-the-answers-are-not-in-the-back-of-the-book

Gavin, L.E., Catalano, R.F., David-Ferdon, C., Gloppen, K.M. and Markham, C.M. (2010) A review of positive youth development programs that promote adolescent sexual and reproductive health. *Journal of Adolescent Health* 46 (3), S75–S91.

Macaulay, A.C., Gibson, N., Freeman, W.L., Commanda, L.E., McCabe, M.L., Robbins, C.M. and Twohig, P.L. (1999) Participatory research maximizes community and lay involvement. *BMJ* 319, 774–778.

Myers, G. (1989) The pragmatics of politeness in scientific articles. *Applied Linguistics* 10 (1), 1–35.

Resnick, M.D., Bearman, P.S., Blum, R.W., Bauman, K.E., Harris, K.M., Jones, J., … Udry, J.R. (1997) Protecting adolescents from harm. Findings from the National Longitudinal Study on Adolescent Health. *JAMA,* 278 (10), 823–832.

Vaughn, N.A., Jacoby, S.F., Williams, T., Guerra, T., Thomas, N.A. and Richmond, T.S. (2013) Digital animation as a method to disseminate research findings to the community using a community-based participatory approach. *American Journal of Community Psychology* 51, 30–40.

Youngblade, L.M., Theokas, C., Schulenberg, J., Curry, L., Huang, I.C., and Novak, M. (2007) Risk and promotive factors in families, schools, and communities: A contextual model of positive youth development in adolescence. *Pediatrics*, 119 (Supplement 1), S47–S53.

Index